In My Mind's Eye

To Laurie

Best wishes,

Jenny Uglow

In My Mind's Eye

MEMORIES OF A CORNISH GIRLHOOD

JENNY LLOYD

Createspace, 2015

In loving memory of my parents Joan and Mif Muir-Smith

For my children Tom Lloyd and Jane Lloyd Ellis and my grandchildren Tabitha and Marlow Lloyd and Nathaniel and Benjamin Ellis

A NOTE FOR BRITISH READERS

I first wrote these pieces for American readers. You will find some American vocabulary, American spelling and punctuation, and some explanations of things you already know, like O Levels and cricket.

CORNWALL

Cornwall is England's toe, arched and stretching warily into the Atlantic, testing the waters warmed by the Gulf Stream and tossed by gusts of the prevailing west winds. On windy days shadows of small clouds whipped across our farm's fields faster than I could run to keep up with them. I called it stripey weather. Stocky trees, hawthorns, hazels, scrub oaks, turned their backs to the wind, forming bizarre asymmetrical shapes as if lacquered by a fanciful beautician. Nothing in the Cornwall of my childhood was tall. The churches had squat square towers and the chimneys of the old tin mines were no higher than necessary. Now wind is an asset

1

and the tallest buildings are huge concrete windmills, standing together in an elegant white grove, their ghostly humming accompanying the harvest of a force of nature.

Squeezed between the English Channel and the Irish Sea, Cornwall is rarely dry. In the green sheltered valleys the light and penetrating rain we called "misty wet" fosters huge rhododendrons, hedges of fuchsias, woods full of primroses and bluebells. The mild and moist climate now makes it the perfect home for the Eden Project, a scheme to collect all the plants of the world in one place, both outside and under geodesic domes. The site was once a mine in a curious industrial landscape of white pyramids and blue artificial lakes formed by extracting china clay or kaolin, Cornwall's main export, an essential ingredient for products ranging from paper and fine porcelain to antacids. Today the debris from mining is backfilled into old pits and the white waste that used to line streambeds and color the ocean in a huge swirl is no more.

Cornwall is also a land of moors, moist spongy empty spaces, punctuated by rocky outcrops, home to sheep and ponies, but few humans. The main vegetation, apart from the stunted bushes, is bracken, an indestructible fern-like plant no grazing animal will eat. Bodmin Moor, a bleak and forbidding landscape straddling the main central highway, had a sinister reputation as a home to witches, black magic, and pirates, the subject of a famous Daphne du Maurier novel, *Jamaica Inn*. Now Jamaica Inn is a tourist stop, and more people look for King Arthur than witches. Dozmary Pool, not far off the highway, is supposedly the place where the disembodied arm gave Arthur his sword Excalibur.

Cornish lanes are maze-like, bounded by high walls of granite lumps. You can't see over them, especially when topped with low hazel bushes. You can't see the granite either since the crannies are filled with dirt so any plant that can thrive on a little soil takes root. I learned the names of all the flowers: coltsfoot, red and white campion, Solomon's seal. In some places where the soil is right, primroses and bluebells bloom in spring and tiny wild red strawberries peer from behind the bracken in summer. The effect is like driving in a green tunnel—sometimes, if trees arch over the top, it *is* a tunnel. Many of the lanes are so narrow that the plants brush the car, and if you meet another vehicle coming in the opposite direction the driver nearest a passing place, usually a field entrance, has to reverse.

Cornwall's glory is its coasts. The north coast is often rugged, high above the sea, dented with inaccessible coves visible from the cliffs above. On the cliffs the springy grass is dotted in season with purple heather and yellow gorse, a prickly version of broom. Booming surf rolls into the north coast beaches, bringing with it a vicious undertow at low tide that drowned one or two swimmers a year when I was growing up. The south coast is softer, with more good harbors for fishermen and accompanying picturesque fishing villages, now filled with tourists, as the pilchards, Cornwall's most plentiful fish, have gone. Everywhere is the sea in its many moods, softly twinkling the bluest blue, shaking its white-topped steely breakers in a storm, turning purple in the setting sun.

Cornwall was where my parents chose to live for most of my growing up. They exiled themselves from the London of their own childhoods, and from the comfortable life they had known. How and why they decided to do so, and the consequences of their decision are the subjects of this memoir.

FINDING THE FARM

As my parents used to tell it, they bought Gunwen Farm on an impulse.

In the last year of World War II my mother, baby brother Michael and I were in temporary exile in Cornwall, away from the bombs falling around our real home west of London. My father, works manager of a factory making life rafts and barrage balloons, snatched a weekend away from supervising by day and fire-watching at night. After a long day's journey on train and bus, he arrived at the shepherd's cottage where we were living, and had to go back the following day. My parents stayed up all night, not to miss a minute of each other's company. This is how they recalled part of their conversation:

My father said, "We're not going back, are we?"

"No."

"We're going to buy a farm, aren't we?"

"Yes."

That, according to them, was that.

As someone who, with my partner, bought the house we live in one afternoon when we were not planning to move, I understand tipping points, the moments when everything coalesces and decisions are not only possible but also almost preordained. We had talked about moving and decided not to, but the conditions that started the discussion in the first place were still there. When we unexpectedly found a house that fitted our needs, we pounced.

Likewise, this was not the beginning of my parents' decision, but the end. Every night my mother had left us children with the shepherd's wife and walked to the red phone box a mile away to talk to my father. As my mother fed sixpences into the slot, they must have discussed their hopes and plans for the future. By then they knew the war would be over eventually, and that the Allies would win. That night, when my father arrived, they already knew what they wanted to do. Their conversation was just the final confirmation of something already agreed.

By the fall of 1944 my parents had been married for six years and lived apart for almost four of them, since my father slept at the factory. My father hardly knew me, aged just five, or my year-old brother. Bombing raids and punishing wartime production schedules had raised my father's blood pressure and caused circulation problems in his legs. My parents may have had idealized dreams of a more leisurely life, although farming hardly proved stress-free. Also, they were deeply in love, so the real reason for their extraordinary decision was the prospect of spending all their time together for the rest of their lives.

My mother and father were both townies, born in London suburbs to parents who grew up in London itself. However, rural Cornwall had a special hold on their hearts as the place where they had been able to escape my maternal grandmother's hostility toward my father. Nonetheless, their only experience of country living until our bomb-induced exile was on holiday, when all inconveniences are fleeting.

My father knew nothing about farming, and, while he certainly needed a break after five years of non-stop work, going from works manager with a steady income to farmer without one was quite a leap. As my mother's wartime contribution, she had helped on a local farm before we left for Cornwall, so she at least knew how to milk a cow. Of the two, she was the more enthusiastic about changing their lives. Keeping house and looking

5

after small children for five years made her realize she wanted more than being a housewife like her mother. Although she had taught kindergarten before she married, she would find it difficult to get work after the war when most schools, like government offices, did not employ married women. Farming would allow her to work without leaving home.

Finding a farm to buy was challenging. Paper was strictly rationed in wartime, so newspapers had little space for advertising, but my mother called estate agents (realtors) and heard of what sounded like a suitable farm for sale in a remote area in the center of Cornwall. Getting there was difficult. No public transport went anywhere near it, and there were no cars or fuel to take prospective buyers to view properties. To confuse any German spies who might be parachuted in, the government required the removal of all signposts nationwide and forbade the sale of maps. Undaunted, my parents borrowed an old map and bicycles and set out for the train station.

A single-track branch railway line took them with their bikes to Bugle, an ugly straggling kaolin-mining town. On a fine fall day without Cornwall's penetrating misty rain, they took off into a world of high-hedged lanes and small farms, stopping at every fork in the road to check their map or ask the way. The hazel leaves were turning russet brown, exposing the ripening nuts, and the last of the ragged robin bloomed in the hedges. Eventually they coasted down a hill to where the land opened out into marshland below a high rocky outcrop the map told them was Helman Tor. Passing a simple Methodist chapel and a row of granite slate-roofed cottages, they turned into one of the narrowest lanes yet, up a hill, and there, as the road veered right, was a gate with peeling white paint and a faint black inscription, "Gunwen." They were triumphant—they had found it! Excitedly, they opened the gate and, full of anticipation, rode down a sandy driveway at the edge of a pasture. They passed a few dark brown cows grazing, then went through another gate, around a corner, and stopped at the edge of the farmyard. There reality hit.

They stood looking at a mass of mud, impossible to bike through, surrounded by a large barn and several other dilapidated buildings. Any romantic notion of rustic country living evaporated. The place needed serious work. They left the bicycles at the edge of the morass and picked their way around the mud to a small gate leading to the house. Knocking at the front door, they surprised the owners, Mr. and Mrs. May, who had no telephone and so no way of knowing they were coming. The Mays, an elderly couple who were retiring from farming, asked them in for a cup of tea and a piece of yellow, raisin-studded saffron cake, a Cornish delicacy, a distinctive and acquired taste, not very sweet and with a hint of caraway.

The farmhouse was as unpromising as the outbuildings. The peeling wallpaper and the musty smell suggested serious damp, and the cold slate floors added to the chill. An ancient coal-fired range provided the only heat, as well as the sole means of cooking. Water came from an outside pump. There was no bathroom and the toilet was a one-hole outhouse up a path several yards from the house. But my parents saw potential in the five bedrooms and large, inviting kitchen. Maybe the challenge excited them, maybe the price was right. In any case, they made an offer.

ANCESTRY

    Settling on a remote farm in Cornwall, my parents became almost expatriates. Their families and friends were clustered around London, a long day's journey away, one they couldn't make together because someone had to milk the cows. At first they had no telephone, and the nearest phone box was more than a mile away, so their only contact with their former life was through the post. My brother and I grew up without much interaction with our relatives, and my parents rarely talked about them.

    The English people of my generation were mostly incurious about their ancestry. Unlike most Americans our recent forebears hadn't crossed oceans to reach a chosen land, and we assumed they had lived in the British Isles much as we did, although with fewer creature comforts. In any case, tracing one's ancestors was a difficult and laborious task involving visiting record offices in different parts of the country, something most people had neither the time nor money to pursue.

Until the Internet. Now all I need is a computer, a subscription to an ancestry site, some research skills (I am a historian), and patience. Also, as I began writing about my parents' early life, I became curious about their families. I began looking for my grandparents on-line in nineteenth-century English censuses. Like many in Victorian Britain, my ancestors yielded to the lure of London, moving from different areas—a small town in the West of England, another in Oxfordshire, Perth in Scotland. Only my paternal grandmother's family were London natives for most of the century. They all settled in the boroughs of Paddington and Camden, then on the edge of the city, neighborhoods of workers and small businesses. All lived within walking distance of where my son would live for several years a century later.

My grandparents were respectable middle-class people. My grandfathers were professionals, an architect and a civil servant, my grandmothers supportive wives. I had assumed that their parents were similar. Not so. The closest to middle class was my great-grandfather James Smith, a piano manufacturer employing thirteen men and ten boys in 1871, but reduced from owner to manager by 1891, when, with the introduction of the gramophone, pianos were no longer required in every genteel home. It is possible that my father's parents met because a piano tuner lived with his grandmother as a boarder, and may have worked in his grandfather's piano factory.

My other three great-grandfathers were a builder who eventually made a fortune in property, an upholsterer, and a coachman who kept a boarding house. My mother's parents lived very close to each other and probably met as neighbors. My maternal grandmother, daughter of the coachman, worked as a milliner before her marriage. A photo of her, possibly for her engagement or wedding, since her left hand with her ring is prominently resting on a chair back, shows her wearing a huge hat, probably one of her own creations, wide-brimmed, adorned with what seem to be whole ostrich tails. My father's mother never worked for a wage, but her mother died when she was a teenager and she kept house for her father and working sisters.

Both my grandmothers experienced hardship that they left behind when they married upwardly mobile professionals, and I never heard of them speak of their early lives. They would have had to admit to parents in

9

"trade," and even to working themselves, jeopardizing their middle-class status. The England my grandparents, parents and I grew up in was intensely class-conscious. "All Things Bright and Beautiful," a popular nineteenth-century hymn I sang at school and in church in the 1950s, included a verse (now omitted) that epitomized the general belief:

> *The rich man in his castle,*
> *The poor man at his gate,*
> *God made them high and lowly,*
> *And ordered their estate.*

I learned from my parents to assess people's class status in many ways, by where they lived and went to school, by how they dressed (nothing too bright or gaudy), by their choice of furnishings (no net curtains), by the cars they drove (Fords were out). But most importantly, I learned to define a person's class by how they spoke. Middle class people had no regional cadences, but spoke the clipped speech that used to be called a BBC accent (most BBC presenters don't have one any more). Even now, when it sometimes seems that only I and the royal family talk like that, I still make that calculation as soon as someone speaks. I do my best to discount that automatic assessment, and it isn't even relevant today, when it seems to me few people care about their accents, but I often can't stop myself entirely.

Beyond the accent, there were also words that were taboo if you wanted to be recognized as middle or upper class. Table napkin rather than serviette. Looking glass, not mirror. Perhaps the most common mistake was to say "toilet" instead of "lavatory" or "loo." When my then husband Malcolm and I were living in Italy our six-year-old daughter Jane shook Malcolm in the middle of the night. "There's a nasty insect in the toilet," she announced urgently. He rolled over, opened one eye, said, "It's not a toilet, it's a lavatory," and went back to sleep. The knee-jerk reaction of classism. I dealt with the nasty insect.

When, thanks to the efforts of the piano maker and the builder, my grandfathers acquired the education that enabled them to become professionals, they had to learn the rules of the middle class. They had to be vigilant, to erase any hint of a London accent, to hide anything that might suggest they came from the upper ranks of the working class. This might explain a mystery I uncovered during my research.

My father's last name was Muir-Smith, a name I myself found burdensome, with the hyphenation that made people unsure how to alphabetize it, and its faint hint of snootiness. I was surprised to discover that his family had been plain Smiths until my father was born, when my grandparents suddenly appeared in the census with the hyphen (there was a Scottish Muir ancestor). Why? It's possible my grandfather worked with another Sidney Smith, a fairly common name at the time, so added the Muir to avoid confusion, but I suspect another explanation. My father was born when both his parents were in their early forties, a much longed-for son after thirteen years of marriage and one ten-year-old daughter. Maybe they didn't want their son to carry on the plain, ordinary Smith, so they tacked on the Muir. A name that was almost unique, that suggested distinction, a whiff of aristocracy. A name I was happy to lose and will probably die with my brother.

What didn't die was our class status. My parents were careful to stop us developing Cornish accents, to teach us middle-class ways, to educate us to become professionals. We were not to suffer for their eccentric choices. We didn't.

CHILDHOODS

Sidney, Rose, Kathleen and Eric Muir-Smith, c. 1910

Frank, Rose, Gordon and Joan Handover, 1920s

In the spring of 1962 I was studying for my postgraduate education certificate in London. Once a week my father and I met at lunchtime for a series of short films at the Mermaid, London's newest theater. One day they showed Roman Polanski's debut, *Two Men and a Wardrobe*, and, then, with no break in the darkness, up came the titles for Chaplin's *The Immigrant*, made in 1917. My father nudged me. "I saw this before," he whispered. "In 1917." He was then seven years old, and had gone to the movies by himself in his London suburb.

My father was born in Mortlake, south of the Thames, but by the time he was school age his parents had bought what must then have been a new house across the river in Chiswick. For most of the year he was an only child, as my grandparents had sent his ten-year-old sister Kathleen off to boarding school six months after his birth. She probably resented my father, especially as my grandmother made no secret of her preference for boys. When Kathleen was home she was his babysitter. In a photo of the two of them he has a mop of blond curls (the blond didn't last), contrasting with her long dark ringlets. Neither of them is smiling.

Although my father's mother had longed for a boy, she was not very interested in raising him. When Kathleen wasn't home she let him roam on his own at an early age— including going to the cinema. He went to Ravenscourt School, within walking distance from home, where he was awarded a prize of Charles Kingsley's *The Heroes* when he was nine—I often read the book as a child but didn't notice the inscription until my son pointed it out. He moved on to St. Paul's Boys' School in Hammersmith, the next suburb closer to London, at that time separated from Chiswick by green fields. My father took the bus there, and he enjoyed telling us how there were rival bus companies racing to get to the bus stops first. He loved the thrill and always chose the bus he thought had the most reckless driver.

My father's favorite times were the summer weekends the family spent at their bungalow on the Thames, where he and my grandfather spent most of their time in boats. My father became expert at sailing and in maneuvering a punt, a long flat-bottomed boat propelled by a pole, notoriously difficult to handle. Later he got his own canoe, built in Canada, and unique on the Thames at that time. In the winter the whole family went on long bike rides. Once they cycled to Brighton, on the south coast, and back, about forty miles each way.

When my father moved to St. Paul's School at age fourteen, his greatest pleasure was playing rugby football, or rugger. Some of his team-mates becoming life-long friends. He also did well academically, and passed his

13

School Certificate when he was sixteen. He didn't join his father in the civil service, but went to work as a management trainee with the Dunlop Rubber Company at their head office in central London. He learned time and motion study, and when I was older and read *Cheaper By the Dozen*, about growing up with Frank Gilbreth, one of its pioneers, my father explained to us some of the things he had practiced.

At sixteen, he was already an adult, earning money, independent, although he still lived at home. He bought a second-hand motorcycle, which was mostly in pieces in his parents' kitchen while he worked out how to improve its performance. When he was twenty, once his training was over, he rode it away to live in Birmingham in the English Midlands, where he applied his expertise to supervising women sewing rubber raincoats. He also played rugger for the company's team, where he acquired the nickname "Mif," short for Muir-Smith, a name that stuck for the rest of his life.

Like my father, my mother was the second child of older parents, with a much older sibling, but her childhood was very different. When her brother Gordon was a baby and my grandfather was still serving his apprenticeship as an architect, the family lived in my great-grandfather's boarding house. By the time my mother was born they lived in Kingston, on the Thames outside London, close to my father's birthplace. Then my great-grandfather on my grandfather's side, a builder and property developer, died and left my grandfather a good sum of money that he used to buy a large house in Wimbledon where my mother spent most of her childhood.

Because my grandparents were well off they didn't send my mother to school, but, like many other affluent parents at the time, hired a governess, who was also her chaperone. She had little contact with other children beyond her cousins. Her greatest enjoyment was her private ballet lessons. I still have two professional photographs of her wearing a tutu and poised on her toes. There used to be more ballet pictures, but much later she tried to burn them, a reminder of a past she preferred to forget. One photo has a slight scorch mark where my father rescued it from the flames.

But in 1930 her tranquil if restricted life was interrupted by disaster. At the height of the Great Depression my grandfather lost all the money he had inherited from his father. The big house was more than he could afford on his architect's salary. Debt collectors began to come to the door, and my grandparents were summoned to bankruptcy court. They couldn't cope with the disgrace. Since their son Gordon no longer lived at home, they forced my mother, aged fourteen, to deal with the debt collectors and to go to court on their behalf. The house was foreclosed, and they never owned one again. My mother grew up very fast and lost all respect for her parents. She never told me any of this. Middle-class people did not talk about family disgrace. Once, when she was an old woman, she talked about it to my daughter, otherwise I would never have known.

For my mother the one advantage was that they could no longer afford the governess and she went to St Paul's Girls' school (not at the same time as my father attended St. Paul's Boys'), where she made friends, played sports, and sang in the choir, enjoying every minute of being away from her gloomy home. When she too completed her School Certificate, her parents expected her to be their home companion, but she also needed to earn her living to help the family finances. She apprenticed at a local kindergarten, and found she loved teaching. She also found independence. Her parents couldn't hold her.

HE NEVER LOOKED AT ANOTHER WOMAN

The girl stood slightly behind her parents at their front door, her face partly shaded by a lilac bush. The first thing my father noticed was two large blue-gray eyes peeping shyly from under straight-cut bangs—what English people call a fringe. Next he noticed the long slim legs under her short school uniform tunic, the same as worn by every teenage schoolgirl— box pleats falling from a square-necked yoke and tied around the waist with a broad sash called a girdle. A photo of her at about the same time, her fourteenth year, shows her much as he remembered, her tunic covered by a white jacket.

The girl saw a tall, heavy-set man with dark wavy hair low on his forehead. She recognized his boldly striped black, white and red blazer that marked him as an Old Pauline, an "old boy" (alumnus) of St. Paul's School. He stood next to her brother Gordon, unsmiling, holding out his hand to greet her parents, then her. "Eric Muir-Smith, but everyone calls me Mif,"

he introduced himself, "I work with Gordon at Dunlop's and we room and play rugger together." "Joan," she whispered.

That was how my father met my mother. He was twenty-one, she fourteen. He claimed that from that moment he never looked at another woman. I believe him.

The group made polite conversation over tea, served in the best Minton bone china. Mif learned to talk loudly and clearly to my partially deaf grandmother. In return, she gently but firmly probed his background and education.

"Are you from Birmingham?" asked my grandmother, probably wondering why he didn't have a Midlands accent but spoke the standard English by then associated with the BBC.

"No, I grew up in Chiswick, where my parents still live."

"What does your father do?"

"He's a civil servant with the Post Office."

"I see from your blazer that you went to St. Paul's. Why didn't you go to boarding school like Gordon?"

"My parents wanted to have me at home. My sister was already married, so I was the only child living with them."

Mif tried to talk to Joan, but could get only brief replies. Yes, she went to St. Paul's Girls' School. She had only just started, but had already made friends and discovered she loved field hockey. They briefly exchanged anecdotes about Gustav Holst, the composer who taught music at both the boys' and girls' schools. When Mif auditioned for the school choir, Holst covered his ears and said, "Oh my God." It put Mif off singing for life, but Joan was enjoying the girls' choir.

My grandparents had no idea that Mif was about to disrupt their lives. They would not have believed he could be interested in a shy fourteen-year-old. Work and rugby kept him in Birmingham most weekends, but by the end of the year, 1931, he had taken Joan out at least once, probably in his canoe. In the first of his surviving letters to her he thanked her for coming and added, "The weather added a touch of adventure to the homeward journey."

The letter began, "Dear Joan (I really couldn't call you Miss Handover, could I?). He regretted that, "Outings such as that on Saturday are far too few and far between." He signed himself Eric Muir-Smith, but then said,

17

"Leave it at Mif." He also hinted at possible parental disapproval. "Please remember me to your people," he wrote, "even if our acquaintance is of a somewhat brief nature. Perhaps I looked rather wild on Saturday, but their fears of my not returning you in safety were happily not realised." Their seven-year courtship had begun.

Mif in the 1930s

THE LONG COURTSHIP

In 1937 my father and mother, aged twenty-seven and nearly twenty-one, went to Cornwall alone on a two-week vacation. They were not married. I always knew this in a back-of-the-mind kind of way, but only recently have I been struck by their enormous daring.

They were driven to it by my grandmother's implacable opposition to their courtship. My grandmother, whom I called Dandan, did not like my father. Most parents would be anxious when a man nearly seven years older than their fifteen-year-old daughter started to take her out on dates, but Dandan's antipathy was also grounded in fears for her own future. She didn't want her daughter dating anyone. Middle-class Victorians like my grandparents expected a daughter to stay at home and look after them in their old age. My mother was their only daughter, and my grandmother's deafness kept her isolated and dependent. She knew that when she had to send my mother to school she would lose some control, but my father was a far greater threat to her expectations.

The other issue was my father himself. He played rugby with abandon, and often appeared at my grandparents' door with a black eye or cuts and bruises on his face and ears. He had fixed his motorcycle to drive

19

considerably faster than the manufacturer intended. He sometimes came to pick her up after rugger games smelling of beer. He was moody, sometimes sullen, and not good at small talk. He was certainly not the ideal suitor.

Dandan tried forbidding my mother from seeing my father, but it didn't work. After dealing with their financial crash my mother had little respect for her mother's opinion. She went out with my father whenever he was in London, possibly secretly, pretending she was meeting her school friend June. The year after she left school my father moved back to London to work and they began to meet more often, at rugger matches in the winter and on river outings in the summer.

I can trace my parents' courtship through their letters. My mother kept all of my father's and a few of her own in an old box file that I never saw while she was alive. Like her ballet pictures, she tried to destroy them, as if determined to erase all evidence of her life. When she sold her house to go live with my brother, he only just managed to stop her from throwing out a drawer full of family photos. She once told me that she saw no point in looking back, so perhaps she didn't want her children to either. At the end of her life, while living in my sister-in-law's residential home, she asked one of the staff to burn the letters, but the staff member, uncomfortable with the request, took them to my sister-in-law, who eventually gave them to me.

The letters, all in their original almost-square envelopes, begin in 1931, when my mother was fifteen, and end in 1938, the day before their wedding. My father's handwriting becomes looser as time passes, while my mother's matures a little. The stamps document the royal drama of the 1930s—first King George V, including one for his silver jubilee, then later one postcard with the stamp of the disgraced Edward VIII shortly before his abdication, then on to the coronation of George VI. The addresses on the early ones also log my grandparents' search for a permanent home after they lost their money—they lived in four different places in three years.

The letters show my father's growing impatience with my grandmother's interference. In one, apologizing for missing my mother's birthday while on a sailing trip, he attached a piece he labeled for her eyes only, perhaps suggesting her mother had read his letters. "I've jolly well got to see you next week sometime. I was absolutely fed up when I left you on

Saturday. That was why I didn't wait until your train went.... I don't think my fed uppedness has passed away yet, and it won't until you get back."

At that time my mother, aged eighteen, was about to escape for three weeks' holiday with her school friend June and June's parents. There she could write freely. She began her letters, "Mif darling," and signed herself "Absolutely all yours." She described watching for his letters, and dreamed of a holiday together, "but I cannot help thinking of the difficulties of parents etc. But still it has just GOT to be." Hardly reassuring to my father were her tales of a medical student picking up the two girls on the beach and a doctor giving them rides in his Renault coupe and buying them chocolate. Yet she insisted that while she was having a good time, it was " only in an innocent way, and I am not likely to do anything else, as I find that—well, I get no fun out of it."

My father was also able to reply more ardently than he could risk when she was home. He opened his first letter with a long quote from the Song of Solomon beginning, "O my dove, that art in the clefts of the rock, in the secret places of the stairs, let me see thy countenance," and wrote of a "sense of emptiness which comes on me when I'm not very busy and even when I am. You're the culprit, darling." He told her, "I am very good nowadays and go straight home after Rugger. Last winter was a bit too gay. Besides, I didn't know you so well."

He too imagined a holiday together. He wrote of "a very tenuous idea in my mind that we might spend a holiday together one day—even next year," but added the cynical, "Provided always that we don't come to hate each other like poison in the meanwhile." Two letters later he was more practical, suggesting they could go away "with my people as chaperones as a start." The previous month they had made a small beginning by spending a few days at New Milton, on the south coast of England. They were not alone, but his mother, with what were surely advanced ideas for her age, had already "expressed surprise that you and I didn't stop on at New Milton together."

The following year, 1935, my mother went back to Devon with June and family, after a year of battles with her mother over her refusal to give up my father. Only half-jokingly, in a letter to my father for his birthday, my mother complained of his "childish & not so childish habits. E.g. making rude noises, biting your fingers, maltreating me, and behaving in a

21

childish manner when crossed." Yet she addressed him as "My darling," and wrote of a time "when you're fat and you snore & browbeat me, and I am an old hag with millions of kids all round me. Perhaps we shan't know each other. That would be worse!" She ended, "O Mif I do wish that I could change into your penknife or something, then I should always be with you."

That my grandmother was doing her best to prevent. She fought back by insisting on a chaperone when my mother and father went out. My father's patience snapped. In July 1935 he wrote,

I don't know how to write this letter but I feel I must.

As far as I can see to go on as we are will only lead to a lot of unhappiness, most of which will descend on you, as your mother despite her protestations quite obviously won't consider your feelings when they conflict with her scruples. At the same time it seems quite plain that she will not alter her views and it is no good my submitting to her, as unreasoned opposition such as this always makes me go into a black rage, as I did yesterday, I'm afraid.

I have been puzzling my head all yesterday and today, and am now too fed up to see any way out but to call it a day until you become of such an age that you can call yourself your own, unless you find yourself someone more amenable in the meanwhile.

It will be said that all this has been brought about through my not getting my own way, and it's true to the extent that in this case, I think, as I have always said, that the only way not to make a mess of a marriage is for the persons concerned to see as much of one another as possible, not as little, and that under fixed conditions, time limits & chaperonage.

I'm sorry, darling, but I feel more strongly about this than anything else, & if your mother persists in winning as you say she always does, then there is no other way.

Yet he ended by suggesting they meet the following day.

He wrote petulant letters to her on holiday. He still addressed her as "Darling," but told her, "I was at one time determined not to write to you at all," and ended, "On Tuesday night (2 am) I dreamt that you had fallen under a bus and I had to fish you out. I laughed like hell." In another letter he was even more bitter: "I suppose you're making the best of things, having a good time and writing glowing accounts to your mother so that she can say 'I told you so.'" But a brief note in December ("Darling, Wednesday ten to seven. Hope you're better love Mif") and another the following year ("Ten past seven. No motor car") show they were still meeting. Letters were risky, since my grandmother might read them, but they could talk on the phone, which she rarely heard and never answered. In the album my father assembled much later, a whole page of photographs of my mother dated 1936, mostly out on the River Thames with no one else present, shows that they spent time alone unchaperoned. By then my mother must have been a practiced liar.

My mother's twenty-first birthday, when she would be legally free of her mother's restrictions, was on August 21, 1937, nearly seven years after their courtship began. My grandmother no longer had any influence on her. My father was buying her clothes and paying for hair styling. In a letter signed Pigface and containing a check, he wrote: "Dearest, Kindly go and buy 1 coat and skirt at Swan and Edgars. Also, if you would like to, have your hair done a la Marie."

This time they seriously planned to go away alone. Perhaps it was not as daring as I imagine since going away unchaperoned seems to have been acceptable among my father's friends. In one letter he wrote, "Every bloke I know seems to have gone away with some girl, mostly one whom they've known for about a fortnight." However, I cannot believe my grandparents knew what my mother was planning. She probably told them she going away with June and her parents again. Instead she and my father left for Cornwall on Friday August 13, 1937, eight days before her birthday.

PORT QUIN

One of the narrowest Cornish lanes leads to Port Quin, an almost secret inlet on Cornwall's north coast. The lane opens out abruptly into a small car park at the head of the narrow bay. At high tide a stream trickles into the salt water. When the tide is out, a small sandy beach is surrounded by rocks containing tide pools, home to shrimp, tiny fish, and sea anemones. Tall gunmetal granite cliffs, one of them pierced by an inviting cave, hem the bay. From the car park a visitor can hardly see the outlet into the Atlantic, angled in such a way that the strong local undertow flows past without entering the inlet. Port Quin is one of the few north coast beaches where it is safe to swim at low tide.

To the right of the car park a row of fishermen's cottages clings halfway up the cliff. Today they are holiday rentals, but tradition has it that

24

its women abandoned Port Quin when the entire fishing fleet was lost in a storm. Another version maintains that everyone left when the pilchards stopped swarming just outside the bay. Whatever the reason, the cottages were deserted by the 1940s, when I first remember them. On the other side, on a small hill perched on the cliff, is one of England's smallest castles, Doyden Castle, a granite building with a crenellated top and two lonely Victorian gothic windows facing the bay. Once famous for a local businessman's wild parties in the safe seclusion of a very private place, when I knew it Doyden had a second life as a tearoom few managed to find. Now it is more vacation rentals.

The Port Quin cliffs are part of the British National Trust's Cornish cliff path, providing views of the Atlantic waves crashing onto the cliffs outside the bay. Walkers who climb up past the cottages or go beyond the Doyden to the headland can see the sweep of the coast for miles. The cliff tops are covered with yellow gorse and purple heather in season, mingled with tufts of small pink flowers we called thrift. On a sunny day the mingling of the soft colors of the flowers and grass and the purple-blue of the sea provide an unforgettable visual delight.

In the middle of August 1937, alone and unmarried, my parents drove into Port Quin and booked at a bed and breakfast in the cottage nearest the car park. There are so many things I never thought to ask them. One was why they chose to go there. My mother had never been to Cornwall, my father only on rugger tours with the Old Paulines. Every spring he packed his kit, climbed on the bus, and spent two happy weeks wrestling with large Cornish miners in the inevitable mud, patching up his bruises and scratches, and ending up every night in the pub. My father was rarely nostalgic, but rugger could bring it out. He occasionally took my brother and me to watch the Old Paulines play. I remember them as wet, windy days. We watched with feigned interest while he regaled us with stories of nighttime pranks and drunken camaraderie.

But the rugger tours were always farther west and mainly inland. The group would never have gone to Port Quin. I suspect my parents were heading for the resort areas a little further down the coast but noticed a sign for the bed and breakfast directing them off the main road and were

25

intrigued. The setting was idyllic, the peace and privacy just what they had in mind.

I have only two photos of their first visit. In one they are sitting on a rock at the edge of the cliff near the harbor entrance. He has his arm around her, and they are looking quite serious, but perhaps they just got caught unawares by the timing mechanism on my father's prized Zeiss camera. My mother's left hand is hidden, so I can't tell if she wore a fake wedding ring. When I took the photo out of the album to scan it, I saw that my father had written "Our rocks" on the back.

The other photo shows a large sandcastle, somewhat like a haystack. My father told me it was my mother's twenty-first birthday cake, a symbol of her freedom from my grandmother's control. It must have taken some time to build and I wonder if they danced around it. My father wasn't much of a dancer, but he might have made an exception.

MARRIAGE

Shortly after they returned from their Port Quin holiday, my mother met my father in central London. He was in one of the silent grumpy moods she had become used to—they were often connected to her parents' disapproval. He said nothing as she got off the train and they boarded a bus. Still not a word as the bus stopped outside a jeweler's in Regent Street. They got off and went in, and at last he spoke. "Choose a ring, whatever you like best." She picked a sapphire surrounded by small diamonds. Their engagement was at last official.

After that my father's letters became much more cheerful, full of planned purchases for their life together, often enclosing checks and telling her where to shop. In November they were looking for a table and cabinet, probably antiques since he described one table as wobbly. He agonized, "I am plunged into the depths of gloom. We can't possibly afford what we want," yet shortly afterwards he sent her a check and suggested they meet to look at china and glass in upscale Harrods. He took her out to dinner, where she ate only the plainest food, drank water, and always asked for an apple for dessert.

Her parents at least tolerated his presence at their house. One photo my father took early that year shows a snowman they built in my grandparents' garden. In another he has a black eye and some gauze on his cheek, but is cheerfully hugging my mother. Another caught my mother, her parents, and their dog on a country walk. But the letters show that the irritation persisted. In my father's very last letter, written two days before their wedding, and enclosing money to pay the church, the last line reads, "Sorry I was a pig last night. I was dead and your ma always gets my goat."

They must have tried not to worry about the world outside. In March Hitler ordered German troops into Austria. The following month he demanded that Czechoslovakia, a country only twenty years old and with few defenses, cede to Germany the German-speaking area called the Sudetenland. The future of Europe was murky.

My parents married on June 4, 1938. My mother wore a simple white lace dress, high to the neck with long sleeves, so classic in style that a quarter-century later I wore it at my own wedding. The clouds of her silk veil almost hid her carefully waved short hair. She smiles happily in all the photos, while my father, handsome in formal morning dress, seems more restrained. My mother was a wolf cub (cub scout) leader, and her troop formed a guard of honor outside the church, holding long poles to make an arch just high enough for my tall father to stoop only slightly.

The wedding reception was on the lawn in the garden of my mother's parents' rented house, an idyllic background of trees and shrubs in full bloom. The English weather smiled. Not so my grandmothers. In the wedding photos the best they can manage is a slightly self-conscious smirk under their wide-brimmed hats. My grandfathers look jollier, but, with their white hair and bald heads, they appear too old to be fathers of the bride and groom, reminding me that both my parents were late babies, born when their parents were well over thirty.

Nana, my father's mother, had befriended my mother during the long courtship, surprising, since she notoriously didn't like girls. However, she loved to make trouble. At the wedding reception she told several guests, "She's only marrying him for his money." I used to laugh when telling this story, saying that neither bride nor groom had any. But when I think about it now, I am letting my later experiences with Nana prevent me from being fair to her. Just as my mother's parents were not happy that their daughter was marrying a beer-swilling rugby player seven years older than she was, my father's parents had probably hoped for a daughter-in-law with a little money settled on her, not the younger child of an impoverished architect who couldn't even pay for his daughter's dresses. Their minimal smiles reflected this reality.

Also, as the letters are witness, my father *did* have money. He was twenty-eight years old, had been working for Dunlop's for thirteen years, and was poised for an upper managerial position. He lived simply, and clearly had savings. Before the wedding he budgeted £150 for furniture, nearly £7,000 or $12,000, at today's retail values. While I don't think this mattered to my mother, and she lived happily in considerable poverty later, my father was indeed a "catch."

For their honeymoon my parents returned to the bed and breakfast at Port Quin. My father snapped a picture of them together on "their rocks," so similar to the one he took the year before that I have to peer at them closely to see that they are in separate years. In other photos they are exploring a local farm. Prophetic?

Their happiness seemed to be matched by better news in Europe. In September the British Prime Minister, Neville Chamberlain, met Hitler in Munich and came back with an agreement that he called "Peace with honour."

Everyone wanted to believe him.

29

TRUBY KING

I was born ten months after my parents' wedding, a gap I counted anxiously as a teenager. I like to think I was conceived in Port Quin, making me a Cornishwoman, proud of the county of my childhood. It is just possible, since their honeymoon lasted two weeks and I was born late. My poor mother was in labor for two days before I finally appeared at eleven thirty at night, still time to make me an April Fool's baby. I selfishly used to wish that my mother had held off for another half hour.

My birthplace was a rented house in a small town outside Birmingham, where my father worked. When my mother told her mother that she was pregnant, my grandmother replied, "I am very sorry." Yet she was there for the birth of the first grandchild she'd actually seen, since my older cousin Penny was born in South Africa. A photo shows her standing in the back garden with a rather grim expression, holding me wrapped in a bulky knitted shawl. I can see that my hair is already problematic, too fine and sticking up in the wrong places.

The following August my parents took me on holiday to Port Quin. Of all the family photographs scattered haphazardly in the top drawer of a small antique tallboy, the ones that embarrassed me most as a teenager were a series of me sitting on my baby potty in front of my parents' car, a small Fiat (called Fifi) with doors hinged in the center so they opened like bat wings. Now I realize that the odd thing is that I was on the potty at all, since I was only five months old.

There was a reason. My mother's doctor had recommended she follow the baby regime prescribed by Dr. Frederic Truby King. Truby King was a New Zealander who trained as a doctor at Edinburgh University, then returned to New Zealand to become superintendent of a mental hospital. He was an avid proponent of breast-feeding, and published *The Feeding and Care of Children* in 1913, still the most used baby manual in 1930s Britain. In a book about his methods his daughter described the "perfectly happy and beautiful Truby King baby" as "a joy from morning to night," and the mother as "not overworked or worried, simply because she knows that by following the laws of nature, combined with common sense, baby will not do

otherwise than thrive." *

King's version of the laws of nature doesn't seem very natural. He recommended feeding every four hours, and leaving the baby untouched in between, however much she or he cried. Night feeds should be discontinued as quickly as possible. Mothers should limit cuddling and holding the baby to ten minutes per day, the baby should be in a separate room from the beginning, and should spend several hours outside, whatever the weather. Perhaps that is why I was outside with my grandmother so soon after my birth.

My mother was young and had little experience with babies. She trusted her own doctor, a woman, who recommended King's regime. However, I was certainly not the serene child King's daughter described. When I was less than two months old my parents moved to London and rented an apartment. I cried constantly for two weeks before my father devised a contraption so he could rock my cradle with his foot while reading the paper. Probably even that small intervention was a breach of Truby King's rules.

King also had rigid rules about toilet training. He emphasized the importance of regular bowel movements and recommended that mothers hold babies over the potty from the beginning. Clearly my mother tried, and she may have been successful, since photos taken when I was approximately eighteen months old show no trace of the telltale bulkiness of cloth nappies (diapers). In one of my favorites, where my mother and I are leaning over a gate at the Port Quin farm, I appear to be wearing panties without nappies.

---

* Mary Truby King, *Mothercraft* (Melbourne: Whitcombe &Tombs, 1934)

My mother believed she was doing her best for me, but later she rarely spoke about Truby King, and when she did it was not with gratitude. A young mother followed her doctor's advice, but it gave her little pleasure. I suspect that in the war years when we were alone at home she cuddled me close, as comfort for us both. When my brother was born nearly four years later she abandoned King's principles, did not let him cry, and kept him in cloth nappies until he was toilet trained.

I now wonder whether my mother's adherence to King's rules was partly responsible for my rather distant relationship with her. Although many people, sometimes total strangers, confided in her, and she was a successful marriage guidance counselor, I never told her anything personal. I even kept my first period from her for a month, when I had to tell her because I had run out of the emergency supplies she had thoughtfully provided in advance. It wasn't the kind of thing we talked about.

Yet my brother's experience suggests that perhaps Truby King was not the main culprit. Recently he told me that he didn't feel he knew my mother at all. We were not a demonstrative family. I rarely saw my parents hug or kiss, although their mutual respect and easy companionship showed that they deeply loved each other. They didn't hug us much either. We all embraced the reticent middle-class culture of 1940s Britain, and later my brother's and my distance from our parents was aggravated by our absence at boarding schools.

WAR

On our 1939 Port Quin holiday, the photo shows my mother sitting tranquilly on the bed and breakfast steps with me in her arms. The sun is out and everyone is smiling. But while we were there Hitler and Stalin signed their non-aggression pact. Two days later Britain allied with Poland, and declared war when Germany attacked Poland on September 1. We left for Port Quin at peace and returned at war.

Yet for the first year war made little difference. People called it the "Phoney War," and the British government, led by Neville Chamberlain, discussed coming to terms with Hitler. In the summer of 1940 we were on our way to Port Quin again—there are more potty photos. We still had a car, and the petrol (gas) to run it. My father could take time off his important job to go on holiday. He may not have been there all the time, since in a photograph of him and me sitting in a field, he is incongruously dressed in a suit and tie, probably about to take the train back to the world of work and war. Cornwall was still a refuge, but a temporary one. Soon there would be no car, no petrol, no holidays.

In the spring of 1940 Hitler launched his Blitzkrieg, occupying Denmark, Norway, and the Netherlands. Britain had to choose, fight or become a German satellite. Winston Churchill replaced the pacifist Neville Chamberlain as Prime Minister and prepared for battle. The prospect looked grim. In May the British army had to be rescued from the beaches of Dunkirk, leaving much of their equipment behind, seriously limiting their ability to fight a land war. France fell to Hitler in June. The war in the air known as the Battle of Britain was beginning and bombs started dropping on London in September.

In the summer of 1939 we were living in the London apartment where, thanks to Truby King, I had cried for two weeks. My father had changed his job. In 1939, about the time I was born, Dunlop's offered him a promotion to work in their Indian company. My parents did not want to go to India. Perhaps my father's pre-war socialism—his "pink phase" he called it—made him uncomfortable with the prospect of life as an expatriate imperialist. Perhaps they simply didn't want to live in a tropical climate. Whatever the reason, they refused the promotion and I grew up in an island tenuously holding out against Nazi domination rather than in an uneasy subcontinent chafing against British rule.

My father moved to be works manager at P. B. Cow, a suburban London company with large military contracts for the production of gas masks. After poison gas had been used extensively in World War I, people feared that if there were another war, gas would be dropped from the air in bombs, so even before Britain declared war Parliament passed a law requiring everyone to have a gas mask. I remember my child's version, its grotesque shape vaguely reminiscent of Mickey Mouse, or so the makers wanted children to believe.

The P.B. Cow factory also manufactured life jackets (known as Mae Wests for their large chests after inflation), essential for pilots forced to bale out over water. Another P.B. Cow product was an inflatable rubber life raft (dinghy) dropped to rescue a pilot afloat in his Mae West. My father's job was essential to the war effort, so he was not drafted into the army. At twenty-nine, he was over the age range of twenty to twenty-two normally called up, but all men up to the age of forty-one were technically liable. I wonder if this was a factor in his decision to take the position.

He did not stay long with P. B. Cow. He moved to another company, RFD, in Godalming, a town southeast of London. RFD manufactured barrage balloons, huge inflatables tethered over major cities. The balloons themselves were useful in obscuring pilots' vision, but the essential parts were the tether wires that made it impossible for dive-bombers to get close to the ground without running into them. My father's main responsibility was the design and manufacture of specially-designed rubber dinghies to be carried under planes and easily dropped to rescue pilots and crews. Winning the war in the air was vital to Britain's survival, so rescuing trained pilots was essential. My father worked closely with a civilian, Uffa Fox, well known for his successful designs of small boats but also for his temperamental character. Lord Beaverbrook, Churchill's Minister of Aircraft Production, visited the factory frequently and my father greatly admired his business sense and emphasis on efficiency.

The London Blitz was not a factor in my father's job changes. By May of 1940 we had taken temporary refuge in Leatherhead, west of London, with my godmother, a friend from my father's rugger days. From there my father could commute to RFD while they looked for somewhere permanent to live. While we were there my godmother's husband was in the force evacuated from Dunkirk. When he returned my mother remembered that he talked for twenty-four hours without a break, a searing account of personal trauma.

Shortly afterwards, when I was one year old, despite the huge uncertainty that loomed over everyone's lives, my parents bought a house in a village about ten miles from RFD. It was a grand purchase for a newly married couple, and showed my father's earning power at age thirty. I have no idea what they paid—clearly not the £1.3 million the house sold for in 2004—but it must have been more than the value of my father's parents' suburban villa, and perhaps comparable to the large Wimbledon house my mother's parents lost when my grandfather's finances crashed.

I am surprised my parents decided to live in East Clandon rather than in Godalming, the closest town to the factory. Perhaps in 1940 they still hoped the war would not prevent my father from making the journey home every night. Perhaps they simply fell in love with the place, and knew they had to have it, as my husband and I felt when we first saw our apartment outside Florence many years later. But soon after they moved in, it became almost impossible for my father to drive home. To prevent German pilots from orientating themselves by looking down, the government imposed strict petrol rationing and a total blackout at night (including car headlights), making most inessential journeys impractical. This was the beginning of my parents' long separation, nearly five years of hurried and infrequent meetings when my father could get away from a factory operating around the clock.

Now the war was real.

THE OLD HOUSE

I lean over to smell the flowers, the hem of my smocked dress rising up behind me as in so many children's book illustrations. My father lies on the lawn, holding my hands ready to raise me in the air on his feet. I run with the careful abandon of a two-year-old across the lawn towards the house. Holding a long broom, I earnestly sweep leaves with total concentration. In these photos I am happy, free, in the first home where I could do these things.

It was called the Old House. It stood on the edge of public land, called the Common, in the village of East Clandon, about twenty-five miles outside London. Built in the sixteenth century, Shakespeare's time, with eighteenth-century additions, it had a typical Tudor exterior, a wooden frame ("wattle") filled in with "daub," a mixture of clay, hair and straw. It probably had a thatched roof once, replaced by tile when the addition was built.

Surrounding the house was a typical English garden, actually several gardens. On one side close to the road, out of sight from the house windows, a tall yew hedge with clipped topiary hid a large vegetable garden, a sizeable barn, and our air raid shelter. By the house was a rock garden with a clump of catnip where our cat sunned herself in summer. There's a photo of me, aged two, sitting on the steps leading to the garden, naked except for my panties, with the catnip behind me, talking to our gardener, clearly a necessary person to keep up such a large space. Near the barn were several apple trees, including a Cox's Orange Pippin, my mother's and my favorite. At the back of the house the formal garden gave way to a large lawn surrounded by shrubs and rose bushes. There I could run freely, shielded from the world by a substantial hedge.

The front door opened to a central hall that we used as the dining room. On the right was the kitchen, the site of a memorable fight with my mother. I sat in my high chair, a round pottery dish with illustrations from *Peter Rabbit* in front of me, refusing to eat my tasteless codfish, while my mother vowed that I would not get down from my chair until I did. I didn't like fish, and I also wanted to win the battle of wills. Wartime food rations were meager so my mother was especially anxious to have me eat what there was. I screamed, cried, sulked, but she stood there, implacable. Eventually she won. I ate the stuff.

Down a step on the other side of the hall from the kitchen was the comfortable sunny sitting room. The step down was the site of a major disaster. I loved to "help," as the broom photo shows, and I once pushed a tea trolley containing my mother's Minton bone china tea set over the step, with the predictable result. A couple of teacups, delicate white with a blue flower pattern, survived the catastrophe and for me always carried a faint feeling of guilt, although I don't think I was punished at the time. My mother's distress was enough. Curiously, when I chose my own china as a wedding present from my godmother, I also picked a very similar pattern of white with blue flowers.

Up the stairs from the entrance hall were three bedrooms and a bathroom, my parents' room at the end over the sitting room, mine next to it with my barred cot (crib) and my stuffed animals, and a spare room at the other end. Reminiscing about his childhood in East Clandon on its web site, a man who lived through the war in the village remembered that there

38

was no electricity, and I cannot see any wires to the house in the photos I have. We must have used candles and oil lamps, practice for our future on the farm.

Outside the protective hedge was The Common, a stretch of open land with free grazing for village residents. There we tethered our roan pony Strawberry, who pulled the two-wheeled open trap, our main means of transportation once petrol rationing started to bite one year into the war. Our car, Fifi the Fiat, veteran of the Port Quin journeys, disappeared from my life in 1940. Maybe my father kept her at work, but she would have been useless without enough petrol to get him home.

Our world shrank to walking distance. A short walk around the corner was a row of cottages originally built for workers on the local grand estate. Mr. and Mrs. Martin, a childless couple, lived in the closest one, and were my babysitters when my mother helped out at the farm across The Common, her wartime contribution. The Martins, seemingly about the same age as my grandparents, were unfailingly kind and always seemed to have a good supply of rationed sweets (candy), saving their share for me.

My best friends my own age were twins, Judy and Mary Allen, who lived in an upstairs apartment in the village center. Judy was a terror, always into mischief. One day she cut Mary's hair off, leaving her own untouched. I preferred the quieter Mary. Even then I didn't like trouble.

If my parents thought of East Clandon as a refuge, they were wrong. Shortly after we moved there, some Canadian soldiers came and parked a huge anti-aircraft gun on The Common. As they were setting it up, my mother went over to ask when they were going to fire it, since she wanted to make sure I was not close by when they did. The sergeant in charge replied kindly, "Ma'am, we are only practicing assembling the gun. If we fired it here your little old cottage would fall down."

The hedge, the topiary, the Cox's Orange Pippins, the lawns were my security from the dangerous world beyond the garden gate. But they were not protection enough. Above us was the air.

THE BAG MEMORY

I still see it clearly. A hand, long and slim, ringless, reaches for a white paper bag. The bag is one of a bunch looped on a piece of white string hanging from a nail tacked to the side of a brown wooden shelf. Connected to this mental snapshot is another picture, much more blurry, of railings (metal, I think), with my feet on them. An elephant's trunk reaches for pieces of a square roll—what the British call a bun. This scene has sound; my father is telling me that this elephant can shave a man.

The hand in my memory is in the shop at Paignton Zoo, and its owner is about to fill the bag with buns. I know more than I see. I am two-and-a-half years old, and both my parents are there with me. I must have added other visual details later since I remember them in black and white, not color. They probably come from one of those photographs my parents kept in a drawer, the ones my father always meant to organize. How else could I step outside my mind's eye to see myself in the zippered furry jumpsuit my father had someone make especially at the factory where he worked? Modeled after those worn by Battle of Britain pilots and occasionally by a very rotund Winston Churchill when he visited airfields, it had an ominous name—my siren suit, conjuring up warnings of air raids. I think I was also wearing a woolen pointed cap like a pixie's. I used to know the elephant's name, but that detail has faded. Female, I think, perhaps Rosie.

Why do I remember this isolated occasion, my earliest childhood memory? Why the hand, why my feet on the railing? What keeps these images in my conscious mind seventy years later when it has buried so much else? Were buns so hard to get in wartime Britain that I remember this one, which I did not eat, as I remember my first banana or taste of ice cream? I doubt it—would we give rationed or scarce food to an elephant? All I can say for sure is that I *do* remember. Images so clear of such an inconsequential event must be genuine, and I suspect that they are the random flotsam of an experience unprecedented in my short existence.

40

In that fall of 1941, two years into World War II, I knew that war was something to fear. My mother later told me that the smattering of child psychology she had acquired in her curtailed training as a kindergarten teacher made her worry about the effects of fear on me. We had an air raid shelter in the garden, but in the nightly air raids I dimly recollect her carrying me downstairs to sleep under the dining-room table, a more familiar and supposedly safe place. Where did she go? She would not have left me to go outside to the shelter. Maybe she crouched under the stairs in the total darkness of the blackout, a lone adult, listening to the muffled explosions, waiting for the all-clear siren. Perhaps I sensed *her* fear—certainly her attempt to shield me from it did not work. I still recall my recurring nightmares from that time of my barred crib being slowly lowered into the dark recesses of a coal mine full of leering, dirty men, a terrifying place from which I woke screaming. The fear of the nightmare was almost worse than the dream itself. I dreaded bedtime.

By day it was easier to forget the war, but days too had their perils, especially when the main roads were blocked by seemingly endless convoys of huge, noisy vehicles with what I saw as menacing poker-like protuberances. For some lost reason I became afraid of anything with three wheels, unfortunately a common but unpredictable sight as steamrollers repaired roads torn up by tanks. My mother had to endure my inexplicable screaming fits, since even if I could have understood my fear I hadn't the words to express it. Like so many other things it was nameless, part of normal life. To my parents, life was abnormal, unpredictable, with no assured happy ending, unlike the fairy stories my mother read to me from a children's book she stood in line to buy, printed on rationed paper.

Although my father was only a few miles away we saw him almost as little as if he had been fighting. His all-female work force worked around the clock in eight-hour shifts, and when my father wasn't supervising he spent the night at the factory watching for fire. He never talked about it, but years later I found an engraved watch he had been given, a reward for throwing firebombs off the factory roof with his hands. The only incident I ever remember him mentioning was a works party where someone spiked the punch, and he had to get several passed-out women home in the blackout. I wonder if my mother worried about him, a man surrounded by so many women? He must have worried about us as he listened to and saw the bombs drop every night. He managed to get home for my second birthday, bringing a balloon he had made from a spare piece of rubber at the factory. Balloons I knew only from storybooks, since there were no materials for such trifles in wartime, and when I saw it lying in state in an armchair, an alluring if lurid orange, I was so excited I bit it. I have hated popping balloons ever since.

My mother's life had different tensions. She had the more mindless tasks of housework and looking after me, which may have allowed too much time to worry. I suspect she took on war work on the local farm not just to help as best she could, but also to get some companionship, although at first it can hardly have taken her mind off events. Our village was on the front line before London in Hitler's expected invasion, and my mother was the community's invasion secretary. She was twenty-five years old. She made arrangements to have children taken to a safe place, and made labels for everyone in the village so bodies could be identified quickly. She took literally Churchill's rousing speech, "We will never surrender." Quite recently my brother told me that she once confided to him that she had contemplated killing me if the Germans arrived, since she had heard they did terrible things to children. She never told me that, but I don't doubt she could have done it. She never flinched from what she decided was necessary. Of course the threatened invasion never came, but the bombing continued as enemy planes going to and from London flew directly overhead, jettisoning their bombs on us if they were attacked. Sleep was fitful and restless.

On that day at the zoo my parents were probably trying to forget that the war was going badly. Hitler controlled most of Europe and was advancing in Russia, and Japan had occupied parts of the British Empire and threatened India. It was before Pearl Harbor, Britain was alone, and seemed likely to become an offshore satellite of a Nazi continent.

Much later I asked my mother why we were at that particular zoo a long way from where we lived. She told me my father had a few days off, and they had tried to get as far from the bombing as they could, staying with friends in this western seaside resort, an unlikely target for air raids. It was one of the extremely rare days when we all escaped the war. My parents had been married less than four years, but their love lasted a lifetime and this brief interlude must have been poignant pleasure. I may have sensed the relief from tension, the short interval when we could enjoy ourselves without the unpredictable threat of the siren, the sinister whine of a night raid, the ever-present context of fear that I shared with my parents, however imperfect my comprehension. It must also have been one of the longest times I spent with my father in the six years of war. Perhaps this is why I do not see or hear my mother in my memory. I was there, in a safe haven, with my father, in the suit he had brought me, listening to him.

"Hold out your hand flat…" I raise my eyes from my feet to the soft pink lips waving hopefully in front of me and offer my piece of bun.

THREE

Another memory.

I'm in the garden of the Old House, running around a tree stump near the hedge, slightly dizzy. I'm wearing a dark blue dress with small white dots. I'm thinking, "I am three." It's my birthday, though I don't know what that means.

Now I realize that it meant the year when the shell of my protected life within the enclosed space of the Old House began to crack. Somewhere around my birthday I got sick, nauseous and throwing up. The doctor diagnosed jaundice (hepatitis). I was put on a strict diet to protect my young liver. No milk, only one boiled egg a week. I lost my taste for milk, but longed for the forbidden eggs, still one of my favorite foods. Nausea became my nighttime companion for many years, although I rarely actually threw up. Even today I will go to huge lengths not to vomit.

The war was going a little better in 1942. After Pearl Harbor, the United States was now Britain's ally, and after Hitler invaded Russia Stalin's army was fighting Germany in the East. I too had turning points. In September my mother decided I needed to spend more time with other children. I was to go to nursery school.

My mother's first choice was a small school run by Anglican nuns in the village. There were few Anglican convents and nuns were a rare sight, so this was an unusual choice, and the school's walking distance from our home may have influenced my mother's decision. I had never seen a nun and something about them, probably their all-enveloping dress and covered heads, terrified me. Perhaps the black habits reminded me of the people in my coal-mine nightmares. I screamed when my mother tried to drop me off, and after a few days she gave up. I suspect it was not the first victory of my cosseted life.

Instead I went to the local day nursery in the village with my twin friends Judy and Mary Allen. We played all day, which was fun, but I was already a budding intellectual and expected more. I somehow knew that you learned things at school, and that was what I wanted, not playing house

44

with the meager toy selection. However, it was convenient and still close enough to walk for my increasingly pregnant mother.

Right at the end of my third year, ten days before my fourth birthday, I stopped being an only child. I remember one of my parents, probably my father, telling me that they didn't want to have another child until they could be sure she or he wouldn't grow up under Hitler. However, when much later I asked my mother about that, she replied, "Oh no, no, it was just that we never saw each other." Neither explanation really works; when my brother was conceived in mid-1942 the war's outcome was still very uncertain, and clearly they *did* see each other at least once! Perhaps on their wedding anniversary, which would fit with my brother's birth.

In the 1940s almost all babies were born at home. On the day my brother was born I went to spend the day with Mr. and Mrs. Martin. My father was home, and when he came to fetch me he said,

"There's a surprise for you at home."

"What is it? What is it?" I asked excitedly, holding his hand as I skipped down the lane past the spring daffodils.

"Wait and see," he said.

I rushed into the house. Nothing downstairs, no present, no sign of a special treat. Upstairs I found my mother in bed, proudly holding a bundle with a small red face—my baby brother Michael. I was hugely disappointed. A baby was useless to me and clearly a rival for my mother's attention. In the few photos of the two of us together when Michael was a baby I am not smiling, although I am sure I was asked to. In one, when we are in the pony trap with my mother, I have a mulish expression.

The following autumn I went to what I regarded as a proper school where we had formal lessons. I looked forward to them, since I knew I wanted to learn. The school was in Guildford, the nearest large town, so my mother had to take me there and back on a bus each day, a trial since she had to bring my squirming brother.

After nearly four years of my mother's undivided attention I was a spoiled child, used to getting my own way and unwilling to try anything I might fail at, a trait that has stayed with me. On the first day of school I sat stubbornly at the edge of the room, refusing to march to music or skip (jump rope) with the other children because they were things I had never done. The principal, a middle-aged motherly woman, called me into her office.

"Why won't you march and skip with the other boys and girls?" she asked gently.

"Because I don't know how," I mumbled.

"Well, you won't learn to do it unless you try."

The principal must have spoken to my mother, because a skipping rope appeared at home, and we practiced marching around the dining room. I began to join in at school.

In class we were supposed to be learning to read, but we had only one reading book each, probably because of wartime paper shortages. It began, "I see a cat. I see a ball. Kitty sees a cat. Kitty sees a ball." I soon had the whole book memorized and thought I could read. I also learned my first poem:

Spring is coming! Spring is coming!
Birdies build your nest!
Weave together straw and feather,
Doing each your best.

Since we never went to church, I sang my first hymn at school, "There is a green hill far away," part of the religious education compulsory in all English schools.

I decided I liked school, and that I could mostly ignore my brother. My life seemed in equilibrium again. But not for long.

Although my parents could not have anticipated it, my brother's birth coincided with the turning tide of war. The Allies defeated Rommel's tank divisions in North Africa, the Russians annihilated Hitler's Sixth Army at Stalingrad, and the Americans were advancing in the South Pacific. However, bombs still fell around us, the blackout remained, and there were shortages of everything. Hitler wasn't going to give in easily. He had a new weapon to plague us.

EVACUATION

Some neuroscientists believe that every time we retrieve a memory we subtly alter it, although the core meaning remains. Yet the vivid memory flashes I still retain from my first four years seem to be immutable, trapped like a dinosaur footprint in rock. A hand reaching for a paper bag. A tree stump. A sock.

The sock is knee-length, gray, with a thin red stripe around the neatly folded down top. It is on the left leg of the boy sitting next to me in the school air raid shelter, a long dark passage with slatted seats on either side. I know the boy only slightly—he isn't in my class. It is daytime and I don't like missing our lessons. I don't think I am frightened, although something made me etch the sock into memory. Nighttime air raids were routine, and no bomb had come remotely near me personally.

But day raids were new. Until the last year of the war, bombing was a nighttime event when German pilots were safer from anti-aircraft attack. But in the summer of 1944, after the Allied D-Day Normandy landings and the liberation of France, Hitler was losing the war but not ready to give in. Hoping to weaken British morale at home while lessening the demoralizing effects of Allied bombing and food shortages in Germany, he ordered the use of a weapon that he hoped would restore German fortunes—the V1 rocket.

The V1s were the first cruise missiles, unmanned and carrying a heavy payload of explosives. The British called them flying bombs, buzz bombs, or doodlebugs, the latter because of their distinctive buzzing drone. The sound still reverberates clearly in my memory. The first time I heard it my mother and I rushed out of the house to see what it was. We peered up at the unfamiliar black object, plane-shaped but too small to be carrying people, as it flew on into the distance. We soon learned from the radio to take cover, not go out to watch. The V1s were aimed at London, but if they had too little fuel or their engines were inefficient they fell around us, twenty-five miles short of their target. If the drone stopped suddenly, the silence meant danger, take shelter, and hope to avoid the direct hit for which a shelter was no defense.

The flying bombs came in huge numbers—seventy to one hundred a day—killing more than six thousand people over the next year, and seriously injuring another eighteen thousand. They failed to dent British morale, but did a lot of damage. Over a million houses were hit in three months, almost as many as in the year-long London Blitz of 1941. Shooting them all down was impossible, but the main defense, radar, the Allies' secret advantage, provided enough warning for fighter aircraft and anti-aircraft guns to destroy some of them in the air before they reached London. That too meant some fell near us.

No sooner had we become resigned to the disruptions of the V1 raids than Hitler replaced them with the next generation, the V2s, genuine rockets, the first sub-orbital ballistic missiles. Because the V2s flew in space they were silent, arriving without warning except for the sonic boom when they reentered the atmosphere at 3000 mph, too fast to give notice of their imminent crash. They were the brainchild of Wernher von Braun, the rocket scientist who later became a hero of American space exploration after being spirited out of Germany by the US Army at the end of the war in something called Operation Paperclip.

The first V2 ever to land in London on September 8, 1944, fell on my father's mother's street, destroying their garage, killing three people and damaging several houses. At first the residents had no idea what had hit them. The government didn't want to cause panic, but by October Churchill had to admit publicly that there was a new weapon. The silence and lack of warning were scary and although the V2s had no effect on the war's result, they had a major impact on our family. This was the first time anyone we knew well had experienced bomb damage and although my parents initially didn't know what had caused the destruction, the lack of warning and the scale of the damage unnerved them. They decided that my mother, my brother and I should evacuate to Port Quin until the danger, whatever it was, was over.

The journey was a nightmare for my mother, who had to deal with luggage, a five-year-old and a one-year old. We had to pass through London to change trains at the height of the V2 raids. I remember the journey from Waterloo Station to Cornwall. The train was so crowded we had no seats for the whole four-hour journey. Rail carriages were divided into eight-seat compartments joined by a corridor on one side, with the toilet at one end. We crammed into the corridor, elbow to elbow with other passengers claiming their iota of space. I sat on our suitcase, with nothing to do except watch the other people, while my mother stood, trying to contain my ever-active one-year-old brother. I was bored, but could do nothing except kick the suitcase. When my brother needed a diaper change my mother passed him down the line to the person nearest the toilet who changed him. They passed him back together with the dirty diaper. No one complained.

When we finally arrived at Port Quin the bed and breakfast was gone, another casualty of war. Mrs. Dingle, who had kept it, now lived with her husband and son Percy in the shepherd's cottage on the local farm—Mr. Dingle was the shepherd. The cottage didn't even have an air raid shelter (or electricity or a bathroom). Here the war was remote, our routine predictable, no sudden interruptions, no silences followed by explosions. Our only problem was the fleas.

LEARNING TO READ

"I see a cat…" Somehow, I thought that repeating those magic words was reading. In Port Quin I learned it wasn't.

Since our stay at the Dingles' cottage was only temporary, my mother had decided not to send me to the local school, a long walk away. Instead she took over my lessons. She wrote words on pieces of paper, and soon discovered I couldn't read them. She decided to take action.

First we had to find a suitable beginning reader, a challenge at a time when print and paper were rationed and books were in short supply. For that we had to go to Port Isaac, home of the nearest shop. We walked the cliff path, today designated an area of outstanding natural beauty. Autumn is one of the best times to enjoy it when both the prickly yellow gorse and the purple heather are in bloom, creating a floral carpet perfectly offset by the light green springy cliff grass and the blue ocean far below. The boom of the surf accompanied us as I skipped along with my mother, excited to be on an adventure with her while my brother stayed behind with Mrs. Dingle.

Miraculously, as I now see it, the village Post Office, also a general store, had one beginning reader, probably a prewar edition still unsold. It was called *Mac and Tosh Go to School,* and even better, the girl character was called Jenny! The story was simple; Jim and Jenny took their two dogs Mac and Tosh to school, where they showed them the normal doings of the school day, and also made a paper kite (Jim) and a paper doll (Jenny). I still have the book, the illustrations somewhat ineptly colored and with various marks I made when I used it to teach my panda and teddy in many childhood games of school. I liked it, and once I understood what reading was, I learned very quickly.

Although my mother was an avid reader she had no time to read for herself while we were awake, and there were no books in the Dingle household. So even after I learned to read I still thought reading was something either my mother or I did out loud. Then we spent Christmas with friends in Polperro, a fishing village on Cornwall's south coast. They had a daughter a little older than I who sat in a chair silently reading, the first time I had seen someone my age do that. I decided to try it myself. She was reading *Alice in Wonderland*, and when she finished she gave it to me to keep. I still have the book, a 1921 edition with the original Tenniel illustrations, a Christmas present to someone called Babe in 1924. I opened its browning pages and began to read: "Alice was beginning to get very tired of sitting by her sister on the bank and having nothing to do." I was hooked for life.

Between September and that momentous Christmas we lived quietly in Port Quin away from the anxieties and tensions of war. We heard planes on anti-submarine patrols from the nearby air base but as the Allies advanced and took over the rocket launch sites neither the flying bombs nor German bombers now reached Britain. The Allies did all the bombing.

We learned the rhythms of farm life. We had arrived in time for the end of harvest when the sheaves were carried into the barn or piled in thatched ricks to dry. Later we watched fascinated as the steam-driven threshing machine turned the sheaves into grain and straw. We saw cows milked, sheep herded, eggs collected. We watched the horses plow the fields for winter wheat. My brother and I had no idea we would one day be doing some of those things ourselves. We did not hear the conversation when my parents decided to buy the farm, although they told us of the decision soon after. I liked Roscarrock Farm, where we were staying, so I thought it would be an adventure.

On fine days we walked down to the beach where my brother did his bum-shuffling (he never crawled) on the sand and tottered on unsteady legs. I poked around in the tide pools, disturbing small shrimp, sea anemones and tiny fish. I sometimes played with the girl my age in the big farmhouse, the only other child nearby, but she was at school during the day and our time together was mostly at weekends.

In contrast, my father's life was anything but tranquil. Although the Allies' advances in Europe made the need for life rafts and barrage balloons less urgent, the factory was still working twenty-four hours, and at the same time he had to arrange to sell the Old House and most of the antiques they had so carefully collected before their wedding. The farm needed capital, so my parents sold almost anything of value, including my mother's engagement ring. I now realize that even if my father had been able to leave his job without risk of being called up to serve in the last push toward Berlin, we could not have done without his salary until the farm began to generate income.

As farmers our petrol ration was larger than for other citizens, so an important purchase on one of my father's flying visits was a car, a second-hand Austin Seven. We left Port Quin in it and, after Christmas in Polperro, my mother, brother and I moved into Gunwen farm. My mother was twenty-eight, I was five, and my brother under two. We had left the sirens and drones of war for the silences of the deep countryside. But I had a new skill to help me adjust. I could read.

FIRST IMPRESSIONS

Gunwen Farm, Christmas 1944

In the twenty-first century it is difficult to imagine the remoteness of the community we joined at the beginning of 1945. Gunwen Farm (the name means "white down" in the almost extinct Cornish language) was in a valley between the rocky outcrops of Helman Tor to the east and the plateau dotted with kaolin mines to the west. The area had no public buildings except a Methodist chapel and the only regular outside visitors were the postman and the milk truck, the latter collecting milk not distributing it. There was no public telephone or transport, no electricity. The darkness on moonless nights was familiar to us, since we were used to the blackout. The silence was not. I don't know whether I was already frightened of the dark, likely after bombing raids, but the isolation scared me. An old Cornish prayer, much quoted on tourist postcards, went,

"From ghoulies and ghosties and long leggety beasties and things that go bump in the night, Good Lord deliver us." I agreed.

Few of the valley residents had gone far from their homes; some had never been to any of the neighboring towns. None had cars—ours was the first—and only a few had riding horses. Most of them were self-sufficient farmers whose few wants could be met by walking a mile or so to Luxulyan, the nearest village. While the shepherd's cottage we had been staying in at Port Quin had no modern conveniences, that had been temporary. This kind of remoteness and lack of any comfortable amenities was far beyond my parents' middle-class suburban experience.

On the day we took possession I had my first chance to open the peeling white gate that led down the sandy driveway to a second gate at the boundary of what we learned to call Entrance Field. The novelty of opening gates was fun at first, but it soon got to be a chore my brother and I fought not to do as soon as he got big enough to take a turn. The farm buildings were out of sight around a corner, and as we drove in, my brother and I first encountered the morass of sticky mud Michael immediately christened "the dirty." Created by years of animal and people trampling through it, enhanced by the soft, damp Cornish climate, the dirty (the name stuck) was our constant companion. At any time of year we rarely went out without the tall rubber boots called Wellingtons or wellies, perennially lined up inside the back door.

Surrounding the dirty was a large old two-story barn and a collection of smaller barns, all built of solid blocks of Cornish granite roofed with slate, the standard Cornish building materials. Behind the large barn was an enclosed area known as the "mowhay" (pronounced mowey—another Cornish word?) with a big open Dutch barn for straw storage at one end. Through a gate on the opposite side of the main farmyard a smaller and less virulent dirty fronted another set of barns.

A gate on the right corner of the main dirty led to our new home, another solid granite and slate building. The pleasantly symmetrical farmhouse front had five large sash windows and a front door facing south, but everyone came in through the back door closest to the main farmyard. The house was larger than the Old House, with six bedrooms, a large kitchen, two living rooms, a cool slate-lined room for food storage known as the dairy, and a "back kitchen" that Americans might call a mudroom—

54

sorely needed. The toilet was an outhouse up a path behind the big barn. The only regular heat was from a coal-fired kitchen range that probably dated from when the house was built in the mid-1800s. Most rooms had fireplaces, but, except for the sitting room, we rarely used them.

We entered the house through the back kitchen, a stark room with a stable door that opened in top and bottom halves. Like the rarely used front door, it had no lock. In front of us as we entered was a hand pump, the only water in the house, and a large sink on the back wall. To the right was the main kitchen where we were greeted by Mr. and Mrs. May, the previous owners, who were staying on for a short time to help us settle in.

The kitchen was the hub of the house, the room in which we spent most of the time when we weren't outdoors. It was a long room with a slate floor and a large window looking out onto the small enclosed yard outside the back kitchen door. The main piece of furniture was a table that stretched the entire length of the room and could easily accommodate a dozen people. A wooden bench under the window stretched along one side. Next to the table, inset into the chimney wall, was the cooking range, with one oven and two hot plates. It required vigilant attention to keep it burning, especially on windy days, and was kept looking good by a weekly, messy coating of what was called black lead.

Off the kitchen toward the front of the house was the sitting room, as my parents called it. It was carpeted, comfortable, and even warm when the fire in the fireplace was lit. Here my parents put the few pieces of furniture remaining from their former life, a sofa, three comfortable chairs, and an antique dresser we called a tallboy with drawers on the lower half and a small double-doored top cupboard. My mother kept it to the end of her life. One drawer held the jumble of photographs whose remnants I still have. My father built bookshelves to cover an entire wall, one side for grownups and one for children.

Down a short passage from the kitchen was the cool dairy, slate shelving around all the walls and a slate floor providing the closest we could get to refrigeration. Through a door to the left of the dairy was the dark and damp front hall, where my mother hung my father's rugger photos. Off the hall was another downstairs room, our children's playroom until we got too old to need it and it became a spare bedroom.

Upstairs were three large and three small bedrooms. My parents slept in one of the large ones, the home of my mother's three-mirrored dressing table, another remnant of her former life. At one time or another I slept in all the others. My favorite was the bedroom over the kitchen with a window seat overlooking the farmyard, a good place to read. It had a large double bed with a lumpy mattress that we bought along with other beds from the Mays. All the bedrooms had washstands with large pitchers for water (cold) and matching basins, soap dishes, and toothbrush holders.

I have no memory of what I thought of our new home. I expect I accepted the change stoically—I had no choice. But I may not have liked the unfamiliarity, the dampness, the isolation. I would have taken comfort in my mother's reassuring presence, even if I had to share her with Michael.

SETTLING IN

Helman Tor

A large house with no hot water, cold water only from a hand pump, no heat except from the old cooking stove, no toilet, no electricity, no telephone, and half a mile from the nearest neighbor. Two small children, one still in nappies. And a farm to run alone. That's what my mother faced when we moved into the farm in January 1945, when she was twenty-eight. She and my father had made the choice; she knew what she had to do. She was up for it.

She could do nothing about the house, since all their resources had to go to stocking the farm. Even an indoor chemical toilet would have to wait for my father to do the necessary work. But she immediately realized that she would need help with us children, since she could not easily or safely

57

take us to milk cows or groom horses. Also, she hated housework. Perhaps her parents had instilled in her the idea that ladies did not clean, although she was never too concerned about ladylike behavior in other respects, and I think she was just more honest about a task that has few appealing features for most of us. As far back as I can remember, and no matter how poor my parents were, she always had someone do the cleaning for her.

She asked around in the immediate local community and found Rosemary Rundle, the eldest daughter of a large family that lived in one of the cottages down by the Methodist chapel. In a remote area with few jobs for women Rosemary was glad to live in, taking charge of me and my brother while also responsible for cleaning and laundry, the latter all by hand, with water boiled on the stove in a big copper kettle. She would have been used to that, since no one in the valley had indoor plumbing. Rosemary was the one who taught me how to make little boats by folding and bending the long rushes that grew by the stream on the moor, something I passed on to my own children, and they to theirs. Sometimes I played with Rosemary's youngest sister Joan, who was about my age. I envied Joan her long curly blond hair and was glad of her company, but I was a bossy child, used to playing alone, and with considerably more worldly experience, even for a five-year-old. I patronized her, and since I did not go to school with her we drifted apart.

School leaving age in Britain was fourteen in 1945, so Rosemary was probably that age when my mother hired her. She was gentle, softly pretty with wavy brown hair and a generous smile. She was the best looking young woman in the neighborhood and all too soon left to marry one of the local young men. To replace her my mother hired her younger sister Margaret. Margaret was an entirely different proposition. Strong-minded and strong-willed, she clashed with my mother frequently, and occasionally openly defied her. Margaret hated ironing, not surprisingly since she had to use heavy and clumsy irons (literally made of iron) that heated on the stove, so maintaining an even temperature was impossible. Too hot, and clothes and sheets scorched, too cold and they stayed stubbornly wrinkly. One particularly bad day she slammed down the iron in front of my mother. "I'm not going to iron another thing, and I'll hit you with this if you make me!" My mother, good at diplomacy, and knowing that firing her was not an option since there were no other possibilities in the neighborhood, calmed her down. "You can leave it for now, Margaret, and come back to it later when you are rested. I'm afraid ironing still has to be done."

Although we feared her temper, Margaret was usually kind to us children. She was the one who taught us about our surroundings. She took us for long walks up to Helman Tor, the local landmark, a ridge on the skyline with three large piles of rocks spread along its back. To get there we went down the lane where wild strawberries, sloes, hazelnuts, and many wildflowers grew in the tall hedgerow, and walked briefly along the road before turning on to the path across the moor, a spongy damp area covered with a few scrubby bushes, mossy grass, and fern-like bracken. We stopped by the stream to make the reed boats and float them down as far as we could follow them, and skirted the pond that Margaret told us would suck us in if we went near. Then we started uphill along a shady lane, hoping we would not meet Mr. Sanders, the local farmer, who scared us with his sudden appearances and booming voice. Finally we came to the gate in a dry-stone wall that led to the tor's ridge.

Up close the tor's rock piles were small mazes of passages and little caves, irresistible places to explore. We played hide and seek, as British children call it, we chased each other, and when we were tired we retreated to a mossy ledge we called the sofa. There we leaned back against the rock wall and looked out over the valley to the farm, a toy home in a Lilliputian landscape. Margaret showed us the two rocking stones, very large pieces of granite worn smooth by the wear and tear of the Cornish climate, balanced on other stones so that if you stood in just the right place even lightweights like us could gently rock them back and forth. She said that if you could rock one of them you would know who you were going to marry. We stood as she showed us, in precisely the right place, our feet slightly apart, and the stone rocked! We felt powerful, even if we got no premonitions about our future partners. "I'm going to marry Trevor," Margaret announced. Later she did. Perhaps they already had an understanding, or perhaps Margaret always got her way. I bet Trevor had his hands full.

Rosemary and then Margaret were my mother's lifelines as she did as much as she could to make the farm viable before the war ended and my father could join us. The Mays had included some animals and crops in the farm's purchase price. There were two horses, Topsy and Peggy, essential in a land of no tractors, one South Devon cow that provided us with milk

59

but none to sell, a few chickens whose eggs were also only enough for our own use, a pig not yet fat enough to kill, and a few sheep. All needed daily feeding and attention except the sheep, who grazed by themselves but had to be checked frequently since they were prone to foot rot, insects burrowing in their wool, and wandering off into places like the end of one of our narrow lanes where they couldn't see how to get out. We had no respect for stupid sheep.

My mother had kept a pony to pull a trap when there was no petrol during the war, and had learned to milk a cow in her wartime work, so at least the chores were not all new. She may have learned something about sheep from Port Quin's Mr. Dingle, but not enough to deal with them by herself. I don't know what she did about spring lambing, but when it came to shearing in early summer she brought in an expert. I have a photo of her holding the hands of my brother and her cousin Betty's son Peter Crawford. They are all looking at a sheep on the ground being sheared. The boys, still toddlers, look nervous, and Michael is sucking his usual two middle fingers. A little later my mother asked if she could have a go. First she had to straddle the sheep and force it down to the ground. Instead, as we watched in horror, the sheep ran off with her on its back into a bramble patch. Our dismay turned to giggles when she emerged, slightly scratched but otherwise unharmed. Shortly afterwards we sold the sheep.

My parents were determined to farm efficiently and profitably, so they made some early decisions. The farm, only sixty acres, was too small to make growing crops for market profitable, so they would concentrate on selling milk, eggs, and fatted pigs. First, they decided to develop a herd of Guernsey cows. Guernseys are small golden brown and white cows with gentle dispositions and high butter fat milk that carried a premium on the market in the days before we knew about cholesterol. My mother sold the South Devon she inherited from the Mays and bought our first Guernsey, a mature cow called, somewhat tritely, Buttercup. After that, all our cows had flower names with initials from their mothers, and the Bs proliferated so much that we had to comb my little book on *The Language and Sentiment of Flowers* (the only flower book we had), to find new names—Betony, for example. Other cow families were descendants of Clover, Daffodil, and Elsie, the next purchases to join the herd.

When we took over the farm some crops were already in the ground. There was a field of mangolds, turnip-like root vegetables good for animal feed, and potatoes in a field called Rocky Park. Harvesting potatoes is back-breaking and intensive, requiring a gang of workers. My mother hired a group of traveling potato pickers, all women, to harvest our field. They made a fuss over me, but I couldn't understand a word they said. I thought it was because of their thick Cornish accents, but much later my mother explained that I didn't know any of the profanities that seemed to be their entire vocabulary. Just as we stopped keeping sheep, we never grew potatoes again.

A few cows, a few chickens, two horses and a pig were about all my mother could handle on her own. But she had one more problem to solve. Where was I to go to school?

THE PLUM TREE

In Britain the beginning school age is five, so I should have been at school in the fall when we lived in Port Quin. Instead, my mother had taught me. Now she had farm chores most of the time, and anyway I missed the entertainment and challenges of school. The nearest free elementary school ("state school," the British call it) was in a small town, Lanivet, a little over three miles away as the crow flies, but further for human travel. Children in our valley had to walk well over a mile across the moor to the nearest bus stop where a local bus took them the rest of the way.

Walking to and from the bus was not impossible—Joan Rundle, the same age as I, did it every day. But the clincher for my parents was the school's record. After nine years of schooling both Rosemary and Margaret Rundle were almost illiterate, and my parents had promised themselves that my brother and I would not suffer educationally from their eccentric decisions. So my mother had to find somewhere else.

Since we had a car my mother could have taken me to a more distant private school every day, although our petrol ration might not have gone that far. But the busiest part of the farm day coincided with the time we would have to leave for school. Once my father joined us and we had a full milking herd, both parents needed to work at morning milking, which had to be over by 8 a.m. so that my father could take our two big churns of milk on the back of the tractor down to the stand at the edge of the moor, where they were picked up by the milk lorry promptly at 8:30. Missing the milk lorry meant taking the churns into Lostwithiel, a few miles away, and the loss of most of the morning. Selling milk took precedence over getting me to school. There had to be an alternative.

Gorran Haven was a typical small Cornish fishing village at a time when the fleets still went out in search of mackerel and pilchards (a small fish a little larger than a sardine). Visitors drove down a hill and stopped outside the only shop, a whitewashed cottage that doubled as the Post

Office and general store. Ahead was the harbor, bounded on each side by dark granite cliffs topped by a fringe of grass. A small sandy beach, an almost invisible seaweed-strewn strip at high tide, bordered the deep-water moorings of a half-dozen sturdy wooden fishing boats, their nets slung over the sides to dry, sheltered from the Atlantic by a strong, solid granite wall. On the left a row of small houses, also granite, slate-roofed and framed by luxuriant fuchsia bushes, lined a steep narrow lane that led to steps down the cliff to a larger beach, Little Perhaver, that I came to know well.

In January 1945 my mother, my brother and I drove down the hill into Gorran Haven and turned right into a sandy dirt lane. We stopped at a large ordinary-looking house with a sign saying The Plum Tree. My mother, eager to detect things I might like, pointed out that the namesake tree was in the front garden. This was St. Goran School. At age five and a half I was leaving home to be a weekly boarder.

The proprietor and only teacher was Phyllis Rapley, a single woman in her early forties, just a little older than my parents. She was of average height, wiry, with short brown curly hair and glasses, interesting to me, since I thought only grandparents wore glasses. Her clothes, like everyone else's in those days of rationing, were serviceable but unmemorable. There was almost always a twinkle in her eye as she had a slightly warped but sympathetic sense of humor. She loved practical jokes, like putting a soft toy in an unusual spot and waiting to see who noticed first.

I don't know if she had any teacher training, or why she decided to settle in Gorran Haven, a long way from her native Hampshire. Perhaps, like us, she was a war refugee since her family home was close to Portsmouth, Britain's largest naval port, and subject to heavy bombing. Trained or nor, she was an inspired, if strict, teacher and Miss Rapley, or s'Rapley, as we called her, was forever dear to all her students. She spent almost all her waking hours with us. She taught us, read to us, played games, some of which she made up herself, comforted us. She had someone come to clean and cook meals, but did all the rest herself. She was like everyone's favorite maiden aunt.

Most people I know are horrified that I went to boarding school so young, although there were one or two other children my age. My usual reply is, "It was a lot more fun than being at home on the farm." For me it was a blessing, a community beyond my own family where I could learn, read, and play with other children. Although I suppose I must have been homesick at first, I don't remember it. I had plenty of time to be on the farm. My mother drove the twelve or so miles to pick me up every Friday afternoon and drove me back every Sunday, and four months of the year were school holidays. Yet I never had a sustained time at home like my brother's more than two years before he joined me at St. Goran School. I never developed a deep understanding of the farm routines—some, like threshing, I rarely experienced because they were in school time. I didn't mind. School was worth it.

In the mornings we did our lessons. Since there were only about ten students we all worked individually at our own pace, with Miss Rapley as coach. The one requirement was that we had to have everything done by lunch. One day she told me to rearrange the letters PRDO into a word. I got stuck on PORD and couldn't think of anything else. Lunchtime came and I was still looking at the letters. I started crying, which got no sympathy. Eventually, when everyone else had finished eating, I managed to rearrange the letters to DROP. "We've had enough of that," said Miss Rapley with a wry smile, as she served me my warmed-up lunch.

In the afternoons, unless it was raining hard, we went for long walks along the cliffs or to the beach, usually Little Perhaver, similar to Port Quin with its rock pools, but sandier. We got used to the long climb down, and the even longer, it seemed, climb back up. Sometimes we spent our meager pocket money in the Post Office, although in 1945, with candy rationed and ice cream non-existent, there wasn't much to buy except the odd pencil.

I enjoyed the company of the other children. My best friend then was Dorothea Dimmock, a daygirl who lived with her mother down the road toward the harbor in a cottage with a garden full of flowers behind a squeaky iron gate. Mrs. Dimmock gave piano lessons. There was no husband—maybe he was away fighting, maybe she was a widow, or perhaps she was hiding from scandal in this rather remote community. Since absent fathers were the norm in wartime—I hardly ever saw my own—I never wondered.

At school there were around six boarders who slept in two bedrooms, one for boys, one for girls. Unlike the farm, we had a bathroom! There

64

were no shots to prevent childhood diseases then, and I got both measles and mumps in my first year at The Plum Tree. The three of us with measles had to stay upstairs in a darkened bedroom to make sure our eyes weren't affected. We weren't allowed to read much, torture for me, and we ate a lot of strawberries that were growing in abundance in the Plum Tree's kitchen garden. Since then I have always preferred raspberries. When I was better my mother gave me a book, *Little Gray Rabbit's Christmas*, one of my favorite series. It had snowflakes all over the cover, supposed to remind me of the measles spots. Every time I looked at it, it did.

VICTORY

The war had not gone away, just become more distant.

My father was absent as ever—they still needed life rafts and barrage balloons. But for my mother, my brother and me, life took on a new rhythm that did not include air raid shelters or even blackouts. No pilot could see the light from one of our candles, and in any case we went to bed early.

Our weekly routine included driving to Bugle, the nearest small town, to pick up our rationed food—butter, sugar, cheese, bacon—from the post office that doubled as a general store, as did so many in Cornish towns. When I was at school I missed the weekly Bugle excursion, but during the Easter holiday I went along. One day, as we drove into the town and stopped outside the post office, next door to the local pub, we noticed several young men in uniform, a rare sight in central Cornwall, especially during the last stages of the war in Europe when all forces were at the front and the Cornish air bases were no longer used for protecting Atlantic shipping. Even more exotic, the uniforms looked odd. The soldiers were not British, but American GIs.

Bugle was a small town and my mother was an attractive woman in her late twenties, slim, with bobbed medium brown wavy hair and a smooth complexion. At once three of the men rushed to the car, opened the door, and asked my mother to come in for a drink in the pub.

"I have my children with me and they aren't allowed in," my mother protested.

"No problem," said the most assertive GI in his unfamiliar American accent. Before my mother had a chance to protest, turning to me, he said, "Here, take these." He gave me a comic and a pack of gum. I had never seen either before. The comic was welcome new reading material, but I mistook the gum for severely rationed candy, sucked it a little, and swallowed it whole. I have never since enjoyed chewing gum.

The men hustled my mother into the pub, leaving me, aged six, to supervise my two-year-old very active brother. I worried about my mother's disappearance and how long she would be. To my relief she came out quickly, but she was concerned that the GIs might follow her to our very isolated home. One did, but she managed to persuade him to leave, I have no idea how. After all her wartime experiences my mother was up for any challenge.

Meanwhile the war in Europe dragged on. Nearly a year passed between the D-Day landings and the fall of Berlin. But finally, on May 9, ten days after Hitler's suicide, German troops unconditionally surrendered to the Allies. I was at school on VE (Victory in Europe) Day, and was looking forward to a day of celebration in the village, including a parade and children's sports like three-legged and sack races. My mother had other plans. My father had time off, so she came to fetch me from school to see him. I was sulky and didn't want to give up certain fun to see a father I hardly knew. Then, to make matters worse, we ran out of petrol on the way home, several miles from any garage, and in any case we had no more petrol coupons. But everyone was helpful at that time of huge celebration, and a friendly lorry driver gave us enough of his fuel to get us home. I don't remember seeing my father. I was still mad at missing the village fun.

Shortly afterwards, when war production ended, my father was able to leave his works manager job. He became a full-time farmer and part of our lives again. When my father had grandchildren he used to say he didn't know how to behave with toddlers since he had missed so much of his own children's early years, but he soon became a normal part of our life, and more inclined to fun than my mother. My mother was delighted to have him back at her side after being apart for four of their six married years. She certainly needed his help.

The war in the Pacific lasted another seven months. I was at home when Japan surrendered. My mother woke me up that morning.

"The war's over," she said excitedly.

I knew that I should be excited too, but I didn't know what she meant. The war had been part of my world for as long as I could remember, and I had no idea what life would be without it. I thought "Japs", as we called them, were a kind of plane. No one mentioned the atomic bomb.

On VJ (Victory in Japan) Day the postman brought us small British and American flags, although we had no one to wave them at. Otherwise nothing changed. My father went to harness the horses to pull a small implement that cut down thistles in the fields so they wouldn't crowd out the good grazing grass for the cows. I left my panda and teddy with the flags in a shady spot by the field gate and climbed on to the seat of the thistle cutter with my father. He held me tight. The horses plodded forward. Now only the thistles would die.

LAMLEDRA

The approach to our new school was up a very steep hill, one of many in Cornwall that I have rarely found elsewhere—maybe a Welsh hillside on the way to see a sheepdog show its paces, or the dirt road up to the monastery above us in Italy. But those came later. Between the ages of six and ten this was the steep hill I knew best. Our car labored as it climbed the rough blacktop, the debris washed down by rain providing welcome traction, as we always seemed in danger of slipping backward.

The entrance to the hill branched off almost secretly from the main road leading to Gorran Haven. It hardly looked drivable. The width of one small car, it was bounded on the right by a tall Cornish stone hedge topped with stubby hazel and hawthorn, on the left by the similar hedges of cottages clinging to the hillside. Only the few who knew where it led ventured up, so we rarely met a car coming in the other direction.

At the top we emerged abruptly from the shelter of the hill into the sudden light of the bare exposed cliff top. The hawthorns shrank to lopsided bushes leaning away from the wind. We passed a farm and stopped by a pond, full of tadpoles in spring, to open a gate. In front of us down a cliff at the edge of a close-cropped grass field, was the Atlantic Ocean, deep blue in sunshine, slate gray on drab Cornish days, the view always catching our breath however many times we saw it. Below the cliff Vault beach curved white and pristine toward the severe, bare Dodman Point. The sound of the sea was always with us, a sigh in good weather, a rumbling boom in bad.

To our left, sat the house called Lamledra, nestled in a slight depression at the top of the cliff just deep enough to protect it from the worst of the Atlantic gales without sacrificing the view. Clad in weathered gray shingles, with a roof of Cornish slate and banks of windows looking out toward the sea, it seemed ageless, but was in fact about forty years old.

Lamledra was my school's new home. Soon after the war The Plum Tree became too small for Miss Rapley's school. Somehow she must have met John and Marjorie Williams, Lamledra's owners. John Fischer Williams, a successful lawyer and later civil servant, built the house as a holiday home, probably paying for it with money he inherited from his grandfather in the opium trade. When he bought the land he was about to be married, and wrote to his fiancée, "It is a beautiful place, very very beautiful, and not like other places—it is to places what you are to other women—just so fresh and life-giving—it sweeps all the rest of the world away."[†] Lamledra and its surroundings are still one of my own ideals of beauty, ever present in my mind.

The Williams family had lived there throughout the war and were active in the village of Gorran Haven's affairs, so they probably met Miss Rapley socially. Now the war was over and they were moving back to Oxford, so renting the house to the school was a perfect solution for all parties. Only in the months of July and August did Miss Rapley pack all the school stuff away, leaving the house to the Williams family while she visited her own relatives.

[†] Jenifer Hart, *Ask Me No More: an Autobiography* (London: Peter Halban, 1998), 25.

The house was just right for a small boarding school. It had twenty-one beds, although I don't think there were ever that many boarders, and a children's wing at the back that became an ideal schoolroom. Outside, a long gravel terrace in the front of the house was surrounded by low shrubs. A high fuchsia hedge inside a stone wall circled the whole area, making a boundary we were not to cross without permission. We played hide and seek, house, cowboys and Indians, or popped open the fuchsia flowers to reveal their frilly skirts. Sugar-deprived because of rationing, we pulled the legs out of the small flowers and sucked the tiny dabs of honey at the ends.

The center of the house was a large living/dining room with a long dark oak table where we ate our meals. There was ample room to play or read on the window seats overlooking the garden and the sea. Just underneath the ceiling a frieze listed in red and black Gothic letters the names of the Williams family, the closest we ever got to them. Under the windows low bookshelves kept their children's books. There I read American books like *What Katy Did*, *Pollyanna*, and *Daddy-Long-Legs*. I only dimly understood that they were set in the United States. Most of the characters in children's fiction had lives so far removed from mine that they all seemed equally remote.

The day at Lamledra started at eight o'clock, when we got up—one of the few rules was that we weren't to make any noise before then so Miss Rapley could sleep. Since she spent almost all her waking hours with us, and we all knew when not to try her patience too far, we lay quietly until the morning bell.

We did our lessons in the schoolroom at the eastern end of the ground floor. Every morning after breakfast the boarders went through a small lobby and into the long room with windows on both sides, one side blocked by tall bushes but the other looking out into the garden and beyond the fuchsia hedge to the sea, a perfect view for daydreaming. The day-children arrived from the village and, like practically every school in England, we began with brief morning prayers from the Church of England prayer book—"O Lord, our heavenly Father, who has safely brought us to the beginning of this day..." followed by the Lord's Prayer. We then settled to the day's work at the desks and tables scattered around the room, each with our own assignment. Miss Rapley moved from person to group and back again, teaching, coaching, encouraging. My favorite part

71

was reading, since I could lose myself in almost any book, although I didn't like an abbreviated edition of *David Copperfield* and I have never enjoyed Dickens much since. Sometimes we came together in groups of similar age for subjects like history, or for art and needlework projects. Once a week Mrs. Moore came in to teach singing. I remember her teaching me to pick out the treble melody for a Christmas carol, "Unto Us A Child Is Born," that she wanted us to practice. That was the closest I came to playing a piano for many years.

Among the few papers that survived my mother's holocaust of memorabilia when she sold her last house is a single school report from St. Goran School for the Easter (spring) term 1947. Looking at it more than sixty years later, I am surprised to find Miss Rapley assigned marks and positions for each subject since I don't remember any competition or even dividing us up into forms (classes). I took my first position for granted but must have been chagrined to lose 120 overall points, especially through carelessness in number (arithmetic) and geography. I am amused that the future historian did best in history.

The report also shows my academic rather than artistic bent. 1947 must have been the last time my singing improved, and I clearly had a slapdash approach to penmanship ("must remember to hold pencil properly") that has lasted. I cannot remember what we did in needlework, or even what handwork was. I am a little surprised at drawing was weak since the next year I won first prize for my age in a Gorran Haven village drawing contest. I drew a fuchsia, a flower with which I had an intimate acquaintance from the Lamledra hedge. I have doodled fuchsias ever since.

We did schoolwork only in the morning. Afternoons were for exercise. Although the report says we did drill (formal exercises) and games, I don't remember regular sessions and am surprised to find that I merited a "Good." On most days, unless it rained hard, we went with Miss Rapley for long walks in the surrounding country, along the coast toward the Dodman Point, down the steep path called the Foxhole to Gorran Haven Village, up the hill to St. Goran Church (the saint has one r, the place named after him two).

Miss Rapley turned our walks into nature study. We scoured the hedges for wildflowers, excitedly pointing out any new ones. Miss Rapley came to see, peering through her glasses at the find. She seemed to know everything, and could always tell us the flowers' names—red campion, bladder campion, herb Robert, jack-in-the-pulpit. In spring we watched the tadpoles in the farm pond grow legs and turn into tiny frogs. We observed the differences in farm seasons, ones I missed at home. Once several of us ran into the field of oats outside Lamledra's gate and flattened part of the crop. The farmer saw us, came running up and took us in to Miss Rapley. She scolded us, especially me, because, as she pointed out, a farmer's daughter should know better. But my distance from the farm made me only marginally a farmer's daughter, and although I felt ashamed, I hadn't known it was bad.

British schools have three "terms," autumn (September to December), spring (January to March), and summer (April to July). In the summer term we almost always went to the beach in the afternoons. Sometimes we took the zig-zag path down the grassy cliff at Lamledra's front to Vault beach, stretching for several miles toward Dodman Point. Vault's sand was coarse and uncomfortable to walk on barefoot, so we usually went there when it was too cold to go in the water. Instead we waded, climbed the rocks, poked sea anemones, tried to catch shrimps in the rock pools, and hunted for shells, especially tiny pink cowries that we found only there.

On warmer days we walked down the Foxhole to the village and then up a hill on the other side to the steep wooden staircase that took us down to Little Perhaver beach. Here the sand was perfect for sandcastles and the sea came in and out in shallow leisurely sighs that made bathing fun for non-swimmers, which most of us were. We changed into swimsuits behind rocks and ran around in the water splashing each other and pretending to bodysurf on the minimal waves. We usually took a picnic tea, with jam sandwiches and Miss Rapley's signature fruitcake, which she made when she felt like it with whatever ingredients were to hand, standing over the bowl with a cigarette in her mouth, its ash dangerously close to falling in. She baked the cake in a slow oven until she remembered to take it out. It was always moist, just fruity enough, and delicious.

I slept in a bedroom at the east end of the house with windows on two sides. My roommates were Anne Hemsley, the eldest daughter of my parents' first farm pupil, Pat Wakeman, who lived in the next-door farm, and Susan Abbot, our vet's daughter. Susan was obsessed with American cowboys— Annie Oakley was her greatest hero. I knew the words to the

73

songs in *Annie Get Your Gun,* at that time playing in London, before most other popular songs. I sometimes went to play with Susan during the school holidays. I was in awe of her very fashionable mother and her family's quite grand Georgian-style house on Bodmin's main street with a curved pillared entrance and a bright yellow door straight out of Jane Austen.

Also in our dormitory was Rosemary Thomas, a little older than the rest of us. I was more friendly with her brother James, and once Michael and I spent a weekend on their parents' farm on the Roseland peninsula south of Truro, Cornwall's capital. The farm's fields stretched down to the estuary of the River Fal, but I was most enchanted by the garden cemetery of the ancient small church of St. Just in Roseland, a controlled wilderness of rhododendrons, fuchsias, hydrangeas, and roses tumbling down a steep hillside toward the river. The granite church nestled halfway down the hill was a poem of whitewashed simplicity. I thought it was the most beautiful place on earth.

At school, in the evenings after supper when the five- and six-year-olds were in bed, the older ones went into Miss Rapley's study where she read to us, mostly quirky books that appealed to her sense of whimsy. I loved them, especially Eric Linklater's *The Wind on the Moon,* the story of two very mischievous sisters who rescue their father from a wicked tyrant with (I much later realized) a marked resemblance to Hitler. Others she read to us that combined magic and realism in the *Alice in Wonderland* mode were Beverly Nichols's *The Tree That Sat Down* and *The Stream That Stood Still.* I loved them all and persuaded people to buy them for me for birthday and Christmas presents so I could read them over and over.

One year Miss Rapley wrote two plays for us to perform for our parents, one for the younger children, and one for us older ones. She wrote characters to fit each of us. The play I was in was a short family drama and I played Selina Potash, a very inefficient and untidy maid, that must have spoken to my daydreaming unawareness as well as my perennial inability to keep my hair and clothes orderly. I can't remember the plot or any of my lines, but Miss Rapley must have liked the character because quite often after that she would appear among us as Selina Potash, disheveled and carrying a broom. Usually she had an ulterior motive, to playfully draw our attention to something she wanted to change, but sometimes it was just for the fun of it. I was flattered that she chose my character to have a longer life.

Miss Rapley also loved practical jokes. I am an April Fool's child. In most years my birthday fell during the Easter school holidays and I suffered no more than my brother's pranks. But in 1949, when I was ten, Easter was late in April and my birthday was in the last week of school. I came downstairs for breakfast almost incoherent with excitement that I was celebrating with all my school friends. I might have realized that this gave Miss Rapley an ideal opportunity, but I didn't.

In front of each of us was a half grapefruit, sprinkled with sugar, a treat in those austere times only four years after the war had ended. I picked up my spoon and dug in. There seemed to be an unusual number of pips (pits), but I carefully picked them out and arranged them around the edge of my plate. I didn't notice any hastily concealed smirks or suppressed giggles from my neighbors. The flesh seemed tough, but it tasted of grapefruit and sugar and I chewed it. Finally I dug in my spoon and pulled out a wedge of cotton, liberally soaked with grapefruit juice. I looked in amazement. This wasn't grapefruit flesh. Miss Rapley had concocted my grapefruit by squeezing the juice from one half. Then she added the cotton, a layer of shredded tissue paper and finally all the pips from everyone else's grapefruits. She had poured on the juice and spread more than she should have of my sugar ration on top. It had worked beyond her expectations—I had eaten all the paper before I pulled out the cotton. I joined in the general laughter at my most memorable April Fool.

One of the pictures hanging in Lamledra's "great" room showed eight children holding hands and dancing in a ring. I imagined that the eight children were we boarders since there were only eight of us at the time we moved to Lamledra. A 1946 photo, which must have been taken shortly after we moved there, shows thirteen children, eight girls and five boys, some of them day pupils from the village. I can still remember some of their names. I am sitting in the front row, my arm around Mary Lou Featherstone, a daygirl I don't remember as a particular friend. My eyes have shied away from the camera and my hair is pulled back from my face showing my widow's peak. As usual, wisps escape from the invisible braids behind me. We are all smiling, as of course you did for snapshots, but I don't think it was much of an effort. Lamledra life was almost always good.

There must have been moments of stress and sadness. Once I remember packing a small suitcase, determined to run away, although I got no further than the gate before turning back, and I can't recall why I wanted to leave. Probably another child had hurt me in some way. I doubt it had anything to do with Miss Rapley. She made school fun. She also made sure we learned. When I moved to my high school the September after the grapefruit episode, my lessons contained little new for a year. Michael stayed at St. Goran School for another two years before he also moved on to his boy's preparatory school and our connection with Miss Rapley loosened. Shortly after Michael left she got an offer to take over a larger school in her hometown and St. Goran School was no more.

HANDYMAN

A pig house and part of the dirty

I wonder if there are "handy" genes?

My father's grandfathers, a piano manufacturer and an upholsterer, both worked with their hands. My father's interests as a teenager were his motorcycle and his canoe, providing him with some experience in engines and woodworking. But construction? I have no idea where he learned that.

On the farm he had a small workshop opposite the back kitchen door where he kept his tools. No power tools, of course, since there was no electricity, but he had a full and well maintained set of hand tools neatly arranged along the wall. The only machine was what he called a fretsaw (scroll saw), operated by a foot treadle. With it he made us amazing toys. I had a replica of a flour mill where I poured peas over the water wheel to make all the processes work. On the roof he painted in careful letters, "The Jennifer Mary Milling Corporation" in my honor. He also made us a farm, and when my brother Michael got big enough he made a garage for his Dinky Toy cars and a table for his Hornby model railway layout. In the austere days after the war, when Britain was broke and there were few luxuries, he cut smiley faces, suns, moons and stars out of plywood and painted them silver to hang on the Christmas tree.

But his main task was to make the farmhouse and buildings suitable for our needs. Neighbors and friends helped out when he needed it, but he did most of the work himself. First we needed an efficient and easily cleaned milking parlor. He chose a barn beyond the farmyard and the dirty and built concrete milking stalls with metal stanchions for twenty cows. He mixed all the concrete by hand in a wheelbarrow. A passage in front of the stalls let him feed the cows while my mother milked them. Next to the milking parlor he set up a small dairy and outside he laid a wide grooved concrete path where the cows came in. He hosed it down twice a day.

In the house, he built on a long narrow room behind the kitchen on a damp outside wall that needed protection. At the far end he put a chemical toilet on a platform, rather like a throne, so we no longer had to make trips to the outhouse. Then he turned his attention to a narrow enclosed wooden staircase we didn't use much that went from the kitchen to the upstairs, a relic of the days of live-in servants. Not long after my father came back to live with us, it was the scene of one of the few occasions when my brother stuck up for me. I was having a tantrum and my father decided to take me upstairs to cool off in my bedroom. As he took me up the narrow stair my brother bit him in the rear from behind, saying, "Don't you hurt my sister!" My father, who wasn't hurting me, couldn't turn round in the narrow space to deal with the assault. Michael and I both ended up banished to our rooms. Shortly afterwards my father blocked off the staircase by building a long tall dresser (as we called it) across the whole wall with shelves above and cupboards below to store all our dishes and silverware.

Quite quickly the miscellany of buildings my parents had inherited from the Mays acquired specific uses. The big barn held calves below, chickens above and behind. The row of small barns on the opposite side of the dirty from the house became pigpens. Opposite them was the open shed where we kept the car and another that eventually housed the tractor, the first in the neighborhood. With the tractor my father tore down hedges to make larger and more efficient fields and cleared lanes choked with undergrowth to make access to the fields easier. He was out of the house from early morning until late afternoon, always with something to do.

One challenge was unexpected. My mother woke in the middle of the night with the feeling that something was wrong. There was flickering light on the bedroom ceiling. She jumped up, went to look out of a window facing the dirty, and saw that the big barn, the one closest to the house, was on fire. A lamp heating day-old chicks had fallen over and ignited the hay and straw. Several calves, our future milk-producers, and the newly-arrived tractor were in the barn. We had no phone, and the nearest fire engine was six miles away. My father rushed to get the tractor out, while my mother grabbed my brother (I was at school and missed the excitement) and herded the calves to safety. She didn't wait to put shoes on, and said that she could always remember how the mud squished through her toes. Still shoeless, she drove as fast as she could to the nearest phone to call the fire brigade.

The firemen didn't know the area and when they could see the fire tried to take a short cut, getting bogged down in a muddy field. Fortunately, our neighbors could also see it and all turned out to help. With an endless chain of buckets to the duck pond they put the fire out before the fire engine arrived. Then my father had to rebuild, putting in a new floor and replacing the slate roof with corrugated iron. Yet another way in which the farm became ours.

DAIRYWOMAN

Dairy cows are demanding animals. They need milking twice a day, every day. Their udders fill and get so big it is difficult for some to walk. Probably the nearest feeling is having to pee so badly you feel as if your bladder will burst. What's more, if cows are left unmilked too long they risk mastitis and other infections.

Our cows, our main source of income, were mostly my mother's responsibility, although my father took the lead when calves were born, sometimes having to pull the calf out with a rope if it was a breech birth. My mother was much faster at milking than my father. Dressed in brown bibbed overalls over a long-sleeved shirt, her feet in the inevitable black wellies, her hands a little raw and chapped from frequent washing in cold water, she looked every inch a dairywoman.

On the farm, milking time was early morning and late afternoon. We were immutably tied to that schedule. My parents could never be away together overnight, and no matter what we were doing in the afternoons, we had to be back for milking time. When we finally left the farm and returned to "civilization," for some time the habit held and we were all still home around five o'clock.

Milking began with getting the cows in from the field. In the early mornings, around 6 a.m., that was my father's job. When my brother and I got old enough to help and were home from school, in the evening it was our task, one of the better chores, at least in decent weather. We walked out to the field, shouting "C'mon," got behind the furthest cows, and started clapping our hands and shouting to get the stragglers to move. The cows came in willingly, since they got fed in the cowshed, but always in the same order, with Buttercup, the senior cow, leading the way, and the others following in an order roughly based on seniority, but also on each cow's personality, dominant or submissive.

Meanwhile my brother and I tried to push each other into the many cowpats (cow pies) in the fields. Because of the omnipresent "dirty," we always wore wellies, but even with their protection it wasn't pleasant to step through the crust into a squishy brown cow pat and have the fermented grass smell on your boots for a while.

The cows came up the concrete slip and into their accustomed stalls, where my father clicked in place the long steel stanchions that kept them there but allowed them to move their heads up and down to eat.

Once they were all in, my mother brought out the stainless steel milking pails and the wooden milking stools, low because Guernsey cows are smaller than most breeds. My mother sat on her stool, leaned her head into the comfortable hollow between the cow's rear leg and stomach, and took firm hold of two opposite teats, squeezing them rhythmically so a solid stream of milk went into the pail she held at an angle between her knees. The milk rattled against the steel bucket. After the stream from those two teats began to lessen she switched to the opposite side and continued to alternate until there was little milk coming out. She then switched to "stripping," pulling her thumbs and index fingers down the teats in turn to get the last drops. The whole process took between five and ten minutes, depending on how much each cow produced, and whether the cow was an easy or hard milker. My mother then weighed the bucket and noted the result on a chart so she could keep track of each cow's yield, before pouring the milk into the milk cooler and moving to the next cow.

When I was about seven years old, as soon as my hands were big enough, my mother taught me how to milk, standing over me, helping me to hold the teats in the right way. I learned on Cowslip, a placid cow whose milk came out easily. I enjoyed the peaceful rhythm of the milk hitting the pail with a satisfying ping, the comfortable warmth of the cow's body against my cheek, the intimacy of the rumblings in Cowslip's stomach, the earthy smell of the milk, and the feeling of satisfaction when the task was done. But I never was very good at it—I was away at school most of the time and didn't get enough practice. My mother could milk five cows to my one, and I rarely progressed beyond Cowslip.

Milk spoils easily and needs to be cooled immediately, so my father installed a cooler in the small dairy attached to the cowhouse. It looked like a washboard made of pipes with cold water from a tank above the dairy flowing through them, pumped by a petrol pump. Each bucket of milk went down over the pipes, and into a large steel milk churn identified by a metal label with our name and identification number stamped on it. The

81

churn from the evening milking stayed cool enough in the mild Cornish nights, ready for my father to take it and the morning churn to the stand on its journey to the milk processing factory.

My mother always poured some milk straight from the pail into a dish for the farm cats who congregated by the dairy every morning and evening and wouldn't drink the milk if it got too cool. She also filled a large pan for the house. None of us liked the creamy Guernsey milk, so the milk simmered very slowly on the stove until the cream rose to the top and my mother carried it to cool on the slate shelves of the house dairy. When the cream clotted she skimmed it off the top with a slotted spoon—the famous Cornish clotted cream. Only my brother liked it, but he made up for the rest of us, pouring a generous portion of cereal into a bowl for breakfast and adding an even greater amount of cream. We called it cereal on cream. If my brother was away at school, my parents usually fed the cream to the pigs.

In the days of food shortages after the war my mother made some of the cream into butter. She held a bowl of cream in the crook of her left arm and flipped it with her right hand until it curdled and then turned into butter. She used two wooden grooved paddles to pat the butter into a rectangular shape. Sometimes, to be fancy, she put some into little brown earthenware pots and decorated each individual pat with a thistle head motif pressed from a wooden stamp. The butter was delicious, and even after commercial butter stopped being rationed she used to make it occasionally for a treat.

Although dairying was a monotonous routine, my mother never showed any signs of tiring of it. She developed a rapport with the cows, who gave their milk to her as they would not do to others, even my father, who occasionally had to take over the task on the few occasions when my mother was away. She sat peacefully, bent over, concentrating yet far away, happy in the rhythm and sensations she loved. When we left the farm, she often said she missed the cows badly.

AUSTERITY

"Rationing" is a negative idea nowadays. Rationing healthcare, for example, suggests unfairness, a lack of opportunity, a hindrance to entitlement. Wartime rationing in Britain was all about fairness, equal opportunity, sacrifice, sharing adversity. Britain had been importing approximately seventy percent of its food for more than half a century and by 1941 Hitler's control of most of Europe and the toll taken by German U-Boats sinking transatlantic shipping meant the country had only six weeks of basic foodstuffs left. Rationing was the only answer.

It's easier to make a list of things that weren't rationed than things that were. We could buy unlimited amounts of fresh fruits and vegetables, but those available were mostly what grew in temperate Britain. No bananas or lemons. A few oranges made it past the U-Boats but most greengrocers reserved them for pregnant women and children, and sometimes even limited British apples to one per customer if they got short before the next harvest. Fish wasn't rationed because the government feared that if it were, fishermen wouldn't feel it was worth it to go out to sea and risk the U-Boats. However, the fishermen were still leery of the dangers and fish was scarce, causing long lines at fishmongers and fish-and-chip shops.

Clothing was also rationed. We were limited to one outfit a year at best, and washing old ones was difficult since soap was rationed. So was paper, confining newspapers to about four sheets and causing empty shelves in bookshops. By 1942 only companies, emergency services and farmers were allowed a petrol ration. Everyone else walked, took public transport, or went back to horses. Almost anything fun disappeared from shops, and even cakes for tea became treats since there wasn't enough sugar to make one very often.

The government issued every citizen a ration book, and people had to register for their groceries with a particular store, which received enough rations for all the registered people. Posters and radio messages encouraged everyone, especially workers, to eat the food ration weekly to maintain their strength and health. Every Friday we drove the three miles into the straggling china clay town of Bugle and up to the Post Office, our registered grocery shop, to buy our rations. The Post Office was set back from the street and a little away from the other Bugle shops clustered around the main crossroad. Inside, a metal grille marked off the Post Office part at the back, while the two sides held the groceries, non-perishables on one side, dairy and cured meats (such as there were) on the other. The husband of the couple who owned the store mostly looked after Post Office business, and the wife handled the groceries. Of course they both knew all the customers.

There was usually quite a line in the store and my mother chatted with other women while my brother and I fidgeted. When it was our turn, first the wife carefully sliced off a quarter pound of bacon per person and cut the weekly two ounces of cheese each, weighing them meticulously on the large brass scale, placing the correct weight on one side and the food on the other. With similar care, since customers watched to make sure they got their full due and no one got extra, she cut two ounces each of butter and lard and four ounces of margarine per person from large slabs, weighed them, and then wrapped everything in waxed paper. Finally, she reached over to the eggs piled in a large dish (paper was too precious for cartons) and picked out eight eggs, one each for my father and mother, six between my brother and me, although, since we had our own eggs on the farm, we didn't really need them. After that she crossed to a similar set of scales, on the other side and measured a half-pound of sugar and two ounces of tea for each person into paper bags.

"Do you want the marmalade, m'dear, or would you rather have the jam or extra sugar?" she asked my mother, using the usual Cornish informal endearment. Since we could have a two-pound jar of marmalade every week, my mother sometimes chose jam or sugar, but that day she asked for orange marmalade, a vital breakfast staple to eat on toast.

"Anything on points?" asked the postmistress. Each person had forty-eight "points" every month that we could use for non-essentials like canned goods if they were available. What we chose depended on what was on the shelves at the time, but my mother generally picked up baked beans, rice, or something savory like Marmite (a salty yeast extract that I disliked) to spread on toast. Finally my mother handed the postmistress our ration books and she inked a large rubber stamp to record our purchases.

While my mother was shopping, my brother and I eyed the tempting glass jars of sweets, trying to decide what to get with our three-ounce weekly allowance. There wasn't a lot of choice, mostly what we called boiled sweets (hard candy). I liked flavors like orange and lemon, especially as I rarely encountered them in the flesh. The postmistress weighed our purchases with the same attention she gave to the food, but instead of stamping our cards she cut a coupon from a sheet for each of us and threaded it on a string, a finicky but necessary process since, unlike the stamped food cards, she had to turn them in to the Ministry of Food to get new supplies of these non-essentials.

We then moved on to the butchers. Meat wasn't rationed by weight but by price, usually meaning about a pound and a quarter of meat each per week. In Cornwall by far the most popular meat was beef, since it could be made to go a long way in meat and potato pasties, the Cornish staple food. My mother generally bought beef for pasties, and stews, or mince (hamburger) for shepherd's pie, anything that could be made to go further with vegetables or become tender if cooked long enough. Sausages weren't rationed for most of the war, but they were so full of bread they hardly tasted of anything. Some people were suspicious that the small amount of meat was horsemeat, but no one asked since the animal-loving British didn't knowingly want to eat horse—even in wartime.

Of course, like all mandatory programs, rationing spawned a black market, but most people saw beating the system as unpatriotic. Ordinary people resented the rich who could afford to eat out, so the government forced restaurants to limit their prices and they couldn't serve more than three courses or have meat and fish in the same meal. Many of the rationed things simply weren't available in greater quantities. Instead, people bartered things they didn't need for things they did. On the farm we had eggs to spare, so my mother found an elderly couple who didn't like cheese and swapped some eggs every week for a meager four-ounce slice of government-controlled Cheddar.

People abandoned their lawns and planted what Americans called "victory gardens" to have more to eat. American soldiers were immensely popular with those who met them because they had supplies of cigarettes and nylon stockings that they knew women craved and were unobtainable in Britain. They gave them out quite freely, although, we heard, mostly to attractive young women.

When the war ended, after six years of fighting Britain was almost bankrupt and couldn't afford to import more than essential food, so rationing continued and became even more severe in some cases. Bread and potatoes, never restricted during the war, were rationed for a time, but civilians could now get a small supply of petrol for private use. As part of the enlarged welfare state the new Labour government provided children with free milk, orange juice, and cod liver oil, supplying essential calcium and vitamins C, A and D. The concentrated orange juice and cod liver oil came in small rectangular bottles and we got a teaspoon of each every day after breakfast, doled out by my mother at home, and Miss Rapley at school. The cod liver oil tasted so awful I shuddered as it went down, but the orange juice chaser was delicious, or so it seemed at the time. Everyone I know who remembers it loved it.

On the farm we escaped some of the deprivation. We had abundant supplies of milk, butter, and eggs, and more petrol than most people. For a short time we grew vegetables in the mowhay, although my parents had little time to tend them. We had chickens we could eat when their best laying days were over. My father didn't like killing things so after a number of frustrating times waiting for him to get up the courage to do the deed, my mother took over. She tied the chicken's legs together, strung it upside down on a nail on the garage outside wall, a procedure that for some reason kept it from flapping its wings. She chopped its head off with a small axe she kept there for just that purpose. It took a few minutes for the chicken to stop twitching before she took it down, plucked and gutted it.

Much later, while doing historical research, I discovered that the open area where my mother did this, its only use as far as we were concerned, had once been the main room of the original farmhouse, and the site of many small Methodist meetings. We never noticed the old fireplace on the wall, almost totally obscured by weeds.

We also had pigs, and every year for several years after the war we killed a pig for our own use. Killing a pig is not for the squeamish. If I was home from school our parents always told me to take my brother for a long walk while the actual killing happened. They strung up the pig from the roof in the car's garage and cut its throat so it bled to death, squealing most of the time. Then, with help from neighbors, they butchered the carcass, salting some of the meat for ham and bacon, mincing other parts for sausages that they encased in parts of the intestines. Extra blood they dried and made into black puddings (blood sausages). For me the best part was the doughnuts my mother deep-fried in the rendered fat, dredged with just a little of the precious sugar. For my parents, starved of meat and deprived of bacon for so long, the distressing process was worth the effort, but once meat rationing ended we killed no more pigs.

Rationing for some items dragged on until 1954, when I was fifteen. When I went to my boarding high school in 1949, sugar was still rationed and we weren't allowed to have it in tea, a useful prohibition since I lost my taste for it and have hated sweetened tea and coffee ever since. Sugar, sweets and meat were the last items to "go off the ration." Before that, gradually some previously unobtainable things had crept back. A tangerine in the toe of my Christmas stocking stopped being a big deal. I had my first banana in the late 1940s, not so great a treat as my parents had made it out to be. At about the same time we went down a small side street in St. Austell, a nearby town, to Kelly's Cornish Ice Cream shop, where I had my first ice cream, vanilla, the only flavor available. I didn't like cream, so that too was a disappointment. I have forever been able to resist ice cream.

Today museums show plates of fake rationed food to emphasize just how little we had to eat. Those of us who can remember rationing view them with nostalgia. We have forgotten what hunger is.

FRIENDS AND PUPILS

In Cornwall we were expatriates. We lived among people who spoke with such thick accents they were difficult to understand. My brother and I made friends with middle-class children like us at school, not in the neighborhood. My parents' main Cornish friends were Bob and Dorothy Nicholls, who owned a large farm close to Lostwithiel. Dorothy was a Kendall, from a well-respected Cornish family, and was thought to have married beneath her. I found visiting them very boring, unless their youngest daughter Cynthia was there. She was older than I was, but willing to show me around and chat, mostly about farming matters. Apart from the Nicholls, my mother and father were on good terms with their native Cornish neighbors, but they mostly spent their meager leisure time with friends who spoke "BBC" English, who had grown up with the same middle class assumptions and prejudices as they had.

Some of them were friends from their former life who joined them in their crazy adventure. Perhaps, like my mother and father, they too were weary of war and wanted to escape to a simpler life. The first were Daphne and Phil Harris. Petite, dark-haired Daphne, a talented painter and dancer, had married Phil hastily on one of his Navy leaves during the war. Phil ignored and sometimes picked on their three-year-old son Rodney, born during his father's long absence at sea, and lavished all his affection on Linda, their baby daughter, born after his return. Phil was volatile, irascible, and unpredictable, and his marriage to Daphne was rocky, so my mother, known by her friends as a reliable and wise confidant, invited them all to live with us while the two of them sorted things out.

The family settled into two of our six bedrooms and Phil worked with my father on projects like the bathroom, while Daphne looked after her children and shared the kitchen with my mother, taking turns to cook lunch. We sat at opposite ends of the long kitchen table as if to emphasize the separateness of the two families.

"Mmm," said Phil one day at lunch, "Joanie's rice pudding is better than yours, Daph."

88

Daphne immediately stood up, knocking her chair over, and stormed out of the room to shut herself in their bedroom for the rest of the day, until my mother later went up and coaxed her out.

Yet they *did* sort out their differences and stayed married until Phil's death as an old man. They bought a house on a large plot at the edge of Lostwithiel, a neighboring town, where Phil started a construction business, and Daphne taught dance, designed greeting cards, and became a pillar of the local Women's Institute. As I write, she is still alive, in her nineties, still living in Lostwithiel, having taught tap dancing up to a few years ago. Phil and Rodney never managed to understand each other, and as soon as he could Rodney emigrated to Australia.

Once Phil and Daphne had settled in their own home, Daphne's sister Pam, her husband Peter Pearks, with their children Peter and Tessa, decided to move to Cornwall as well. Pam and Peter bought a farm in our valley, then sold it and ran a restaurant in Fowey, a nearby harbor and port. Even closer, in the next farm, my parents' friends Mary and Jim Wakeman joined the group. Jim had a bad case of Bell's palsy, freezing one side of his face, perhaps making him unfit to be called up in wartime. The young Peter Pearks and the Wakeman's daughter Pat went to St. Goran School with my brother and me. I was a year older than Pat but in the school holidays the age difference didn't matter and most days one or the other of us walked the short distance down the lane that linked our farms to play. The only time I ever saw a snake in Cornwall was when we disturbed an adder in some long grass and ran screaming to Pat's parents for comfort.

Once my parents were confident they knew how to farm, they decided they could earn a little extra money and get some help with farm chores by teaching others. They advertised for pupils who paid for instruction in all aspects of running a farm from the daily chores to managing the finances. The fee also covered the cost of their room and board with us in the farmhouse. The first to sign up were Alex and Faith Hemsley, who moved in with their four children, John, Anne, Elizabeth (always called Tootoos, I can't remember why), and Bruce. Alex had been a doctor in Fiji, but something had gone wrong, I never knew what, and he had decided to try farming. Faith and my mother got on well, and I, always glad to have some company other than my brother, enjoyed playing with Anne, who was my age, and showing her simple farm chores like collecting eggs. However, at the back of my mind I can vaguely remember rumblings of jealousy when she joined me at St. Goran School, as she seemed prettier and better at sporty things.

I definitely benefited from having a doctor in the house. One day I ran out of the back kitchen door straight into the big copper kettle full of boiling water standing just outside, ready to mix with the cats' lunch of old bread and crumbled meat cube. My right leg somehow plunged directly into the kettle as it spilled over. I screamed, everyone came rushing out of the house, and Alex took charge. He immediately treated my leg with a salve he had with him and wrapped it in a huge bandage that he sniffed every day to tell how the healing was going. It would have taken at least a half hour to get me to the nearest hospital, so I was very lucky to have Alex there. When the bandages finally came off after several weeks my leg emerged without a scar.

Alex quickly learned the rudiments of farming and the family bought a farm close enough to Phil and Daphne Harris for Faith and Daphne to become life-long friends. Faith was an earth-mother type, always happy with a baby in her arms, and the family grew to ten children, some adopted. They had enough pasture for ponies, another reason for me to envy Anne since most girls of my age were pony-mad, but we needed all our grazing land for the cows. Eventually Alex went back to medicine and emigrated with the family to Australia where he signed on as a flying doctor in the Outback.

The next farming pupil was Karl Dunger, whom my brother called Dunghy-Dunghy, a name that stuck for all of us. Dunghy was a Polish Jew, which meant nothing to me in the late 1940s, except that he spoke a pleasantly accented English. We loved Dunghy. He was a gentle, loving bear of a man, immensely kind to us children, although we must have been daily reminders that his entire family had died in the death camps. I knew nothing about the Holocaust, which did not even have the name then, and didn't know about Dunghy's loss. I don't know how he survived—perhaps he had somehow got out of Poland and enlisted in the Polish army that formed in England. Later he too bought his own farm, and married Gladys, a similarly kind woman, as garrulous as he was quiet. I suspect he knew her before he came to live with us, and married when he was able to support a wife. They had no children and after Karl's early death from a heart attack, Gladys left for Israel.

Our last pupil, William, lived in Guernsey, one of the Channel Islands off the coast of France, coincidentally the original home of our breed of cows. His family grew tomatoes, Guernsey's main export, but William wanted to diversify and keep a milking herd. He was young, even quieter than Dunghy, and good-looking, but so self-effacing I can remember little about him.

After William left, my parents recruited no more pupils. With more jobs available in the 1950s for men who had had their lives disrupted by war, farming was less attractive as an alternative and no one answered my parents' advertisements. However, they now had an alternative source of help. They decided they needed more land and bought a neighboring farm, Gurtla. Since they didn't need Gurtla's farmhouse, they rented it to Willie, a middle-aged bachelor who lived with his aged father and paid a reduced rent in return for helping my parents with their expanded space.

Somehow, although Willie rarely left the farm, he met and courted Pearl (he always said Pearrrl in his strong Cornish accent). They married and went to St. Austell for their honeymoon—it was eight miles away, but Willie had never been there. Pearl was very good to Willie's father and, when he died, he said that Pearl should have everything that was his in the house, which included a large sum of money under his mattress. The rest of Willie's family contested this and between them they spent the entire amount on lawyers.

Gurtla never provided the extra income my parents had hoped for, and eventually they sold it. Willie and Pearl moved away, and we managed without extra help. However, we kept in touch with all the people who had shared our home, and especially enjoyed visiting Dunghy and Gladys.

PARTNERS AND PARENTS

I always knew that my parents loved each other best, and their children came second. They were each other's partners in everything, and we were very welcome but not altogether necessary adjuncts. While they were unfailingly loving, occasionally stern when our behavior deserved it, they never seemed to regret that they saw little of us for most of the year. They welcomed us home, but not effusively, and expected us to fall back into farm routines with no fuss. I certainly never felt unwanted, and I am sure my mother and father chose to have children, but their deepest fulfillment came from each other.

Like most British people of our generations, we were not a demonstrative family. I rarely saw my parents embrace and we children got the occasional hug and a kiss goodbye when we were leaving for school. My mother was more distant than my father, practical, busy, down-to-earth. Her day was more regimented, defined by cows and meals. Yet we still spent plenty of time with her, going to and from school, shopping, helping with meals, time when we could chatter about our days, our friends, what we were reading, rarely our innermost thoughts. She always got us to bed when we were home from school, read to us when we were little, took us to spend our pocket money. On rainy winter afternoons she played snakes and ladders or draughts (checkers) with us, and we sat by her as she listened to her favorite afternoon radio programs in the lull before milking time.

I never saw or heard my parents fight. Admittedly, my brother and I were away at school for two-thirds of the year, so we didn't witness most of their day-to-day interactions, but we were home for weekends and school holidays, and I don't think they could have faked their marital harmony. The most my father ever said was, "But Joanie…" in a slightly plaintive tone if she had suggested something he really didn't want to do.

Once, in the middle of a deluge of rain when we could hardly see beyond the windows, my mother suggested that my father go out to do some farm chore she thought essential. "But Joanie," he remonstrated, "It's coming down in bleeding buckets." I was shocked—I had never heard him use even faintly bad language. My mother relented, and "bleeding bucketing" became the family name for heavy rain.

Probably my parents didn't argue because they agreed about most things. If they didn't, my father usually did what my mother wanted. He adored her and almost always let her have her way. The one thing she could only rarely make him do was waste his time on social contacts with anyone other than their friends. I remember a carpet salesman who had managed to find his way to the farm. My father met him at the gate to the dirty, and just shouted "No" until the poor man retreated in defeat.

Another person he disliked was the Church of England vicar who occasionally walked the considerable distance from the parish church to the farm in a vain attempt to get us to attend services. Fortunately the vicar, who was elderly and fat, moved slowly so we could see him coming across the fields. This gave my father time to escape to a supposedly vital chore in a remote corner of the farm before the priest came puffing up to the rarely used front door to be greeted by my mother, who offered him tea and listened without commitment.

Although my father avoided strangers whenever possible, he was unfailingly congenial with friends and loving to my brother and me. He enjoyed having fun with us. When we were little he used to play a game where he stretched his legs apart with his hands locked in front and we had to unlock them to come in to get a big hug. For a long time he persuaded me that his gold pocket watch opened if I blew on it. (I was a gullible child, not good for someone born on April 1.)

My father encouraged us to try the unfamiliar—his mantra was "Suck it and see." When he had a beer, he encouraged me to take a sip so I would acquire the taste since, he pointed out, my future dates would probably not be able to afford mixed drinks in a pub. He was right—later my university boyfriends were both surprised and pleased that I was happy with a half-pint. As we grew older, my father took us on trips to learn about things other than farming. Once we went to one of the few remaining Cornish tin mines and saw a beam engine, a pump with a huge wooden beam dating back to the eighteenth century, the beginning of the age of steam. Another time he took us to see the very ancient sport of Cornish wrestling, with its own idiosyncratic rules. I was proud that my annual school magazine

93

accepted a piece I wrote about the wrestling match, my very first publication.

Unusually for a woman, my mother was the family driver. Even when my father came with us, which was rare since someone usually had to be home to keep an eye on the farm, she almost always drove. She drove as fast as the car would go (not very) round the narrow twisty Cornish lanes with their high hedges, but never had an accident. She was the one to take us on outings to the beach in summer, where she watched us as we poked around in tide pools, built sand castles, or bathed at the water's edge—I didn't learn to swim until I was eleven, at school. My mother never went in, and I never saw her in a bathing suit. Her pleasures were on the farm—she loved almost everything about it, and hated to be away.

Many people confided in my mother, who had the gift of listening without judgment, a strength she put to good use later as a marriage guidance counselor. Absolute strangers would tell her their life stories if they had the opportunity. When we were shopping my brother and I would stand around fidgeting while my mother listened to one of her many acquaintances telling her their latest problem with a husband, child or neighbor. "Yes, I quite understand." "I am very sorry, is there anything I can do?" Our neighbors always knew they could trust her for help, especially if they needed to be driven to the doctor or on some other vital errand.

My mother reached out and made friends. Yet she wasn't a joiner, never wanting to attend meetings of the local Women's Institute. Uncharacteristically, she, Faith Hemsley, and all of us children once went to the church fete in the vicarage gardens. On one of his visits the vicar may have pressed her to come. As we arrived the vicar came forward, hand outstretched, to welcome us. At that precise moment my mother's knicker (pantie) elastic broke, a common female mishap in the days before stretch fabrics, and my mother ran hastily behind a large rhododendron, leaving the vicar and Faith very puzzled. She emerged, smiling, with her knickers safely in her handbag, but we never went to the fete again.

In contrast to my mother's aversion to formal meetings, my father's social life revolved around what he saw as civic responsibilities. Before the war he had been a socialist as the family bookshelves still bore witness, with books by Bernard Shaw, G. D. H. Cole, and other left-wing writers of the 1930s, although curiously not George Orwell. Then, when Winston Churchill visited the RFD factory during the war, my father developed a great respect for him. He switched allegiances and joined the local Conservative Association, where he soon became an officer.

My father was also chair of the county Guernsey Society, which gave a trophy to the best Guernsey herd in Cornwall. In my teens I helped him do the calculations to decide the winner. We sat together at the kitchen table with statistics of milk yields and calving numbers, my father using his treasured slide rule whose operation I never mastered. We quickly realized that we could weight the numbers in various ways to make anyone we chose win, so we picked the herd we personally thought the most deserving, based on my father's knowledge of all the Society members.

My mother didn't do much with the Guernsey Society, but she did help the Conservatives at election times, distributing literature and canvassing door-to-door, where her friendly and persuasive manner was very useful. She stopped at nothing, and before every general election (once every five years) she went into to the local gypsy encampment to make sure they registered to vote, and to show those who were illiterate where to put their X—for the Conservative candidate, of course. When I got old enough to vote I never dared tell my parents that I voted Labour.

I didn't tell my parents much, which seems odd since everyone else confided in my mother. But perhaps the reason they chose her for their confidences, apart from her non-judgmental attitude, was because she *wasn't* their mother. And I am not sure what I would have told her if I had wanted to. Before I was ten I had little to confide, and a lot of teenagers never tell their parents much. I was a self-contained child, unwilling to be vulnerable. I kept my fears and disappointments to myself. I probably learned that from both parents.

MY MOTHER'S SIDE

My mother's parents were my favorite people after my own parents and Miss Rapley. When I was little, the closest I could get to saying "Granny and Grandpa" was Dandan and Poppa, and so they remained to me and, later, Michael. They epitomized for me how old people should look. Poppa's light hair barely covered his balding head, while his wire-rimmed glasses on his wide face gave him look that suited his name—Frank. Dandan's almost white wavy hair was pulled back into a bun, revealing a soft expression, while some loose curls hid her large hearing aids.

Not long after we bought the farm, when I was six or seven, my mother took me on the long train journey to Dandan and Poppa's rented house in Coulsden, an outer London suburb, leaving me there to come home by myself on the train since she had to get back to the farm. Their house backed onto the South Downs, a range of white chalk grassy hills stretching across southeast England. I went walking along the top with my grandfather. He strode along with his knobby wooden walking stick, knocking away stones that might trip me. Below us was the valley with the roof of my grandparents' house easily distinguishable in the clear early summer air. It was breezy up at the top, still a little chilly, and I could smell the smoke coming from a few late-season wood fires. As we walked I picked the wild flowers.

"What's this one, Poppa?" I asked, holding up a dainty nodding blue bellflower I had never seen in Cornwall.

"That's a harebell. They like chalk soil."

We walked along in companionable conversation about what we saw around us. Poppa never got impatient with my chatter.

Although Dandan's deafness meant she didn't leave the house much, on that visit she took me to the London Zoo. There were no zoos in Cornwall, so I was very excited about seeing all the exotic animals. In particular, I was dying to see Ming, the panda—my favorite soft toy was my panda. I knew about Ming because, as my father often reminded us, her bamboo meals were grown in a village a few miles from the farm. The pub there was called The Panda, and the bamboo groves shivered in the wind behind it.

Dandan and I walked around the zoo, admiring the architect-designed penguin enclosure, laughing at the monkeys' antics, oohing at the lions and elephants, taking in the unfamiliar earthy smells—straw and animal dung, but not like the ones on the farm. I was skipping along, holding Dandan's hand, talking loudly so she could hear me. But then, "It's getting time to leave to catch the train," said Dandan abruptly.

"Please let's see the panda first," I pleaded. My experience shopping with Dandan made me realize that she probably didn't like to ask the way, afraid she might not hear the answer. "We have a few more minutes," she replied, so I asked a nearby keeper, who directed us, and there was the panda in the outside enclosure! At that moment Ming ambled around and turned a somersault right in front of me. I jumped up and down with excitement. Dandan was happy too, and let me stay an extra minute to soak it in. The image has never left me.

I enjoyed helping Dandan with household tasks like setting the table. She was very particular about the correct placement of silverware and I learned the differences between soup and dessert spoons, fish knives and meat knives, niceties we rarely observed at home. After meals I enjoyed playing their old-fashioned games like *bezique*, a card game for two that was all the rage before World War I. After we had cleared supper away the three of us sat around the dining room table playing *Counties of England*, its cards representing manufacturing towns, illustrating a Victorian industrial era fast disappearing in the aftermath of war. Someone my grandparents knew must have spent time in the East since they had a fascinating somewhat battered model Chinese wedding procession, some Japanese *netsuke,* and some tiny hollowed-out red beans that contained even tinier carved ivory elephants. These things normally lived in a glass cabinet in their sitting room, but I was allowed to play with them. Later my favorite piece from Japan was a set of enameled coffee spoons, each a different flower. I inherited them from my mother, and have them still.

In the late 1940s Poppa, an expert in building restoration, was appointed chief architect for the reconstruction of Plymouth's churches. Plymouth was (and is) a major naval harbor and dockyard just over Cornwall's border with Devon. The city was nearly flattened during the war, with almost the entire center eliminated, and most of the churches damaged or destroyed. My grandparents settled into a two-bedroom apartment in a suburb that had escaped most of the bomb damage, and I was able to visit more often. They still had the card games, the Chinese wedding and the tiny elephants, and I still set the table.

Now the three of us walked on the Hoe, the long stretch of cliff top where, in the time of Elizabeth I, Admiral Francis Drake heard the Spanish Armada had been sighted. We saw the statue of Drake at his bowling game, which he is supposed to have insisted on finishing before leading his fleet out to fight the Spanish. At the end of the Hoe was the long stone jetty where the Pilgrims left for America. Behind, the rebuilt city center had a department store, Dingles, (there were none in Cornwall), with an elevator and an escalator, also new to us. We went there once a year to buy school supplies before visiting Dandan and Poppa. On one occasion my brother spent an hour repeatedly going up the escalator and down the elevator while my mother and I shopped.

Once we were on the farm my father never saw Dandan and Poppa again. They never came to the farm. My mother visited them occasionally, but, I believe, more from duty than affection. My grandmother's long years of hostility during their courtship had taken their toll, but since I knew nothing about that then, I didn't notice any tension.

Dandan and Poppa died within days of each other when I was fourteen. According to my mother, they snobbishly refused to join the National Health Service, and continued to go to their private doctor, who misdiagnosed some simple and curable ailment of Dandan's. My mother was there when Dandan died, and she told me that Poppa had no will to live without his wife and gave up trying. Since my mother never mentioned that Poppa had been ill as well, I have sometimes wondered if he committed suicide.

My mother was the only family member at their funerals— I never went to any funerals until I was grown up and married. But I had loved Dandan and Poppa and I missed them.

I also sometimes stayed with my great-aunt Annie and great-uncle Adrian, Dandan's sister and her husband. They had no children of their own, but adored my mother. Uncle Adrian was Italian, and when my

98

mother was a child they used to take her with them to the Italian church in London. My mother always called them just Uncle and Aunt, so to me they were Uncle and Aunty, no other names. They kept a genteel boarding house on a pleasant leafy street in Sutton, another outer London suburb.

Uncle had met my aunt when he was a boarder in their home. He had come to England as a foreign correspondent—family lore said he came to report on Marconi's activities while Marconi sought uninterrupted access to the Atlantic for his radio signals. Shortly after Uncle Adrian married Aunty Annie they emigrated to Vancouver for a while. They told stories about bears walking down the streets. I am not sure they fitted in very well, as I have a photo of them looking very Edwardian, Uncle in a three-piece suit and Auntie in a fairly formal dress, posed with their dog against an unruly Canadian hedge barely contained by a wire fence. Nor am I sure what they did there, but whatever it was it didn't work out and they returned to Britain in the 1920s. Since Dandan and Aunty had grown up in my great-grandparents' London boarding house, it must have seemed a natural choice to open one themselves.

By the time I knew them, Uncle had become first an exile, then technically an enemy alien. He had owned family property in Torre Pellice, a town on the Italian-French border in the foothills of the Alps. Like most Torre Pellice residents, Uncle was a Waldensian, a much-persecuted non-Catholic religious sect originating in the Middle Ages. He too suffered persecution, although not for his religious beliefs. In the 1930s Mussolini's government confiscated all his property, which my mother was to have inherited, because he was a nonresident. Then during World War II, despite his long residence in England and his obvious dislike of Mussolini, he was kept under house arrest in Britain as an enemy alien. None of this affected his or Aunty's good humor, which suffused the whole atmosphere of the boarding house.

When I visited Aunty and Uncle I showed off my table-setting prowess when it came time to serve meals at the long dining table. It was my job to learn each resident's napkin ring and make sure they were all in the right place. Once I had done that, Uncle took me around his beloved flower garden, talking fast in his Italian accent, and making me learn the names of all the flowers. He was especially proud of his mammoth dahlias.

99

I also had a whole boarding house full of residents to spoil me. My favorite was Mrs. Dixon-Smith, who had the prime room upstairs at the front with a bay window. The window seat held a collection of soft toy animals. I particularly liked the tiger, a somewhat meek-looking example, sitting down with a long tail stretching behind it. The first time I visited, when it was time for me to leave she gave me the tiger to keep, and it joined my panda and teddy as my favorites. For several years I made a Christmas card for Mrs. Dixon-Smith and reported on Tiger's health.

Aunty Annie told me how much she loved wild primroses. Primroses like acid soil, and didn't grow in the farm hedgerows, so in springtime I grabbed a wicker basket and walked about a mile to the other side of the farm valley, where I knew there was a hedge full of the pale yellow flowers. I picked a basketful, wrapped them in water-soaked moss, bundled them up in brown paper and mailed them to my great-aunt. I can't imagine what happened to the very soggy parcel en route (no plastic wrap then), but I never doubted that it would get there, and Aunty Annie never failed to thank me as if they had arrived intact.

Uncle Adrian died before I was in my teens, but Aunty Annie lived long enough to come to my wedding. She crocheted a set of tablemats for a gift. I never use them now, but I can't part with them either.

Aunty and Uncle in Vancouver

MOD CONS

For a while bath time at the farm was a once-a-week performance.

First my father filled the big copper kettle and all the pans we used for scalding milk with cold water from the hand pump in the back kitchen. He put the kettle and pans on the black-leaded kitchen range to heat and when they were almost boiling, poured them into the large oblong tin bath in front of the range, the warmest place in the house. He added cold water until the temperature was just hot enough to bear. We then took turns in the bath, my brother Michael and me together, one at each end, squirming and kicking each other, each claiming the other took too much room. I dried myself, my mother dried Michael, keeping us warm by the range until we were in our pajamas. Then my parents sent us up to bed and my mother and father, one after the other, bathed in lukewarm water and our soap scum, with my father taking the final shift. Then they had to carefully carry the heavy bath into the back kitchen and bale it out into the house's only sink.

The copper kettle held about five gallons of water. It got a lot of use, boiling water for dishwashing, laundry, and everyday sponge baths. In the mornings we washed in cold water at the washstands in each bedroom. Every bedroom had a chamber pot under the bed that we each had to empty into the chemical toilet every morning. I quickly trained myself to wait until morning so as not to use the pot.

Mrs. Hore, my mother's household help, did the laundry by hand in the back kitchen sink. That too was a performance. Those were the days before detergents, when people saved the last pieces of bars of soap, put them in a wire cage rather like a small bird-suet container, and used them for laundry or doing the dishes. Mrs. Hore rubbed the clothes with the soap remnants or a big bar of laundry soap, then rinsed them and wrung them out with her large and capable hands. Everything dried outside on the clothesline in the mowhay, although they took a while in Cornwall's damp climate.

Millions of people in Britain lived this way in the 1940s, including all our neighbors. Most of them had known nothing else. Estate agents (realtors) used the abbreviations "mod cons" (modern conveniences) to indicate that homes had electricity and bathrooms. In their former middle-class lives my parents had been used to such amenities and they soon started to modernize. After the barn fire, when my mother had to drive a distance to contact the fire engine, they installed a telephone, the first in the valley. There were no nearby wires so installation took a while, but eventually the squat black dial-up telephone was a fixture on the kitchen windowsill. I can still remember the number, Stenalees 336, Stenalees being the name of the local exchange. All calls outside the exchange had to go through an operator—no direct long-distance dialing. When I visited the farm in 1996, although the number had become much longer, it still had 336 at the end.

My parents quickly became known for their generosity, and our farm became the neighborhood phone booth for emergencies, mostly calling the vet or doctor. Eventually our neighbors the Wakemans got a phone, so ours became a party line, and we had to listen before dialing to make sure they were not already talking. Sometimes we were tempted to join in the conversation, but most of them were strictly about boring farm matters.

Next and best, my parents replaced the old coal-fired range with a new solid-fuel burning Swedish Aga cooker (stove). An Aga was, and still is, a prized asset, with a probably unmatched record for reliability and longevity. The one my parents installed was still there in 1996, fifty years later. It sat, cream-colored, in the recess where the range had been, emanating a wonderful even heat day and night, suffusing the kitchen with warmth. On top were two hot plates, one for fast and one for slow cooking. Below the hot plates on the right were stacked the hot and cool ovens, perfect for all baking requirements. The Aga ran on coke pellets, coal baked at high temperatures to remove the volatile elements, an almost smokeless fuel. Twice a day my father used a special hooked tool to pry up a lid in the middle of each burner to give the Aga its daily meal of coke from a long cylindrical shuttle. The rattle of the coke was one of the normal daily sounds of farm life.

Running along the front of the Aga at adult waist level was a chrome rail where we hung dishtowels and oven gloves. I loved to lean back against it, the warmth seeping into me, drying out after being out in Cornwall's "misty wet." Apart from the occasional fire in the sitting room, the Aga provided the only heat for the whole house. Although Cornwall's climate is temperate (it practically never snows), winters were chilly and the wind blew in through the sash windows. In winter we went to bed with ceramic or rubber hot water bottles (ceramic held the heat better), and at first we even had a copper warming-pan, a long wooden handle attached to a round lidded pan in which you placed live coals to warm the bed. But with the advent of the Aga, we had no coals to put in it, and it became a wall-hung decoration.

The Aga could also heat water, and my parents decided to turn the smallest upstairs bedroom into a bathroom. First, we needed a reliable water supply. My father and Phil Harris installed a small petrol-driven motor in the garage that pumped water from the well to a tank high on a stand in one of the fields, providing enough downward flow to the house. They must also have constructed a septic system before the actual installation. While Uncle Phil, as we called him, was putting in the pipes, he had a ladder leaning against the wall where he had chiseled holes out of the granite. Initially we couldn't understand why several cats that were not allowed in the house were appearing in the kitchen. Then one day I caught Stripey, the most persistent cat, in the act of climbing the ladder. We closed the hole.

When the bathroom was nearly finished Uncle Phil, a handsome, brown and lean former sailor, marched through the kitchen holding a toilet like a tuba and tootling a marching song. We all joined in the celebration, tootling after him down the passage and into the room where Phil was about to replace the chemical toilet. Now we too had the mod cons that I was used to at school. No more chamber pots. The tin bath rusted in the mowhay.

My parents made these improvements in the first few years on the farm. However, they believed it would never be worth the local power company's expense to bring electricity to our remote community of scattered farms. Instead we had three paraffin (kerosene) Tilley lamps, two for indoors and one with a handle so it could be used as an outside lantern, very helpful when cows calved in the night. After filling a lamp's tank with paraffin and doing something mysterious with a flat metal pricker, my

103

mother lit a wick and then pumped vigorously on a long syringe-like protuberance at the side of the tank. There was a pop and whoosh and the round muslin mantle at the top of a small pipe inside a glass shade became full of an incandescence that lit up the room almost as well as an electric bulb. When I was in my teens I was allowed to do it. I discovered the process was not as easy as it looked, and had to pump hard and long before getting the satisfactory whoosh.

My brother and I were never allowed to take a Tilley lamp to bed because my parents were very conscious of fire risks, especially after the barn fire. We had candles to light our way upstairs, but my parents took them away when they kissed us goodnight. Reading in bed had to be by torch (flashlight), for which we had to buy our own batteries from our meager pocket money, so they were usually dead.

Eventually, when I was in my teens, an electric company representative came to ask if we were willing to have electric lines across the farm. Of course we were! Now we could control our own light. My mother could get a milking machine. We bought a washing machine for Mrs. Hore to use. It was a twin tub, one tub for washing in hot water, the other for rinsing in cool. Mrs. Hore loved using it and washed any clothing we happened to leave lying around regardless of whether it needed it or was even washable. To protect my wool sweaters from certain shrinkage I became much tidier.

With electricity we might even have been able to get a television except that we couldn't afford one and anyway there was no reception, just snow, even in towns like Bugle, where Mrs. Hore had a set that usually only managed a fuzzy picture. That was one mod con we never had.

ST. AUSTELL

Once most food rationing had ended and we no longer had to shop where our ration books were registered, we started to do the weekly shop on Fridays in St. Austell, a nearby town on the route to and from St. Goran School. There we first got the week's groceries, and then turned to our greatest pleasure—changing our library books.

My mother parked in the lower part of the town and she, Michael and I climbed the hill to the High Street, where most of the shops clustered closely on both sides. Unlike Bugle, where we had shopped during the worst of rationing, St. Austell had a greater variety of shops, including Truscott's, the shoe store, with its fascinating x-ray machine that showed our toes inside our new shoes. We didn't know then, in the decade of Hiroshima, that it gave us unnecessary doses of radiation.

Nearby was Grose's, the department store, where we bought underwear and school uniforms and ordered the embroidered nametapes that my mother or I, when I got old enough, had to sew on all school clothes. They came in a long string, neatly held together with a rubber band, and we snipped off one as needed. Our long last name, Muir-Smith, made sewing more tedious, and we compensated by choosing the smallest print possible and using initials only for our first name. Even those we sometimes folded under.

We only occasionally stopped at Grose's and Truscott's, and even less often visited the dentist across the street, whom we dreaded because he didn't use an anasthetic. Normally we moved from the grocer to the butcher and then around the corner to the greengrocer, my mother's favorite, since she loved fresh vegetables. Sometimes, if we had pocket money to spend, my brother and I stopped at Woolworth's, full of affordable temptations like sweets and cheap toys.

Once we had done the grocery shopping, the real fun began. My parents belonged to two subscription libraries where they paid a membership fee, one in the chemist (drug store) Boot's and one in the stationery and bookstore W. H. Smith's. First we stopped at Boot's, hurrying through the chemist area to the library, carrying last week's borrowed books up the wide wooden stairs at the end of the store. Upstairs the room was lined with shelves of books, all with little green shields saying "Boot's" on a string threaded through the top of the spine to use as a bookmark.

My mother, with her usual charm, had the Boot's librarian well trained. My parents read the book reviews in the *Sunday Times*, picked out the ones they wanted to read, and gave the list to her. She ordered them and kept them for my parents to read first. "You're my best customers," she explained, "and most people want to read what you like." My father almost never came shopping, so my mother chose books for both of them—one fiction and one non-fiction each per week. For fiction they mostly chose mysteries, a taste they passed on to me, while for non-fiction they liked biographies and memoir, and my father read anything to do with seafaring. The hilariously funny books by Gerald Durrell about his adventures as a zoo animal collector became a major family favorite, especially *My Family and Other Animals*, his memoir of growing up on the Greek island of Corfu.

The children's allowance was one book a week, so I headed straight to the junior shelves. I liked adventure stories, mostly about children whose parents were either conveniently absent or considerably more permissive than any parents I knew, and whose experiences were far beyond anything I could envisage for myself. At that time the most popular British children's author was the prolific Enid Blyton, who wrote in almost every genre and for every age group. Her adventure stories—Famous Five books or the "Island of Adventure" series—were good, I thought, but her school stories less so, perhaps because the schools were like my own, if only a little more exciting. The school stories I preferred were farther from my own experience, set in exotic places like Switzerland or obsessed with odd passions like folk dancing. I sometimes read pony stories, also aimed at girls, but since the farm didn't have enough grazing for a pony, they reminded me of my disappointment and were not my favorite.

From Boot's we moved on to the stationers, W. H. Smith, where the selection was not so good and the librarian less well trained. My parents used Smith's library as a supplement so they did not run out of reading material during the week. They eventually dropped the subscription. Smith's was the town's only bookseller and I liked browsing the shelves for

106

ideas for Christmas and birthday presents and possibilities to look for in the library.

Our last stop was the public library, where we could take out three books for free, one fiction, two non-fiction. Since it had a larger clientele, popular or newer books were usually already checked out, so, although we had a larger allotment, it was harder to pick books we actually wanted to read. Here I discovered Jane Austen and the Brontes, and also lesser and long-forgotten series like Mazo de la Roche's Canadian family saga of the Whiteoaks of Jalna. I don't remember ever failing to come out with my full complement of books, and reading them all before the week was up.

The final treat at the end of the afternoon was on our way back to the car. Close to the car park and the public library we stopped at Peter's Cakes and each of us chose a delicious cream-filled treat—a chocolate éclair, a cream horn, a puff pastry layer—as well as a larger cake to slice at tea. We called the owners Mr. and Mrs. Peters, although their real name was Musitano—perhaps to avoid any bias against Italians after the war, the shop was named for their son. They always greeted us with smiles and chatted with my mother. They did well from the cake shop and owned a fancy fast car. One day Mr. Peters overtook on the brow of a hill and crashed into an oncoming vehicle. Neither party was injured, but after that my father called overtaking on a hill "doing a Peters."

Saying goodbye to the Peters, we drove the loaded car home. Since reading at night without electricity was difficult, we had to take advantage of all available daylight. The family rule was that we could read through breakfast and lunch, our major meal, but had to be social at tea, the evening meal, when it was usually getting dark, in winter at least. I also read most of the day except when I had to do chores. My library allotment was never enough, and I soon graduated to reading my parents' books, although, to my father's regret, I never warmed to the sea stories.

CARS

The other farmers in our valley had always managed without a car or tractor, walking considerable distances to the nearest shops or bus. My mother had other ideas. She needed to get to shops and my school. Even before my father joined us after the war, my parents had bought a second-hand Austin 7, the British equivalent of a Model T Ford. I can still recall its number plate, AKP 731. Like the Model T, it was black, with a boxy body, slightly curved at the back. It had two large doors, allowing access to both front and back seats, and running boards (steps to help you get in). Its wheels were spindly, the tires about half the size of today's, and its bumpers were minimal strips of metal. The single wiper was attached to the area above the windshield.

AKP 731 was in good condition when my parents bought it, but it soon deteriorated. It lived in a barn near the farmhouse, and it had to go through the dirty to get in and out, meaning it was usually covered in a generous coating of mud. Once we had to go to Bodmin, the home of our vet, a town a little closer than St. Austell, and famous in our family for its large mental hospital, mentioned when anyone did something crazy—"Oh, he'll end up in Bodmin." The shopping in Bodmin wasn't good and the vet always came out to the farm, so we didn't go there often. This time we had some quick errand—perhaps to see a lawyer about the purchase of our neighboring farm. My mother parked illegally while we dashed into the office. When we came back a policeman was getting ready to write us a ticket.

"We were only here for a few minutes," my mother protested in an aggrieved tone. He ignored her, probably typecasting her by her middle class accent as an annoying tourist, despite the state of the car. He calmly walked to the front of the car to write down the plate number. He looked down at the caked mud over where the plate hung low before the apology for a bumper.

"Your number plate's unreadable," he remarked, and wrote out another ticket. My mother was furious, although she paid both tickets. My brother

108

and I were humiliated. We were reminded of it every time we went to Bodmin after that. We hated the place.

As well as being caked with mud, the car had other idiosyncrasies. It started with a handle stuck into a hole at the bottom of the oval-shaped chrome-grilled radiator, just above the illegible number plate. The handle had to be turned with a strong jerk. My mother could usually do it, but on very cold mornings when the engine needed an additional burst of energy, my father did it for her. As the car got older it needed an even bigger boost, so we carried a bottle of petrol to fill the carburetor before turning the starting handle. It was known simply as "the bottle of." Soon we were carrying another larger bottle of water because the radiator sprung a leak and needed topping up before every journey. Eventually someone told us to put ground ginger in the radiator tank, which miraculously fixed it.

Other dilapidations accrued gradually. We somehow lost the chrome wing-shaped radiator cap, replacing it with an old and rusty rag. The yellow arrows that sprang out from just before the door hinges to indicate left or right turns stopped working, so my mother relied, somewhat spasmodically, on hand signals. My parents sometimes used the back seat of the car to take young calves to market. They covered the seat, but as my father pushed a calf in, it struggled and kicked the windows, cracking them in several places and giving them a yellow tinge.

As I grew older I became ashamed of AKP 731's muddy and dilapidated state. Very occasionally one of my parents drove the long distance to Exeter to visit me at my high school. As they turned into the driveway in front of the boarding house I could hear my friends' suppressed giggles at the car's state.

One evening my father was taking me to the station to catch the train back to Exeter. We were driving along one of the narrow, one-car-width roads that surrounded the farm when we heard a loud knocking underneath the car.

"What's that?" I asked my father.

"Oh, the wheel's going to fall off," he replied, jokingly.

A few minutes later one front wheel *did* fall off, shearing through at the axle. We were blocking the road, but managed to hold the wheel against the axle to push the car into a nearby field entrance (now I can't imagine how, but my father was ever resourceful). We then had to walk quite a distance to a phone box to get my parents' friends, the Nicholls, to rescue us. My father suggested that I stand at the side of the road and try to get someone to give me a ride to the station, but I vetoed the idea, delighted to miss a day of school.

That was the end of AKP 731. To replace it my parents bought CAF 352, an Austin 12, a larger and more dignified car that had belonged to two elderly sisters who had hardly used it. It was in pristine condition, black, like AKP 731, with four doors, the back ones opening forward. It had more room inside, an internal starter mechanism, and two wipers attached at the bottom of the windshield. Even the bumpers were more substantial. We had stopped trying to get calves into the car, and CAF 352, while still usually generously spattered with mud, never deteriorated as badly as AKP 731 and I was less nervous about my schoolmates seeing it or even riding in it.

CAF 352 lasted until after we left the farm, when it was about twelve years old and had taken us many miles. It didn't have the character of AKP 731, but it didn't die either, merely traded in for a snazzy red Riley.

THE OUTSIDE WORLD

The farm was three miles to the nearest shop, six miles to the nearest town, with no public services except the postman. Few people came through our valley since it was on the road to nowhere in particular. Going to school took my brother and me into another, wider world, although it also meant we were never fully part of the local community. My parents breached the isolation through newspapers and the radio.

Newspapers arrived with the mail, the local *Western Morning News* on the same day, the London *Times* a day late. Both were generally regarded as non-partisan, but leaned towards conservatism. In those days *The Times* indicated its Victorian seriousness by refusing to have any headlines or pictures on its front page, instead running its classifieds there. I sometimes looked at the less forbidding *Western Morning News*, but rarely read anything in *The Times* until my mid-teens, when I started to do the crosswords.

My parents also subscribed to *The Farmer's Weekly*, full of articles on animal husbandry and new machinery. I read parts of it to feed my print addiction, but found it very boring. For some time my mother also took a slim grayish magazine called *The Lady*, a curious Victorian relic where people placed advertisements for governesses and ladies' maids (I am amazed to discover it is still published in a much revamped form). I don't think my mother's subscription signified nostalgia for a ladylike existence, since she loved farm work. I suspect it was a gift from her parents, indulging in wishful thinking. The magazine had sections on knitting and crochet, neither of which my mother did, and nothing in it seemed to fit her daily life. Its fashion tips provided a stark contrast to wellies and overalls:

> *The smart woman always prefers to have just one good outfit which she constantly wears, one in which the coat can be deliberately lined, coloured to the dress she wears below.*[‡]

[‡] The Lady, "Secret of Smartness," 31st August 1950.

My mother rarely wore anything other than farm clothes, and when she did, she picked from the few outfits that remained from her former life.

The radio was an essential farming tool. Our fabric-covered battery-powered set with two knobs, one for tuning and one for volume, sat on the kitchen dresser. The BBC had a monopoly on all broadcasting, and we sat around the long kitchen table, my father at the end, my mother close to the Aga, and Michael and I on the long bench with our backs to the window, our books closed, listening. The most sacred time in the morning was the weather forecast, vital in Cornwall's changeable climate. My parents also listened to the shipping forecast since it could be more accurate than the land weather forecast in an essentially maritime county. The shipping forecast was a monotonous incantation of names followed by a very brief report for each area. "Rockall, Shannon, Irish Sea. Winds north to northwest, strong. Light rain."

To save batteries, we listened only to essentials like the weather forecast and things we really liked. There were three BBC channels. The Home Service provided news, sports, mainstream classical music, theater productions, quiz shows like "Twenty Questions," and local broadcasts. The Light Programme played popular music, radio sitcoms and a few of what we would now call talk shows. The Third Programme was more highbrow, with classical concerts, book reviews and philosophical discussions. The whole family's favorite was the comedy ITMA, standing for "It's That Man Again," that man being the comedian Tommy Handley. The half hour was full of characters with catchphrases like a lugubrious charwoman (cleaning lady) who always said, "It's being so cheerful as keeps me going." We rarely missed a weekly episode until Tommy Handley died suddenly of a heart attack when I was ten. In the later fifties we listened to *Hancock's Half Hour*, with Tony Hancock, whose perpetually depressed outlook kept us laughing, and the iconic *Goon Show*, zany and irreverent, precursor to sixties' satire.

The Light Programme broadcast a daily lunchtime soap opera called "Mrs. Dale's Diary," days in the life of a doctor's wife. My mother was addicted to it, and we had to keep quiet for her sacred fifteen minutes. It was followed by "Women's Hour," which my mother listened to if she had time. I liked it too, especially the last quarter hour when a well-known actor read from a serialized book. I particularly remember *Nothing Is Safe* by E. M. Delafield, a best-selling author, about the effect of divorce on children, although it never made me worry about my own parents' marriage. Then at 5 p.m. my brother and I listened to "Children's Hour," a mix of information, fiction and music, a kind of aural *Sesame Street*. My parents did not listen to another popular soap opera, *The Archers*. It was billed as "an everyday story of farming life," and was originally intended to disseminate useful information to farmers, but no farmers we knew listened to it. My parents despised it, thinking it romanticized farming and showed little of the daily grind.

In the evening we listened to the six o'clock news over our evening meal. It started with the six high-pitched beeps or "pips" of Greenwich Mean Time, followed by Big Ben striking the hour. In the late forties the news was dominated by the beginnings of the Cold War. I still remember the BBC newscaster announcing solemnly, "King Michael has abdicated," referring to the communist takeover in Romania. I was eight at the time. I don't know why that made such an impression on me, since I recall nothing of the Berlin airlift or similar tensions.

We didn't listen to a lot of music on the radio. We enjoyed call-in request shows and *Desert Island Discs*, where a celebrity chose the six records and a book they would take with them to a desert island (I believe the show is still running, and I still sometimes idly pick my choices). In the summer my parents occasionally listened to the London Promenade Concerts from the Albert Hall, and on Sundays they sometimes turned on an hour with the Palm Court Orchestra, a kind of British Lawrence Welk, a string ensemble playing popular tunes and light classics. The one thing we couldn't hear in the age of Elvis was rock'n roll—the BBC, faithful to its mandate to educate and enlighten and not to "corrupt," had a policy not to play it. If as a teenager I wanted to hear the top twenty I had to tune into the European Radio Luxemburg at eleven o'clock on Saturday night, (well past my bedtime), and I could only do that when I got my own radio, half-way through my teens.

For music at home we had a wind-up gramophone with a ragtag collection of 78 records, some of them dating back to my parents' courting days. Several of them were piano dance music played by Charlie Kunz, a popular musician and bandleader in the 1930s. One of them stuck halfway

113

through and endlessly made a sound we interpreted as "toodle-pup, toodle-pup." Michael and I found this extremely amusing and played it often. When I was about ten my father started telling me about the Gilbert and Sullivan productions he had gone to with his parents when he was growing up. He caught my interest and through Christmas and birthday presents over about four years I slowly collected the whole of *The Mikado*, my father's favorite, on 78s, one at a time. In my teens my father bought our first LP, Handel's *Water Music*. Of course we had to buy a new gramophone to play it, and by that time we had electricity, so we said goodbye to winding up and the toodle-pup record lost its appeal.

We rarely went to the cinema because film times usually conflicted with milking. My parents made sure we saw the latest Disney—I thought that the Disney *Cinderella* was the funniest thing I had ever seen, especially the king bouncing on the bed. The only non-Disney film I can remember seeing while we lived on the farm was when my cousins Alan and Sylvia took me to see Danny Kaye in *Hans Christian Anderson*.

Once we were old enough, my mother or father took us to the local pantomime, a British Christmas tradition. Despite its name, it was not silent, but a unique mixture of music, slapstick comedy, romance, villainy, and audience participation. The plot was always a traditional tale—Puss in Boots, Cinderella, Dick Whittington, and Aladdin were some of the most popular. The main male character was a glamorous woman, called the principal girl, and the main comic character role was a male comedian in drag. Only the principal female character was not gender-bending. We sang along with the songs, shouted out when told to, and laughed uproariously. It was the only live theater we saw in Cornwall, and we looked forward to it every year.

Once I went to high school I had a few more opportunities to go to films and see live performances, but reading still provided my main window on other worlds. I read about children who ran their own theatre, danced, skated, rode horses, joined the Girl Guides (Scouts), lived away from their parents on an island in the Lake district, solved crimes without police help. I envied them, but I knew that was not my life, and I was usually content with that. While I also knew that the farm was confining and I didn't want to grow up to be a farmer's wife, I could wait.

MRS. HORE

She looked like the person she was. Solid, strong. Not fat, but sturdy, with muscular arms, stocky legs, not much of a waist. Her dark hair hung in a medium-length bob round her chubby face, her cheeks red, her mouth often in a grim line that belied her innate cheerfulness. I almost always saw her in a flowered working smock pulled over her wide shoulders and ample bosom, her hair covered by a tightly-tied headscarf. And she was always working.

Mrs. Edith Hore (even my mother never called her Edith) became my mother's household help after my brother got old enough to join me at school and we no longer needed someone around all the time to watch us. Mrs. Hore's husband Fred was a china clay worker and they lived in a small granite row house in Bugle—kitchen, living room, two upstairs bedrooms and an outhouse. Her accounts of life with her husband were fascinating, revealing marriage as the battleground quite unlike my parents' harmonious relationship.

"You'll never guess what Fred said yesterday," she'd say to my mother. "He told me my saffron cake was too dry. I told him he didn't have to eat it, and I wouldn't pack it with his lunch tomorrow. He soon decided it was all right after all." In her telling, she always won.

At first Mrs. Hore came a couple of times a week, but later she came daily, even turning up without being asked on weekends if she thought we were especially busy. For the first few years, most days my mother fetched her in our car after milking, but sometimes she came on her bicycle, a two-and-a-half mile ride. We watched anxiously from the kitchen window as she came wobbling into the dirty on a bike that was too small for her large frame. She never fell off.

Mrs. Hore cleaned, washed the breakfast dishes and our clothes, did the ironing, and often cooked lunch. She liked everything very tidy so we had to spend time after she left finding things she had put away in unsuspected places. Like many Cornish men and women, she was a strictly teetotal Methodist. My parents kept a bottle of gin for the occasional celebratory

115

drink, so, before she did her daily chores, Mrs. Hore always went into the dairy and checked that the gin was still wrapped in newspaper to hide the sinful temptation.

Mrs. Hore worked to better herself and her family. To give herself more freedom she bought first a motorized bicycle, then, after passing her driving test, a very old car. She was a terror in both, pushing them to their uppermost speed, which fortunately wasn't very fast. She came roaring into the farmyard, through the dirty, spattering mud in every direction, and screeched to a halt just short of one of the barns. She loved driving.

From her earnings over the years she paid for improvements to their house—indoor bathroom, new living room furniture, a television. She spent her money quite independently of Fred's opinion. She told us that Fred (whom we did call by his first name, following his wife's example) disapproved of what he thought was unnecessary expenditure on the new furniture. When he wanted to watch the television, which he did appreciate, he carried one of the old armchairs in from their garden shed and sat in it.

The main objects of Mrs. Hore's concern and ambition were her two sons, Owen and Colin. Owen, the elder, was too old to take advantage of the free secondary education made available to all by the end of the 1940s. However, he did well at elementary school until he was fourteen and got a good job in a farmer's supply company, where he eventually rose to become the manager. He married Margaret, a local girl from a family rather higher up the social scale than the Hores. At the wedding Mrs. Hore was very insistent that my mother wear her fur coat, inherited from my grandmother, and sit in a prominent position so Margaret's family would notice. Since it was a very cold day and the Methodist chapel was unheated, my mother would have worn it anyway, having few clothes suitable for weddings. But my parents were puzzled to see Owen sweating profusely. They put it down to nerves, partially true, since Owen discovered later when he went to change that he had been so stressed in the morning that he had put his wedding suit on over his pajamas.

Owen did well in his white-collar job, avoiding the hard, messy and sometimes dangerous work in the china clay mines that was the fate of most of the town's young men. However, Mrs. Hore had even higher hopes for Colin, who was young enough to be able to go on to the free secondary school, where he was a star pupil. From there he went to an agricultural college and became a farm manager before emigrating to the United States with his Cornish wife and children. He became a Kansas chicken farm tycoon before dying of a heart attack in his forties. His mother was devastated.

Here's the part I'm ashamed of. Although my brother and I liked Mrs. Hore and she was never mean to us, with the almost unconscious cruelty of children we sometimes treated her very badly. I am glad we were too sheltered to understand the sexual overtones in the name Hore, which must surely have mortified her and might well have made us snigger. One day Mrs. Hore by accident pulled the tail of Mandy, one of our outdoor cats, when shooing her from the house. We made up a rhyme about her that we certainly sang within her hearing, I hope not too many times:

> Mrs Hore
> Scrubs the floor.
> She pulled Mandy's tail
> And Mandy did wail.
> Horrid Mrs. Hore.

We reserved our most despicable behavior for Colin. In the school holidays Mrs. Hore sometimes brought Colin, who was about my brother's age, with her. We got tired of her telling us how wonderful Colin was, and Colin himself tended to boast about his success. However, that was no excuse for our actions. We, with our middle-class accents and boarding school education, felt superior to Colin, and wanted to put him in his place. I have blocked from my memory exactly what we did, but I know we teased him mercilessly about anything we could latch on to, from his Cornish accent (which he later lost) to his choices in reading. Once we pushed him off a wall, I can't remember why. He wasn't hurt, but complained to his mother, who told my parents. We had a lecture about proper behavior to others, and Mrs. Hore stopped bringing Colin. He must have hated us.

Perhaps Mrs. Hore feared for her job, but I think she genuinely loved my parents and was willing to overlook our rotten behavior. She never said anything about our teasing her. She continued to treat us like the family we almost were. She was very sad when we left the farm, and I kept in touch with her for many years. She wrote every Christmas until she died in 2009, aged ninety-four, never failing to say that she remembered how mercilessly my brother teased *me*. Since he didn't tease me much in front of my parents, and, like Colin, I rarely complained, she was the one who saw it. I appreciated her memories and belatedly regretted ever calling her "Horrid Mrs. Hore."

PITCHING IN

Harvest began one July morning after milking time with the sound of the metallic clack of the binder, a siren song for our small farming community. The men straggled in through the gate in battered felt hats, collarless grubby shirts with sleeves rolled to the elbow, and assorted stained pants held up with binder twine, tucked into boots as protection against the stubble. They brought their own two-pronged forks and headed straight for the field where they could hear my father already at work driving the tractor, towing the rented binder that went from farm to farm.

They understood that they worked for each other without pay until all the grain was in, and each farmer sowed his oats and barley to ripen at a different time from his neighbors'.

In our thirteen years on the farm the group changed little, but it represented a divide between locals and "foreigners" that had started when my parents arrived in 1944. The "praaper" Cornishmen were Mr. Spry, Mr. Sanders, Willie, our tenant, and Fred Hore, who took time off work to help. Mr. Spry's and Mr. Sanders' families had farmed in the valley for generations, and my parents acknowledged their seniority in the formal address. Mr. Spry, rotund and ruddy-complexioned, was a fervent Methodist who had quarreled with the local chapel and built his own behind his house, where he preached to a congregation of one, his wife. My father respected his farming experience, usually asked his advice about when the grain was exactly ripe, and occasionally borrowed his horse to do some hoeing—it was the only horse left in the neighborhood, kept for sentimental reasons when others bought tractors. Mr. Sanders lived on an unproductive hill farm close to Helman Tor. Gruff, loud, illiterate, often carrying a shotgun, he scared us children when we met him on the moor. Many years later my mother told me that the large and unresponsive baby his timid wife so frequently needed to take to the doctor was not hers, but the result of her husband's incest with his fourteen-year-old daughter.

The "furriners" included lean Jim Wakeman, the friend my parents had persuaded to join them in farming, and another newcomer, gentle and shy Mr. Clemence, who had done the same on his own initiative. My parents, the first intruders, were the link between the two groups. They had earned respect for their hard work, their lack of condescension, and their generosity with their car and telephone, so when it was harvest time there was no division. The community held together as it always had, and our neighbors gathered congenially in each other's fields each fine day until the work was done.

The women arrived a little later than the men and headed for the kitchen to help. The first task was the mid-morning meal, mysteriously called crib, perhaps an echo of the almost dead Cornish language. We piled a large basket with slabs of bread and cheddar cheese, added brown mugs and filled a huge brown enamel teapot with strong tea mixed with milk and plenty of sugar. It had handles on both sides so two people could carry it

120

between them out to the field. Work stopped, and everyone sat on sheaves and took a break.

Meanwhile, the kitchen was a frenzy of activity. Mrs. Hore, plump and flushed, was making dough, Mary Wakeman peeling potatoes, my mother cutting chuck steak into cubes. As the potatoes were peeled Mrs. Spry, potato in one hand, knife in the other, effortlessly reduced them to a pile resembling wood chips. The harvest midday meal never varied, and Cornish people ate much the same food every day of their lives. First there were meat and potato pasties (pronounced with a short a), one for each person, including children. The dough was rolled out and cut into large circles with a sure turn of the hand. On each of them went a good portion of potato and a smaller portion of meat seasoned with salt and pepper. Once the top of the pepper pot came off over one of them, spilling half its contents. "Give it to Fred," said Mrs. Hore, "He'll never notice." He didn't, either. A pair of experienced hands pulled the two sides of the circle together and crimped them to enclose the filling so nothing would leak out. All that was left was to pierce holes, one on each side of the seam, and put the pasties on trays in the top oven of the Aga for an hour. The kitchen filled with a savory aroma of piecrust and gravy, resulting in a delicious blend of potato and meat, the potatoes perfectly cooked in the gravy. Pasties kept their warmth for hours if wrapped in a towel, and were strong enough to make plates and eating utensils unnecessary.

Dessert was apple pasties, made the previous day with a filling of apples and sugar, and cut in half and served cold with clotted cream to pour into them. We carried it all out at about one o'clock, together with lemonade and more tea. Most Cornish people were strict Methodists and never drank alcohol, in public at least, and no one ever served any.

After lunch everyone pitched in to help. When I was too small to be helpful I used to watch how the binder's sharp teeth sliced through the bottom of the stalks so they fell in a shower onto its moving platform. Inside they were mysteriously transformed into sheaves that the binder spat out at regular intervals. One group of workers followed behind, rhythmically tossing the sheaves with their forks to make three rows into one. My father had small forks made so my brother and I could help, and we prided ourselves on our harvest blisters—a row at the base of the fingers and another at the first knuckles.

121

Even earlier we had learned another task, "shocking up," as it was called around us. We worked along the lines of sheaves in pairs, each first choosing a sturdy-looking sheaf to start, picking it up carefully by the twine around its middle to avoid thistles, and placing two together firmly, meeting at the top in an inverted vee. Two more sheaves made another vee at a right angle, and four more filled in the gaps, making a miniature teepee, the shock. Soon the field was dotted with them, carefully lined up so the tractor could get between them. It was hard work, with a lot of bending; the sheaves were quite heavy, and the stubble nipped our ankles. We looked forward to the break at teatime, with more tea and saffron cake.

Harvesting just one field generally lasted until our shadows were long in the setting sun. I tried to avoid the last few moments, although we could hear what happened all across the valley. There were always rabbits trapped in the small amount of standing grain, and as they ran out the farmers would aim their shotguns or send in their dogs. Rabbit stew was traditional post-harvest fare.

About five days later if the weather stayed fine, or whenever the sheaves were dry enough to bring in to store, everyone returned. The shocks were taken apart and the sheaves pitched into a wagon where two men caught them and arranged them in rows. Pitchers had to be strong and agile, since wagons were loaded about twelve feet tall or more, and catchers needed skill to distribute the weight evenly. When Michael and I were quite young we learned how to stop and start the tractor so that we could drive it around the field, stopping every few yards, a tedious task for an adult but unaccustomed power for a child. We had to give way to a grownup when the wagon got nearly full, and towing needed judgment and experience. Our parents sometimes let us ride on top of the wagon on its way into the yard. Usually they were packed so well there was no danger, but once one toppled over when turning a corner. It keeled over in slow motion, twisting the tow bar like wire, and landing with a thudding sigh. No one was on it, but the incident stopped our joy-riding.

When the wagons came into the mowhay where the open-sided grain barn stood, the men pitched sheaves from the wagon on to the rick, built by my father and Mr. Spry with the casualness born of long experience. If the barn overflowed, as it did in a good year, the outside rick was finished with a carefully graded sloping top, and in the next day or so my father thatched it with reeds cut from the moor. There the sheaves sat for a month or so until they were dry enough to be threshed, another communal occasion. We were usually away at school by then, but I have some recollection of the noisy, dusty threshing machine, much more mysterious than the binder, turning the sheaves tossed into its maw into neat bags of grain and piles of straw, the latter tidily packaged by the accompanying baler.

By the time I was a teenager the binder and thresher were endangered species. One by one, my parents' friends with larger farms rented combine harvesters, and we went with awe to watch them. But the lanes in our community were too narrow for combines, and the binder survived, increasingly anachronistic, as long as we did.

MICHAEL

Michael, my mother, and me in Fowey harbor

My brother Michael has always been a mystery to me, an alien being with whom I have little in common apart from a shared childhood. And even that was not really shared. We overlapped at St. Goran School for two years before I left for high school, the most time we ever spent together. When he started school, before he was five, I did pay him some attention, helping get him to bed and reading him a bedtime story. But he didn't need me. He soon had his own friends, his own life. At school we had as little to do with each other as at home, and after I was ten we were at home together for about sixteen weeks a year. We mostly treated each other with indifference, but beneath the surface a subterranean sibling rivalry always simmered.

We always called Michael by his full name—no one in the family ever called him Mike, although now everyone else does. He and I are nearly four years apart, and I don't remember taking much notice of him when he was a baby. He was less than two years old when we moved to the farm, where there were endless opportunities for danger. He loved the dirty (he named it) and took every opportunity to escape into it. He had a comforter, a cloth diaper we called his cuddly, that he took everywhere with him, and one of my perennial cries was, "Mummy, Michael just dropped his *clean* cuddly in the dirty!"

One day my mother looked out of the farmhouse dairy window and saw Michael crawling around in front of Freddy the bull going "Wuff! Wuff!" The tethered bull was looking interested as he got closer and closer. My mother called to Michael softly, and for once he came to her and she snatched him up out of harm's way. His worst accident was tripping over a jutting stone and cutting his chin near an artery. I was at school when it happened and missed the drama when my father had to drive several miles to the doctor while my mother pressed hard to stop the blood. I wasn't very sympathetic when I saw the stitches and was mostly sorry I had missed the excitement.

When he was learning to talk Michael developed his own words for things, words that became part of the family vocabulary for many years. Apples were "what-whats," pencils "poncties," and a ladder was an "eeyong." He would watch my father climbing a ladder, chanting "ee-yong, ee-yong" in time with my father's steps. When he was a little older he developed a ritual greeting. He would say "Eeny, beany, biney, bo," and you had to reply, "Buddly buddly bye." This later got shortened to "eeny been" and "buddly bye," and eventually there was no need to reply. It became so ingrained that, even when my parents were in their seventies, if one passed the other in the kitchen entrance, they still said, "Eeny bean."

Since I was at school during the week, Michael had my parents and the farm to himself for more than two years before he joined me. He took advantage of my absence. Once, when my parents found he had destroyed a small bush in the garden, he told them the culprit was "little girls," one of my father's affectionate phrases for me.

We were complete opposites. I played school with my soft toys, he played with his Dinky Toy cars, and, later, his Meccano set, a collection of metal girders and gears that you assembled with tiny nuts and bolts. Although I, like everyone else, classified them as boys' toys, I liked Dinky Toys and Meccano too, and occasionally spent my pocket money on a Dinky Toy car. Sometimes Michael let me make something out of Meccano, but I don't remember us ever collaborating on a model and mostly when we played together one of us would try to boss the other. He always stood his ground and I left in tears of frustration.

When he was quite little it was obvious that Michael had a scientific and mechanical mind (he became an engineer) and he loved our old and temperamental Ford tractor. By the time he was ten he could drive it as well as my father, and was better at reversing an attached trailer round a corner. It is now illegal for young boys to drive tractors, but there were no rules then for what you did on your own land and Michael never drove the tractor on the road. The only farm chore we usually did together was getting the cows in for the afternoon milking, which we managed to do fairly amicably, especially since it was a responsible job and we didn't want to upset the cows.

When he was about seven or eight Michael gleefully learned how to exploit my innate desire to please, to do everything right. There was one indoor chore that we both had to do—the after-lunch washing-up. My parents left us to get on with it while they went out to do farm chores.

"I won't do it at all unless you let me wash," Michael announced. I preferred washing too, but I knew that he meant it, and I was too conscientious to walk away with the dishes undried. Since he never did anything I wanted him to, I had no hope of appealing to him to give me a turn. He fetched a stool so he could see down into the deep sink in the back kitchen where the dirty dishes were stacked. He picked a milk jug, put in a sliver of soap, reached for a cloth dish-mop, and pumped it up and down in the jug. "I am a washing-up machine," he chanted. But he didn't wash any of the dishes.

"Get on with it," I pleaded, well aware that he was teasing me but too law-abiding to call his bluff. He took no notice. I stood in frustration, wondering when I could get back to the book I was reading. Eventually he realized I was thinking of something else and finally decided to wash some dishes. He played this game often. I complained to my parents, but he never did it when they were around, and they probably thought I was whining. Michael himself doesn't remember it at all.

Although my parents never showed any favoritism, as we grew up it seemed to me that Michael outstripped me in the things that mattered. He was better looking, with blond hair that had a slight wave, contrasted with my very straight mousy flyaway wisps. His face was leaner and his nose

126

straighter. He inherited every sports gene my parents had, most of which skipped me. He excelled at any sport he tried—football (soccer), rugby, cricket, rowing (crew). This was not immediately apparent at St. Goran School, where we played no organized sports, but he blossomed when he moved on to an all-boys boarding school when he was eight.

My father took my cousin Penny and me to Michael's final end-of-year prize-giving when he was fourteen. He was called to the prize table eleven times, mostly for sporting trophies. Since he had also grown several inches in a few months, his pants were too short and his shoes too small for him to wear socks, so every time he went up the steps he showed an embarrassingly (to us) wide expanse of bare leg. My main emotion was neither pride nor embarrassment, but jealousy. I did get school prizes for academic excellence, but my school awarded them every two years. I would never get this kind of glory.

Michael also did well in school, and some of those prizes were for academic achievement. Here I could at least equal him, and he thought me superior. He used to refer to me as "My brainy sister." I took it as sarcasm, but he meant it and I think envied me. To me it didn't mean much, since being good at sports counted for more than getting high marks for schoolwork in my own all-girls' school. It seemed to me that Michael was the golden boy and I the silver runner-up.

LUXULYAN VALLEY

The gristmill hadn't changed for centuries. Outside it was a tall granite building with a large wooden water wheel on one side, the mill's only source of power. Inside a man hoisted up sacks of raw grain and poured them into a hopper so the corn (in British English the term for all grains is corn) fell between two huge round granite millstones. The top stone turned lazily as the ground grain came out through grooves in the bottom stone and down a chute into sacks on the mill floor. Occasionally my father took us with him to watch the corn we harvested being ground into cattle food, but our visits dwindled to nothing as we began to use the whole grain oats and barley from our fields for the chickens and bought commercial feed for the cows.

The mill was in Luxulyan (pronounced Luxillian), our nearest village. A combined post office and general store with a very limited stock served two streets of small granite cottages with slate roofs. The cottages' men worked as laborers on local farms or walked a couple of miles to the nearest bus to the china clay pits whose white slag hills were visible in the west. Their wives spent their days on the unending tasks necessary in homes with no electricity or indoor plumbing.

The most prominent building in Luxulyan was the fifteenth-century church (Church of England), also granite and slate, with a castellated porch, small pointed-arch Gothic windows, and a squat square tower with a round turret on one corner. An unkempt graveyard surrounded the church, including an exotic tree called a monkey-puzzle with very prickly needles all over its long limbs and trunk, named because it would cause problems for any monkey trying to climb it. Few of the village residents went to the established church since Cornwall became almost entirely Methodist after John Wesley visited the county in the eighteenth century. Most of them went to the Methodist chapel in Bridges, the next closest village. We weren't Methodists, but we didn't go to church either, so I wasn't in Luxulyan much.

Most Methodists were teetotalers then, ensuring that Luxulyan had no pub, but there was a village hall for social occasions. Once I won a raffle there at a local Conservative Association gathering. The prize was Milly, an almost life-sized doll that had previously belonged to me. My parents had donated her after taking her to what was then known as a doll's hospital to be rehabbed, although she was already in good shape since I had never liked dolls much, and she was just too big. I didn't want her back.

Although Luxulyan was small, it had an office for the local Conservative Association, ensuring that my father went there once a month for meetings. The Association president was the parish's most prominent resident, Captain Maxwell-Hyslop, retired from the navy. He lived a mile or two outside the village in Prideaux, a house large enough to be a mansion but too small for stately home status, At home we irreverently called the rather snobbish family the Maxslops, but in public on the rare occasions when we children met them, we were very respectful. My father was chairman of the Association so he had to work closely with the Captain and often met with him to plan activities. It was when Michael and I rode with him on the way to Prideaux for one of those meetings that we discovered the secrets of Luxulyan Valley.

The valley wasn't new to us. We occasionally drove through it as a back way to Par and the main line railway station. From the village the narrow road dipped steeply down, enveloping the car in a cocoon of huge rhododendrons and stands of smooth-trunked beeches and lichen-encrusted birches. The only sounds came from birds and the stream bubbling along to the side. The road curved gently along the valley floor in the dim light. It felt restful, detached, a secret oasis of Cornish beauty.

About half way along a very tall granite viaduct, a bridge carrying train tracks, loomed suddenly above the treetops, spanning the valley from edge to edge. That day my father let us out just before the viaduct to explore. As soon as we left the car we heard water gushing far more strongly than the stream. To our left a waterfall was crashing down the side of the valley and going under a small bridge into the stream beyond. We found a steep path beside the waterfall and climbed up to see where it came from. At the top we saw an open sluice gate from a very narrow canal that ran along the top rim of the valley. The canal's sides were coated with china clay, residue from water flowing from the nearby pits. We followed the stream to the top of the viaduct.

The viaduct was clearly no longer used, with tufts of grass and a few wild flowers growing along its sides and between the granite slabs spanning its bed. We walked across, leaning over the side to thrill ourselves by how high up we were. When we turned to go back I suddenly noticed a glint of light between the slabs under our feet. We looked closely, and there was water flowing underneath! It wasn't just a viaduct, it was also an aqueduct! We immediately called it the *aque-via-duct-duct*. When my father picked us up we told him excitedly about our discovery. He didn't know about it, nor did anyone else we knew. We thought it was our secret.

Now I know it wasn't. Joseph Treffry, a local entrepreneur who wanted to exploit the mineral resources on his various landholdings, built the viaduct in the 1840s. Horse-drawn trams went across the top, and he needed the water for his copper mine the other side of the valley. The viaduct was still in use until the 1870s, and I am sure people still knew about it in the 1950s. Someone opened and closed that sluice.

Now Luxulyan Valley is a World Heritage site, and people come frequently, often after visiting the nearby Eden Project, where they marvel at the attempt to collect every plant on earth. I'm sorry about the increased traffic. But for a time the place was our secret.

PETS

There was no space in our lives for frills—everything on the farm had to be useful. That included pets.

Jemima the goat's role was almost entirely functional. The mowhay, the enclosed grassy yard behind the big barn, had been a place to store hay and straw and grow vegetables away from the greedy eyes of pigs and cows, a safe area for chickens to roam, and a convenient place for the clothesline and the outhouse. The hay and straw remained, but my parents had no time for vegetable growing. They moved the chickens into the barn, and abandoned the outhouse for indoor plumbing. The mowhay's grass and weeds were out of control. Jemima was the answer.

Jemima's appetite was prodigious and she ate anything she could see. Since she could jump over the hedge into the fields or fill herself up on the hay and straw, my father tethered her to a long rope in a different spot each day where she mowed down all the vegetation within reach. She ate anything else as well. Once, my father had to go to a Guernsey Society meeting in London, so Mrs. Hore washed his only good shirt and hung it on the clothesline to dry. Unfortunately she hadn't noticed Jemima was within range. After she came back to get the shirt to iron it she went to get my mother as fast as she could (Mrs. Hore didn't run.)

"Jemima's eaten the shirt collar and cuffs!" she told my mother breathlessly.

My mother soothed her, but meanwhile my father had to find time for a hasty visit to a clothing shop on the way to the station before he boarded the train.

Like Jemima, farm dogs were more utility than pet. When we first moved to the farm we inherited a dog, a lab mix called Sally who worked with the sheep. I have a photo of my mother, my brother and I and two other children holding Sally's litter of four puppies. We kept one of them, Joey, who became Sally's successor when Sally died. But by then we had no sheep and Joey had no function. Instead he started to wander off the farm and was seen several times outside the school in Bugle, perhaps looking for Michael and me while we were away at school. My parents were afraid he might get among other farmers' sheep so they gave him away to someone who needed a working dog.

My father then decreed, "No more dogs." My parents stuck to this decision until I was in my mid-teens. But then my father's camera was stolen from our unlockable car (the reason why there are very few photos of my adolescence), and they decided to get an English bulldog as a thief deterrent. We called the puppy Chloe, a name I had suggested as a joke after having recently survived the minor humiliation of pronouncing the name I had seen only in print "Ch-low." It stuck, with the right pronunciation. Chloe was the one farm animal that had no function other than human companionship and occasionally guarding the car.

However, her breed was intended to bait bulls by weaving in front of their noses. When she was very young she got among the cows and started baiting them, zig-zagging around trying to nip their noses. Michael and I saw her and tried to call her away. She was too engrossed and wouldn't come. Suddenly, to our horror, one of the cows had enough and ran at her with its horns down. Then the entire herd began to stampede behind her. We took refuge behind a four-foot hedge and watched in growing alarm as Chloe hurtled toward us, an army of enraged cows with horns close behind. She was so scared she jumped higher than ever before or after and landed safely on the other side of the hedge, panting and exhausted. We hugged her in happy relief. The cows stopped at the hedge, also exhausted—the milk yield was probably down that night. After that, Chloe left them alone.

The main farm pets were the cats, a shifting population of anywhere between ten to twenty. Their function was to keep down the rodent population, including rabbits, and they did it well. The matriarch was Fluffy, a black and white Persian mix, most of the time the only cat allowed in the house, making her the official household pet and indoor mouser. She didn't really merit the honor since she had an uncertain temper and allowed you to pet her only when she felt like it. If she didn't she would purr deceptively and then turn and bite you. I never learned when this might happen.

Many farmers never fed their cats, believing it kept them hungry and more likely to catch mice and rats. We disagreed and fed the cats three times a day. In the morning and evening my mother gave them a large bowl of milk warm from the cows. For lunch I prepared a large roasting pan full of bread pieces, crumpled a couple of meat extract cubes over them and soaked everything well with hot water. Once it had cooled enough I opened the back door, called "Wuddy, wuddy, wuddy," the family language for "Pussy," and those who were not already waiting came running out of barns, through the mowhay, around the edge of the dirty, or from the cowhouse area. They crowded around the pan and ate voraciously, purring loudly. This was the time to check on who was expecting kittens, and keep an eye on whether they had given birth. Sometimes there was a surprise new kitten, something I always loved to see.

My parents couldn't afford vet fees for cats and nobody we knew spayed their cats or dogs. Fluffy had over one hundred kittens in her long life, but my father broke most of their necks immediately. He wouldn't drown them, the usual method for dealing with unwanted kittens on most farms, after an experience when he put some in a sack, dropped them into the water trough and they survived.

Initially we needed more cats so we kept one kitten from Fluffy's first litter, unimaginatively called Stripey for her black and gray striped short-haired coat. Stripey was the opposite of her mother, ever friendly and never biting. Unfortunately for her, my parents wanted only one indoor cat, so she was banished outdoors. Her main aim in life was to get indoors again, so she stayed close to the house and slipped in through the back door at every opportunity— there were plenty as people came in and out all day.

After a while we got tired of putting her out and she won the privilege of second—and much friendlier—indoor cat.

The outdoor cats were all descendants of Fluffy and Stripey in various complicated and incestuous relationships that I tracked as well as I could with genealogical zeal. Most of them had been kittens born in barns and hidden from us until their eyes were open, when my father refused to kill them. Even then, only the hardiest ones survived what we called cat flu, a herpes viral infection endemic on the farm. It started like a cold, then the kitten's eyes became full of pus, after which it usually died. I hated to see kittens die.

Most of the outdoor cats were tame enough to be petted, and all of them had names. Some of their names were as unimaginative as Stripey's, like her daughter Smokey, who had a beautiful pewter gray coat. Smokey was the farm's champion rat catcher, so valuable that she was the only cat I ever remember taking to the vet. She had been out in a field chasing a rabbit in long grass when she got caught in the hay cutter and lost part of her tail and one foot. My father took her to be patched up and, despite her disability, she returned to form catching rats. She couldn't run as fast, but she made up for it in cunning, lying in wait for her prey in well-camouflaged hideouts.

My favorite cat was Orlando, our only male, a marmalade colored shorthair named after a cat in one of our favorite children's books. He was Stripey's son and, I assumed, father to most, if not all, of our kittens, although there were some other stray males around. He was as friendly as his mother, came when I called him, and was happy to follow me around the farm. I missed him so much when I went to my boarding high school that I talked about him constantly and bored my schoolmates dreadfully. Eventually they sent me a fake letter telling me Orlando was ill and I had to go home. I was distraught and went to the housemistress to find out how I could get home, after which they had to confess it was a hoax. From their point of view it worked since it made me shut up about my cat, but I felt hurt and betrayed.

To me, more than anyone else in my family, the cats were individuals, each with its own personality, its own place in the cat hierarchy, its own genealogy. I loved them, watched over them as best I could, and mourned when they died. They were family.

CELEBRATIONS

I was an April Fool's baby. I woke up every birthday morning with an anticipation lightly tinged with dread —what had someone thought up to try to fool me this time? The day when Miss Rapley fixed the fake grapefruit was the most memorable, but I have received a dead frog wrapped as a present, been told of catastrophes that never happened, given news of friends that was untrue. My son still occasionally tries to fool me. A couple of years ago he e-mailed me that his partner was pregnant with twins again (they already have twins). It caught me for a brief moment before I remembered the day.

Unless Easter was very late, pushing the school holiday well into April, I usually celebrated my birthday at home, saving me from the pranks of my schoolmates and leaving only Michael to torment me. My mother made my favorite birthday cake, a Victoria sponge with jam filling and vanilla icing. When we first moved to the farm in wartime there were no birthday candles and my mother crystallized violets we picked in the hedgerows as candle substitutes for the three of us in the family with spring birthdays. We sang "Happy Birthday," even though there was nothing to blow out.

When I was at home I sometimes had a birthday party with my cousins, my friend Pat Wakeman from up the road, and some of the Helmsley family, children of our former farm pupil. We played games I have always associated with birthday parties like Musical Bumps, dancing to music on the wind-up gramophone, and when an adult stopped the record we had to sit down as fast as we could, and the last one to sit down was out.

Another game was Musical Chairs, when chairs were arranged in a row, each facing the opposite direction from its partner, and one fewer chair than the number of people playing. We walked clockwise around the chairs and when the music stopped we had to sit down in the nearest chair. One person was left without a chair, and was out, while the grownup removed another chair for the next round.

A favorite was Pass the Parcel. My mother wrapped a small prize in many layers of paper, and we passed the parcel around the circle. When the

135

music stopped the person holding the parcel tore off one layer of paper, accompanied by shrieks from the rest of us. To make it more exciting my mother put small strips of paper in some layers with forfeits printed on them. These were things the recipient had to do, like sing with a nut in their mouth or pick a penny out of a mound of flour with their lips. The one I hated to get, because I found it so embarrassing, was "Bow to the prettiest, kneel to the wittiest, and kiss the one you love the best." The choices were all difficult, since you were bound to offend someone, but the worst was the kiss, both embarrassing and sometimes hard to decide. I don't remember ever evading the issue by kissing my mother.

Everyone in the family had birthdays that had some significance beyond our appearance in the world. Michael's, March 21st, was officially the first day of spring. Mine, April 1st, was April Fool's Day, and my father's, April 19th, Primrose Day, the anniversary of the death of Benjamin Disraeli, Queen Victoria's favorite Prime Minister. She sent primroses for his funeral, remarking that they were his favorite flower. Disraeli's statue in London is still decorated with primroses on that day. My mother's birthday, August 21st, was also Princess Margaret's.

Michael's birthday was usually during the school term, so he didn't have a party at home. My mother always mailed him a fruitcake covered by a thick layer of marzipan, his favorite topping, with a minimal amount of icing. One year he stripped off all the marzipan and made a ball that he kept in a sock and used as a weapon as he ate away at it.

I was usually home for my parents' birthdays and spent some time making them birthday cards with glued paper and colored pencils, showing my minimal artistic talent. I don't remember them buying presents for each other, although I expect they did get token gifts, but we had a special meal with birthday cake. My father and brother weren't good at remembering my mother's birthday without prompting from me, and once, in my teens, when I was away visiting a friend, nothing happened at all until, in desperation, at tea my mother served them something she clearly announced as birthday cake. They were appropriately shame-faced.

England is short on celebratory holidays. There is no holiday celebrating national pride like Bastille Day or the Fourth of July. While churches have harvest festivals, there is no nationwide Thanksgiving. Even

136

New Year's Day wasn't a holiday when I was growing up (it was in Scotland). Since England is officially a Protestant country (no saints' days), the Mondays after the two "movable feasts," Easter and Whitsun (Pentecost), were bank holidays when workers had the day off, as they did on the first Monday in August to give them a brief respite between Whitsun and Christmas.

Easter and Whitsun were times when the Church of England expected us to go to church, but my family didn't. On Easter Sunday my parents gave us chocolate Easter eggs (never bunnies), which we devoured immediately. We usually had lamb for lunch. I knew nothing about Easter egg hunts until I learned about them from Americans as an adult and organized them for my children. Whitsun coincided with school half term, so we were home, but did nothing special to commemorate the day.

Christmas Day was an official holiday, immediately followed by Boxing Day, named because it was the time when Victorians gave Christmas "boxes" to their tradespeople. Christmas on the farm was a fairly low-key affair since cows still had to be milked, pigs and chickens fed, and eggs collected, but from the moment I got home on the last day of school I was in a fever of excitement.

In the year after the war when there were no decorations to buy we decorated a tree with the stars, moons and faces my father had made with his fretsaw and painted silver. We continued to hang them every year, adding a few glass balls when they became available and other pieces my brother and I made in various school craft projects, including the gold star I made out of cardboard and foil from chocolate wrappers. It always got the place of honor at the top. We attached real candles in tin holders and lit them on Christmas Day. My parents didn't worry about the tree catching fire, and fortunately it never did.

On Christmas Eve we hung up our stockings (knee-length school socks) at the bottom of our beds. I don't remember a time when I believed in Father Christmas, but that didn't dim my excitement. My parents had to get up so early for milking that they went to bed around 8 p.m., so I was often awake when my stocking got filled. Ever the dutiful child, I pretended to be asleep as I listened to their muffled footsteps on the stairs and their stealthy entry into my bedroom, all in total darkness. They might have been Father Christmas for all that I could see through my half-closed eyes.

I slept fitfully until very early when I could no longer wait for my parents' alarm clock to ring. Since we had no electricity and were not allowed candles in our bedrooms, I emptied my stocking and felt all the objects, trying to guess what they were. The tangerine in the toe and the few walnuts and brazil nuts were easy, as was the pencil, especially as we got them every year, but the rest I had to guess by feel—a chocolate bar? What kind? Was this a small toy?—until my parents got up at 6 and brought a light. It was the most exciting part of Christmas Day, one that lost much of its magic when, in my teens, we could just flip a switch. I often wish my own children could have experienced the delicious anticipation.

The next excitement came after breakfast and milking, when my father handed out the presents from under the tree. We had one present each from our parents, and a few others from relatives and godparents. When my aunt and cousins started to spend Christmas with us, that swelled the number of gifts, but we never had more than one from each person. My parents usually gave me a toy, or, as I grew older, a book or one of the *Mikado* 78-rpm records I was collecting. No one ever gave clothes. Still conditioned by wartime shortages, we recycled the same Christmas paper year after year, unwrapping everything carefully and smoothing the paper out ready to be stored. In the days before Sellotape each package had to be tied with string or ribbon, making preserving paper easier, but over the years the sheets gradually got smaller and more wrinkled, with a litany of crossed-off names.

It was always hard to find presents for my mother and father, who seemed to have no needs or wants, at least that we could afford. Sometimes I had made something in art or sewing class that I could give to my mother, like a slightly leaning glazed clay vase in the year we did pottery, but I usually chose bath salts, smelling strongly of lavender or roses, or handkerchiefs, the latter a staple item in the days before Kleenex. Gift handkerchiefs, embroidered with flowers or initials, came in flat square boxes with photos of flowers on the lids. My mother must have had a very full supply. I had quite a few myself. My father also got his share of less-fancy men's handkerchiefs—he didn't have a lot of use for ties. Once

Michael and I together had a lucky find in a local store— an extra large teacup that my father used every day from then on.

Christmas dinner, at lunchtime, was chicken, roast potatoes and brussel sprouts. Chicken was a treat for most people then, but not so much for us since we ate one of our own quite often. My mother also made bread sauce, a medieval concoction of breadcrumbs soaked in milk that had been flavored by an onion stuck with cloves, and served hot. I never liked it much. For me the real treat was Christmas pudding, a steamed mountain made with suet and lots of dried fruits, rather like a hot fruitcake. My mother made it several weeks in advance. We each got a turn to stir the batter and make a wish before she steamed it for hours on top of the Aga and then set it to mature in the cool dairy.

On Christmas day she wrapped several silver threepenny bits (coins) in waxed paper so they would not contaminate the food, and pushed them into the bottom of the pudding. She then resteamed it until it was hot and turned it out onto a plate, put a sprig of holly in the top, doused it with a little brandy, and set it alight. We oohed until the flame went out. When we were little we ate the pudding with custard, a thick yellow sauce made with Bird's custard powder and milk. Later we graduated to brandy butter, butter creamed with brown sugar and a little brandy. We left the threepenny bits we found in the pudding on our plates and saved them for next Christmas, since they were no longer minted and we couldn't easily spend them. Later we used silver sixpences instead. These were worth getting since our pocket money was usually sixpence a week.

After lunch we listened to carols on the radio until three o'clock, time for the King's, then later the Queen's, speech on the radio. Like practically everyone else in the country, we stood up for the national anthem and, seated, listened attentively in silence to the fifteen-minute address, briefly uniting a nation as it had been in wartime. The message was always one of peace and goodwill, and included some domestic details about the royal family. The Queen always began, "My husband and I...," a phrase lampooned by comedians in the irreverent sixties.

Then it was teatime, our normal mid-afternoon meal of bread and butter with jam, but with Christmas cake, a fruitcake my mother had also made in advance. She covered the cake with marzipan and then with white icing fluffed up and dusted with icing sugar so it looked like snow, although snow was very rare in Cornwall and we never had a white Christmas. Nestled in the icing were a small plaster snowman and a Father Christmas, also saved from year to year, and a couple of sprigs of real holly from a bush in one of our hedges. After I had stripped off the marzipan and given it to Michael, the cake was another of my favorite parts of Christmas.

The one peculiarly English annual celebration was November 5, Guy Fawkes Day (Bonfire Night), commemorating the failure of a 1605 plot by the Catholic Fawkes and others to blow up the House of Lords during the State Opening of Parliament, when King James I, his ministers, and the country's aristocracy would all be present. The plan was to replace James with his nine-year-old daughter, who would be raised a Catholic. One of the lords was warned in an anonymous letter, the plot was foiled, and the conspirators executed. People celebrated the hated Catholic plot's failure with bonfires, which became a tradition, as did firework displays. Children made "guys," stuffing clothing with straw and using a turnip or other vegetable as a head, and paraded them round the streets, chanting:

Please to remember
The Fifth of November,
Gunpowder, treason and plot.
We see no reason
Why gunpowder, treason
Should ever be forgot.

They collected "pennies for the guy" from passers-by, and eventually burned the effigy on top of a bonfire. While Guy Fawkes Day wasn't an official holiday and no one got time off work, most people joined in the nighttime celebrations.

While we were still at St. Goran School we celebrated Guy Fawkes Day at home on the closest weekend. We stuffed old clothes with straw and burned the guy on a bonfire on the mowhay. Anyone could buy fireworks in those days, and my father set off rockets from bottles, lit Roman candles, and attached Catherine wheels to boards so they whirled around scattering sparks. Firecrackers scared me (we called them "bangers"), but I loved to wave sparklers until they died.

PENNY

Growing up, I had little contact with my extended family. We saw my grandparents infrequently. Both my mother and father had only one sibling, each considerably older than they were. My father's sister, Aunty Kathleen, lived in a London suburb with her mother, Nana, and her children who were ten years or so older than I was. Those four cousins occasionally came to the farm but we had little in common.

My mother's brother, Uncle Gordon, had moved to South Africa with his wife, Aunty Hilda, before my birth. Their three children, Penny, Nick and Richard, were all born there. We knew them through Christmas letters, the occasional photograph, and annual food parcels of staples like sugar and tea and bags of candy that were welcome treats in ration-bound Britain. They were like characters in one of my books, similar enough to us to be recognizable but living an exotic life beyond my imagination. I never expected to meet them.

Then, in 1948, my uncle divorced my aunt and married a redheaded South African beauty. He announced the divorce to my mother in a letter. She was always ready to help anyone in need, and I am sure her first reaction, after the shock, was, "What can I do?" Divorce was rare in 1940s Britain—just over three percent of marriages ended that way. Although my aunt was, as far as I know, blameless, to be divorced was a disgrace, especially for the wife. There was little future for her as a rejected woman in the stiffly conventional expatriate South African community, so she and the three children, aged eleven, seven, and two, embarked for Britain on a passenger liner, the Warwick Castle.

After the long voyage up the coast of Africa, through the Suez Canal and the Mediterranean, they arrived in drab, rainy, Britain, with its bomb cavities and post-war shortages. Aunty Hilda knew she could expect no help from her father, a wealthy man, who abhorred divorce, no matter the cause, and refused to meet his only child and grandchildren off the ship. My parents stepped in. My mother went by train to Southampton, a day's journey away, to meet them, and brought them back to the farm. I was excited to meet these cousins we knew only from letters, and looked forward to better companionship than my brother offered.

The farm's Spartan environment must have been a shock to them. Penny talked about how they used to live in a big house with several servants, surrounded by bougainvillea and mango and granadilla trees. But I don't remember anyone complaining, and they settled in quickly. For Michael and me it was a delight, instant brothers and sister in our isolated existence when we were not at school. Penny started attending the boarding school where I was due to go the following year, and Nick joined Michael and me at St. Goran School. Conveniently, our school cook, a glamorous war widow, had just left to marry one of the richer men in Gorran Haven, so my parents persuaded Miss Rapley to replace her with Aunty Hilda, who had never worked a day in her life but had learned to cook from my mother and needed a job, although I can't believe she relished the prospect. She moved into Lamledra for the school terms and she and toddler Richard became part of our daily school existence.

Once I joined Penny at our all-girls' high school the following year we developed two different relationships. At school, where she was two years ahead of me, we kept to our own circles of friends, but in the holidays, when the whole family reunited on the farm, we did most things together. We liked the same books. Penny introduced me to Arthur Ransome's stories of children camping and sailing in the Lake District, which I devoured with the same enthusiasm as other books about things way beyond my own experience. We spent at least a year poring over old fashion magazines like *Vogue* and *Harper's Bazaar* that someone had given my mother, and drawing, coloring and cutting out copies of *haute couture* for our paper dolls.

Very occasionally one of the children said something about their life in South Africa, mostly about foods they missed like pawpaws (papaya). Penny had brought with her some old school books where I was fascinated to see her beginning efforts to learn Afrikaans. Yet, although on the farm Penny and I shared a bedroom and sometimes a bed, we never spoke of the divorce. At first I didn't know about it. If my parents had mentioned it, I hadn't understood. For a couple of years their father, Uncle Gordon, who had moved with his new wife to Rhodesia, appeared on the farm each summer alone, huge and ebullient, his booming voice telling us, "In Rhodesia we always drive in the middle of the road," as we cowered on the floor in the back of his rented car on a trip to the beach. Later, when Aunty Hilda and the children spent their summers in a rented seaside caravan (trailer), he brought a woman with him, whom we called Aunty Pip. No one told me who she was, and the title "Aunty" meant little, since it was an honorific I used for many of my parents' friends. Several years later someone at school mentioned that Penny's parents were divorced. I vehemently denied it. After all, I *was* her cousin. But it was true. I was embarrassed to be probably the last to know.

Another reason why I never asked Penny about her parents' split was my own reticence. I had no experience with introspection, and little with empathy. The ethos of the British middle class was the "stiff upper lip," a stoic refusal to show emotion, never revealing your own feelings and not asking others about theirs. I learned it at home and at school and have never managed to erase its effects. I am still reluctant to ask personal questions and, when asked about my own feelings, I cannot describe the incoherent jumble I never "got in touch with." So I never talked with Penny about what it meant to have no home of your own, nor realized that it was I who had the enviable life.

For while I loved Penny like a sister, *I* envied *her*. Her friends would not believe I was her cousin. She was pretty, popular, good at sports. I was the unathletic "brain." Her perfect wavy dark hair contrasted with my never-tidy, determinedly straight, mouse-colored wisps. She managed to look graceful in a school uniform designed to make us as unattractive as possible, while I looked as if I was wearing a sack. As she grew out of her clothes they were handed down to me, so when we changed out of our uniforms at the end of the school day, I wore Penny's cast-offs. Although no one ever said anything, in my jealousy I imagined the smirks of people contrasting how Penny had looked in them.

When I was in my early teens, every summer Aunty Hilda rented a caravan on top of a cliff close to Polperro, one of the most visited touristy fishing villages. Michael and I used to spend weeks there with the family in the summer, roaming the village and the cliff paths, or walking up to snoop around Killigarth, the local stately home. In the evenings Penny and I used to go down into the village, where I watched in amazement as the local boys surrounded her or catcalled and Penny laughed and enjoyed the attention, while keeping them at arms length. I had no idea how to flirt like that, even if any of the boys had shown any interest in me, which they didn't.

Nick, Richard and Michael all went from St. Goran School to Rosehill, a boys' boarding school two counties away. The year that Michael and Nick, aged fourteen, were leaving Rosehill to go on to their high schools my father took Penny and me with him for the final prize-giving. He snapped a photo of us on a bench. It epitomized the differences between us. Penny is looking at the camera without smiling, composed, calm, self-assured, serene in her sleeveless dress and matching shoes. She already had one of the young schoolmasters lusting after her. I, merely my successful brother's older sister, am more animated, but my smile is a little tentative, my body nervously twisted, arms tense, my feet apart in shoes too heavy for my print dress.

On that day Penny was about to leave school for secretarial college. Aunty Hilda's father had died and left her enough to live on without working, so she bought a house in Dartmouth, Devon, a fishing harbor and home of the Royal Naval College. When I was at university in my twenties Penny married John, a slightly older, very handsome man. As her closest female relative, I was chief bridesmaid at the wedding in Dartmouth, a major tourist spot with very narrow streets. The ceremony was in a picturesque chapel on a point at the end of the harbor overlooking the sea, with the reception at a nearby hotel. Penny and John were to leave for their honeymoon by boat across the harbor to the train station. When Penny and I went upstairs for her to change, she suddenly started laughing helplessly.

"Oh, Jenny," she giggled, "All my going-away-clothes are back at the house!" I didn't drive, but the best man and I fought the bumper-to-bumper traffic back to the house, and then struggled through it again on the way back just in time for them to leave to catch their train. From that moment our lives diverged; we were never that close again.

NEW SCHOOL

Par was a straggling street of granite houses and shops with none of the picturesque charm of most Cornish seaside towns. Its beach was wide and sandy, but without the rock pools Michael and I enjoyed poking around in, and with sea so shallow you had to wade out a long way to cover your knees. West of the beach was the main port from which the kaolin (china clay) was exported throughout the world.

Par was a gateway in another sense. Its railway station provided the connection to the branch line to Newquay, the most popular beach and surfing resort on Cornwall's North Coast. For this reason Par was one of the few stops in Cornwall for the Cornish Riviera Express, the fast train that ran along the Great Western Railway from London's Paddington Station to Penzance, Cornwall's westernmost city. It was that express that was to take me the other way, to Exeter, to my new school.

The station itself was a modest rectangular stone building with a slate roof. A projecting canopy with a tooth-like wooden decorative edge over the up (toward London) platform provided some shelter from the Cornish rain, and a bridge over the tracks led to the down platform and the Newquay connection. Passengers went through the main door, bought their small green tickets at the single window on the right, mostly ignored the small and uninviting waiting room on the left, and emerged onto the platform. They listened for the whistle, shriller than the foghorn-like blast of modern diesel trains, and watched for the smoke of the steam engine. Steam engines were thrilling sights, with gleaming pistons, smokestacks billowing white smoke, and a special immediately-recognizable sound merging hiss and chug. When I hear it on nostalgic British TV programs it takes me right back to Par.

Par was the farm's nearest station for the express train, and from my eleventh year I came to know it well. Six times annually for seven years I stood on the up platform to catch the train to my high school in Exeter, two and a half hours away in the next county, coming home only for half term weekends and the school holidays.

Miss Rapley took pupils only until the age of eleven, so I had to move on from St. Goran School. Many girls' boarding schools at the high school level educated their students to be young ladies, teaching good manners and domestic skills and de-emphasizing academics. Both Miss Rapley and my parents knew that would not do for me. I needed an academic challenge. My parents could find no suitable school in Cornwall, so they chose the Maynard School in Exeter, academically demanding but within their modest financial means. The Maynard was primarily a day school, with a separate boarding house for thirty girls. That was to be my new home away from home.

First, though, I had to be admitted. The school was selective, with an entrance exam, so one spring day in my tenth year my mother and I took the train to Exeter so I could take the exam and see the school. I wasn't worried about passing the test. If Penny had passed, I knew I could. I spent the morning alone in a small room working on the exam, then my mother and I went over to the boarding house to see where I would live.

Tregear, the boarding house, was on the edge of the school grounds with its own separate entrance off a side street. A square, flat-roofed, ivy-covered three-story brick building, it had castle-like crenellations on the top and an imposing entrance porch that the boarders never used. This time, however, my mother and I rang the bell and went in through the front door. An elderly, stout woman came forward to greet us, her gray hair pulled severely back into a bun, wearing a brown high-necked dress and laced shoes with a small heel. She smiled graciously and shook both of our hands. "Welcome. I'm Miss Hyndman, the housemistress," she said. She spoke with an odd accent.

'Are you French?" I asked timidly.

"No," she laughed, "I come from Belfast in Northern Ireland."

I always hated being publicly wrong, so I was mortified by my mistake, but Miss Hyndman didn't seem to mind.

She introduced us to Matron, a younger dark-haired woman who would look after our health, and then showed us the rest of the house. We looked into the large airy dining room with long pocket doors separating it from the study where older girls could relax, play, and chat. Younger girls like me, however, would spend their leisure time in the much smaller playroom, uncarpeted, with a single window and dominated by a bank of square

147

lockers with no locks, just fasteners. Upstairs was a landing with a baby grand piano where we had our evening prayers, and six dormitories on two floors. It all seemed very different from friendly, beautiful Lamledra.

Not long afterwards I learned I had been accepted. I wasn't excited about going so much farther from home, or leaving St. Goran School, but I knew it was what I had to do, and Penny seemed to enjoy the Maynard. Ten-year-olds have few choices, and I wasn't presented with any.

The letter included a list of clothing and other necessities that I would need to bring with me in September. It was long and detailed. Almost all British schools had uniforms, and, once again, I just accepted the inevitable. My mother and I spent a while in Grose's and Truscott's in St. Austell, checking off the items, although some things had to be specially ordered and mailed to us. We then spent hours sewing on the compulsory nametapes, so necessary when we all wore the same things.

For daily wear I needed to have a navy blue gym tunic, a sleeveless pinafore (jumper) with box pleats falling from a breast-height yoke and tied like a sack around the waist with a wide ribbon-like girdle that we stiffened with fake whalebone called petersham. Tunic length had to be four inches above the knee when kneeling at a time when fashionable hemlines were at mid-calf. At the beginning of every term we had to kneel in a line along the school hall's platform steps while the gym teacher came along with a ruler to enforce compliance. I checked mine at home to make sure I would pass.

Underneath we wore navy striped blouses that had to be bought from a particular store, and a school tie we had to learn to tie like a man's. For gym we took off our tunics to show our thick navy blue knickers (panties) with another white pair of knickers we called linings invisible underneath the navy pair. Younger girls like me wore knee-length navy socks and navy Mary Jane shoes, older girls wore black lisle stockings. We also had a school sweater, v-necked with a lighter blue stripe, and lighter-weight school dresses and knickers for summer. We had to have a pair of black lace-up outdoor shoes to wear for the two-minute walk to school from the boarding house, wearing our brimmed navy felt school hats and navy blazers or coats if it rained. The hats had striped red and blue hatbands with the school badge in the middle, a shield with three hands and the meaningless Latin motto "Manus Justus Nardus," translated as "Hand, Just, Spikenard." (Spikenard was a perfumed ointment.) They were the shield and motto of the school's sixteenth-century founder, Sir. John Maynard, who chose the Latin words because they contained his name.

All the Maynard girls wore the uniform, but for some reason that was never explained to us and put our parents to a lot of extra expense, boarders had a totally different uniform for church on Sundays. Sticking to the navy theme, we wore navy suits that we called costumes. These were often handed down from older to younger girls, saving some expense. With them we wore white rather than striped blouses, grey gloves and lisle socks or stockings, and a black velour hat with just the badge, no hatband. We even had to have a second pair of lace-up shoes. This was also the uniform we had to wear when traveling to and from school.

In September of 1949, when I was ten and a half, I stood on Par station in my costume, handed down from Penny, waiting for the train. My brown trunk, packed with all the clothes on the list, down to a dozen handkerchiefs had been sent ahead and would be there when I arrived. I was not alone. The Cornish contingent, as we were generally called by the rest of the boarders who mostly lived closer to the school, included Penny, Anne Hemsley, and Daphne Brooks, whose mother kept a large pub and hotel in nearby Fowey. I was trying not to show any nervousness, but I was both sad to be leaving my familiar world and anxious about the future. Although I was used to boarding school, I had never been away from home for more than two weeks at a time. The six weeks until half term, when I would come back for a long weekend, seemed like an eternity. I didn't say much to my companions. I watched for the smoke.

The train journey was a no-man's-land between home and school. We sat together in one eight-seat compartment, chatting somewhat nervously about how we spent the holidays, all of us aware of the looming term ahead. Sometimes we read, sometimes we looked out of the window at the spectacular, but in time very familiar, scenery.

The Great Western Railway, built by Isambard Kingdom Brunel in the 1830s, was a marvel of engineering, traveling through the ever-changing Cornish landscape. Once we boarded the train at Par we immediately went through a long tunnel and then over a series of viaducts crossing Cornwall's valleys and rivers. At Plymouth we craned our necks out of the window, risking soot in our eyes, to see the massive tubular steel Saltash Bridge high over the River Tamar estuary, the only bridge to cross it for more than a hundred years. Someone told us Brunel had committed suicide by jumping off it. Many years later I checked. He didn't.

At Plymouth the Cornish contingent waved out of the window to Lois and Sandra, who joined us there, then the train skirted the rocky coast, a spectacular ride beside the ocean, punctuated by the sudden roar and darkness of several tunnels. Once my mother, on her way to some school event I was involved in, had to sit for some time while the train driver waited for the track to emerge from the pounding waves.

After the tunnels the railway curved inland and drew into Exeter St. David's Station. There, on my first school journey without an adult, I somewhat apprehensively grabbed my small personal suitcase and followed the other girls to the bus stop. We got off just down the street from Tregear, walked in the back entrance, hung our coats in the cloakroom, and emerged into the main hall. My new life had begun.

Outside the main school building, 1949.

150

ENDLESS COMPETITION

On my first day at Tregear all the new girls, five of us, followed Matron up two flights of stairs and along a corridor. The last room was the Sixth Dorm, for the youngest boarders. Six beds with orange striped bedspreads crowded into a rectangular room with sash windows on two sides, one of them opening onto a metal external stairway, the fire escape. The only other furniture was six chests of drawers and a fireplace (unused) with a mantel. There were no pictures on the wall, and one mirror for the six of us. The room was lit by one central light that Matron turned off every night at seven o'clock (half an hour later on Fridays and Saturdays).

Matron had a stern expression and was all business. "You can choose your own bed," she said. "Your trunks are all here. Unpack them and put your clothes in the chest of drawers nearest your bed. Your games and books go in a locker downstairs in the playroom, and any food ("tuck") you have brought with you goes into the tuck cupboard in the dining room. You can eat it at tea on Wednesdays and Saturdays. The bathrooms and lavatory are on the other side of the corridor, and there is a bath list pinned on the notice board for when your bath night is. Teatime is at five in the dining room."

I hung back from picking my bed, not wanting to be too forward with people I didn't know. Anyway, all the beds looked the same to me. Eventually I put my small suitcase on the one nearest the door. Our trunks had been hauled up to the corridor outside, and I unpacked mine, trying to place my clothes in the drawers neatly, glancing at the other girls, Susan, Kate, Anne, and Lois, as I did so. I already knew from Penny that boarders did not usually make friends with the daygirls and that even in the small boarding house we would spend most of our time with the five or so people of our own age. Anne Hemsley I already knew, which was some comfort, but these girls would have to be my new friends, and I wanted to make a good impression. At that point we didn't say much to each other. We were all coping with the feeling of abandonment that is the onset of homesickness, although we knew enough not to show it. I felt alone, out of

151

place, tearful. This was not friendly Lamledra, with Miss Rapley to tease us and home only a few miles distant. Now Matron was stern and the farm half a day's journey away.

As I got used to the new routine I sorted out the differences. Everything seemed to be a competition. There was a silver cup for the tidiest dormitory, so we had to keep our drawers neat for Matron's random inspections. The neighboring dormitory, anxious to win, began pulling back their bedclothes in a tidy roll to air their beds during breakfast. We cursed them, because this meant we all had to do it if we had a chance of beating them.

We were expected to keep ourselves neat, never easy for me, especially as I wore my hair in pigtails (braids) that I could never pull tight enough, so they always had wisps escaping from them. Over in the main school on the other side of the grounds our gym teachers monitored our tidiness and posture—we practiced walking with books balanced on our heads. Girls who walked well and looked neat got special grey girdles known as carriage girdles to go round their gym tunic waists, clearly setting them apart from the rest of us whose navy blue girdles were far less visible. Miss Ryan, our headmistress, presented the carriage girdles at our end-of-term ceremony. For years I longed for a carriage girdle, but my untidiness defeated me and I never got closer than an honorable mention when I was sixteen. It was supposed to encourage me, but by then I hardly cared.

Schoolwork was also competitive. On a Thursday morning every two weeks after morning prayers three hundred and fifty girls (mostly day pupils) filed into the gym to hear Miss Ryan read out the class lists. Every one of us had an average score of all the marks (grades) received over the fortnight. She didn't announce our individual scores, but for each form (class) we were divided into first, second and third classes and fail. To fail was the ultimate indignity, and in a school where we all had taken an examination to get in, it almost never happened. I didn't mind class lists, since I was always in the first class and never expected not to be. When we boarders went back to Tregear for lunch, Miss Hyndman asked us to raise our hands to show the class we were in. She encouraged boarders to think we were superior to the daygirls and had to do better than they did.

To promote the competitive spirit everyone in the school belonged to one of four houses—Armourers, Goldsmiths, Haberdashers, and

Merchants— named after medieval London guilds, since Sir John Maynard had been a guild member in the sixteenth century. I wanted to be a Goldsmith, the house that seemed to win everything. Penny was a Goldsmith. But I had no choice, and was assigned to be an Armourer. I sewed the guild emblem, an embroidered green helmet, to the right side of my tunic yoke without enthusiasm. The Armourers were usually last in all sporting competitions, which may have contributed to my adult conviction that any team I favor always loses. There was also a cup for the house with the best academic performance, based on the class lists. At least I contributed to that, although I don't remember us ever winning that either.

We also competed in our free time. After school we went back to the boarding house, changed into our own clothes, and had recreation time before tea and homework. If the weather was nice we went outside and played competitive games of catch. The three-story brick chimney on the side of the boarding house was conveniently divided into four horizontal areas by lighter-colored bricks. We threw a ball into each area in turn, highest to lowest, and tried to make it impossible for our partner to catch the ball before it bounced. With so much practice I, the klutz, became quite good at catching. At weekends we ran around the school grounds chasing each other in long games of what we called Acky One-Two-Three (I have no idea why), a mixture of tag and hide and seek.

Indoors, we younger girls spent our free time in the playroom, spartanly furnished with lockers, a wooden table and a few chairs. We competed in endless games of jacks on the playroom's linoleum floor. We even turned jigsaw puzzles into a competition, seeing who could complete a corner first. We compared the progress of the silkworms we kept in glass jars with perforated lids and fed on mulberry leaves from a tree in the school's vegetable garden. Getting them far enough along to unwind the silk from their cocoons (which killed the moth inside) was a great achievement.

We did not compete in disobedience. It wasn't worth it. During the school day teachers gave out order marks for misbehavior, such as persistent talking in class or while in line moving from room to room. Even worse (and rare) were conduct marks for major sins like talking back to a teacher. These too Miss Ryan announced to the whole school on class list day. Conventional and obedient as I was, I never got an order or conduct mark. If we broke the boarding house rules, being late for meals for example, we lost privileges like the weekly shopping trip to spend the pocket money our parents provided and Miss Hyndman doled out in small amounts after lunch on Thursdays. One rule we broke regularly was the ban on talking after lights-out at night. That was the time when, under the cover of darkness, in loud whispers we exchanged confidences, told stories, and, later, shared what we knew about sex. Sometimes Matron caught us, but mostly she didn't bother. Nothing in her bag of penances would have stopped us.

Breaking rules worried me, but I went along to be like everyone else. I wasn't good at disobedience, and I wasn't good at sport, the thing that mattered. The one aspect of school where I shone, academic work, didn't seem to be valued by my peers. In any case every two weeks for seven years I was effortlessly at the top of my class. It didn't feel like competing since I and everyone else took my academic success for granted. If some of my friends envied it, I never knew.

THE FACTS OF LIFE

Somebody once commented to me that because I grew up on a farm I must have learned the facts of life early. Well…a child might have developed a twisted view of sex.

Cows need to calve once a year to keep up their milk yields. We kept an eye on the herd for any cows that were, as we put it, "looking for the bull," that is, mounting on another cow. For a short while we kept a bull, Billy. If a cow needed Billy she was let into his pen for "service," something I don't remember ever seeing. I doubt I would have forgotten if I had.

Bulls are dangerous animals, even relatively placid Guernseys. Every day my father had to go into Billy's pen and hook a pole through a ring in his nose, staying as far away from him as possible. He then led him out to the pasture by the pole, and attached it to a chain on the end of a stake deep in the ground. Even that wasn't foolproof—if the mood took him Billy could uproot the stake and run around the field with it flying in the air like a trophy. When we heard that our farm pupil Karl Dunger's bull had pinned him to the wall and broken several of his ribs, my parents had had enough. Billy was sold.

He was replaced by a man in a van. When a cow started looking for the bull my mother or father called the AI (artificial insemination) man who came as soon as he could in his small white van. The AI man was preferable to (and much less dangerous than) Billy because his services greatly lessened inbreeding, and because we no longer had to have a dangerous animal around. It probably cost more than maintaining a bull, but it was worth it for the lack of trouble. While we were waiting for the van, we isolated the cow in the cowhouse and the AI man inseminated her with a large syringe, something else I don't remember witnessing. I doubt my parents would have stopped me, so I must not have been curious about the procedure. I don't remember wondering what was in the syringe or how it got there. I did know that the end result was a calf.

A cow's gestation period is roughly the same as a woman's, and since we always knew the date of insemination we also knew when a cow was due. That often happened at night, and sometimes my father stayed up with the herd to make sure there was no trouble. Most cows gave birth easily and we would find the calf in the field in the morning, wobbling on unsteady legs and already sucking from its mother's udder. It was rare for us to call the vet, but if there was any danger to the cow he came out. Adult cows were worth more than calves—it was always preferable to lose the calf rather than a productive milking cow.

The most common reason for difficulty was a breech birth. If that happened, my father reached up into the birth canal to put a rope around the calf and pull it out. Once I watched as he plunged his arm up through the cow's vagina, holding the rope, hooked it round the calf's buttocks, then pulled as hard as he could. Out came the calf, covered with slime like my father's arm. The mother started to lick the slime off and the calf struggled a little, then stood up. I was both fascinated and slightly repelled. It didn't occur to me to equate it with human births.

Farming is a business that doesn't leave a lot of room for sentiment. We allowed calves two days with their mothers before we separated them into the calf pens in the big barn to stop them from suckling and drinking our livelihood. Both mother and baby mooed plaintively for a day or so before they accepted the rupture and settled down to the usual cow activities of eating and chewing the cud. We fed the calves their mothers' fresh milk from a pail. When I helped with this I dipped my hand in the warm milk and then put it into the calf's mouth. The calf sucked lustily on my hand, which I then lowered into the pail so it sucked in the milk at the same time. I enjoyed the feel of the calf's tongue, warm and muscular with a scratchy rough surface. Calves quickly learned to drink from the pail by themselves and soon moved on to eating grass, although they could not go out with the herd until they had been totally weaned off milk.

We didn't keep many calves for ourselves, especially since on a small farm our pasture was limited. Bull calves went to the market straight away to be sold and fattened for veal. Heifer (female) calves we kept longer. We raised a few from especially good milk-producing mothers to fill gaps in the herd from deaths (rare) or sale of low milk-producers. The rest we sold as yearlings to other Guernsey farmers at a cattle auction. We gave the heifers names, but never named the bulls except once, when two day-old calves, one bull, one heifer, kept pressing against each other in the pen. My

156

brother and I had just been reading *Belles on Their Toes,* the sequel to *Cheaper by the Dozen* about growing up with Frank Gilbreth. In it, Ernestine, the eldest sister, dated a guy called Al, who greeted the family when they first met with, "Meased to pleet you. Press the flesh." Michael and I found this exquisitely funny, and named the flesh-pressing calves Al and Ernestine.

If sex for cows involved a man in a van, pigs went for walks. Cows' essential function was to produce milk, for which calving was a necessary sideline, but for pigs reproduction was the reason for their existence. We raised pigs for bacon and pork, so each of the three sows we kept had to have two litters a year—gestation time for a pig is four months, and we gave the mothers a little respite. We never kept a male pig (boar—also a dangerous animal) and there was at the time no AI for pigs. A neighbor at the far side of the valley had a boar, so my parents used to herd the pig out of the farmyard and walk her across the moor to the other farm for sex. Once a pig ran away on the moor and it took my father and mother hours to catch her since she kept running straight at them and making them jump out of the way. Eventually my father stretched a net between his legs and caught her as she ran through the gap.

Pigs had litters of ten or twelve piglets or farrows. One was usually much smaller than the others, the runt, which often spent a few days keeping warm by the Aga and being fed warm milk like the calves before going back into the pigsty. Sows are generally good mothers, contentedly (we think, at least) lying on their sides while the piglets squeal and climb over each other to get a teat. After about a month the farrows were weaned and put together in a pen apart from their mother. Despite my mother's affinity for the cows, the pigs were her favorite animals and she loved to check on the piglets' progress. I liked the pigs too. I admired how they kept their sties clean with one corner reserved for dung, and I loved to scratch their scaly, bristly backs while they grunted with pleasure.

Raising pigs for market required vigilance and care. They had to have the right ratio of fat to lean and be at a certain weight to get an optimum price. We fed our pigs specially formulated food and kept a careful watch on their progress, measuring their girth with a piece of string at frequent intervals. As with most animals on the farm, slaughter took place elsewhere, and when pigs reached the right measurement, off they went. The pigs we planned to sell lived fairly restricted lives within their pens, although they always had room to move. The breeding sows had much more freedom, allowed to go out into the dirty and sometimes into a field, although they made a mess of the pasture, rooting it up with their snouts. They loved the dirty, lying in the mud to keep cool and turning over with satisfied grunts.

Eggs were as vital to the farm's economy as milk and bacon. Each week the egg man came in his van to pick up the week's worth of cleaned and neatly stacked eggs. He paid cash, which in turn bought our groceries and other miscellaneous expenses. Chickens had no opportunity to reproduce, and their lives were dedicated to laying eggs. We got them as day-old-chicks (it was a day-old chick lantern malfunctioning that had caused our barn fire). Since farmers only want egg-layers, the-chicks were all female—exceptions were very rare. We took that for granted and not until I was an adult did I find out that people made good money as chicken sexers. My brother became friends with the Australian world champion sculler Sam Mackenzie, who financed his rowing that way. He had somehow learned to look at a just-hatched chick and instantly know its sex, an odd but immensely useful skill. I never asked him how or when he learned it.

Initially we allowed the chickens to range freely and fed them outdoors. I remember pouring the food from a bucket to spell out a word that I imagined a passing pilot would read as if we were on a desert island—not that we had many passing pilots. But collecting free-range eggs was time-consuming and often difficult, as not all hens wanted to lay in the nesting boxes we provided, and my parents didn't have time to search for eggs in other places. When I was home I often did the egg search, warily, since sitting hens could peck viciously.

Next we put the chickens in a barn with what was called "deep litter," a layer of compost-like material that absorbed waste. Collecting eggs was much easier, but the chickens had little daylight and got bored with no grass to search for seeds so pecked each other, often to death. Finally, my parents bought a "battery," a three-tiered factory farm for chickens. The battery was on the top floor of the large barn, with daylight and air. However, each chicken was confined to her own cage with a wire floor through which waste dropped on to a conveyor belt covered in strong paper that could be pulled off and discarded. The hens had their own food and water, and their eggs rolled down the slightly sloped floor into a rack at

158

the front of each cage where we collected them daily. It was very efficient, and we could easily identify which chickens laid every day and which didn't.

Just once sentiment triumphed over economics. My brother loved chickens—he had his own free-range bantam flock—and he adopted a poor bedraggled pullet that had been pecked almost naked in the deep litter. She looked like the extinct Dodo, so that became her name. Under his care, she started to grow back her feathers. Since we were about to go back to school, he decided she would be better off in the battery. Dodo flourished in the safe environment, and one day I went into the battery to find that she had laid a small and slightly misshapen egg! It was her only egg, but she was a privileged resident who was allowed to die of old age.

Although the battery was cruel to the hens, I am ashamed to admit that it appealed to my tidy and calculating mind. During school holidays it was my responsibility. As I walked into the dusty barn the hens greeted me with a crescendo of cackles and clucks as they realized they were about to be fed. While doling out the measures of food I kept track of the eggs by marking a little chart in front of each cage. I rewarded the regular layers with an extra food morsel and gave lectures to poor producers, warning them that they would be Sunday dinner if they didn't do better, a very real threat. The yuckier task of removing the paper full of droppings from the conveyor belt I left to my father.

Another advantage of the battery, in my eyes, was that it greatly cut down on a task I didn't enjoy, washing the eggs for sale, a tedious job that my parents thought well suited to children. While I knew it needed to be done, I hated the monotony. I had to wipe each egg entirely free of any dirt with a damp cloth before placing it in a large indented tray stacked on top of the ones we had already cleaned. Since battery eggs rolled away as soon as the hens laid them, they were far less likely to be contaminated with chicken droppings, the hardest to wipe off. The main danger was that their shells were brittle or thin and broke easily, making clean-up worse than ever, but we tried to deal with that by feeding the chickens calcium.

Perhaps my mother thought that we *did* learn the facts of life on the farm. My one conversation with my mother on the topic, in my mid-teens, consisted of:

"You do know about sex and where babies come from, don't you?"

159

"Yes."

I did, although not from school biology class, when, aged fifteen, we were told about rabbits and expected to extrapolate. By that time it was old hat for most of us. My information came from my peers talking in the dormitory after lights-out, and they mostly got it from older siblings. It was fascinating and reasonably accurate and, for us boarders in the mid-1950s, totally theoretical.

MATRON

We always called her Matron, although we knew her name was Mrs. Sheila Hagen. She was younger than Miss Hyndman, slim, with dark brown wavy hair. I spent more time with her during the year than I did with my own mother, but I never thought of her as motherly. She was brusque, efficient, and somewhat distant. She rarely smiled. Matron, a trained nurse, was responsible for our health and much of our daily routine. She rang the bell to get us up in the morning and made sure no one was late for breakfast. After breakfast we stood in line to get our daily spoonful of the free government-issue cod liver oil and orange juice and any other medicines we needed. Our dentist had given me some chalky pills, probably calcium, to build up my teeth. I hated them and, rule-bound though I was, often threw my pill away.

During the morning when we were at school, Matron checked our dormitories and our clothes drawers to make sure we were keeping our things tidy. She made the list of which nights we could bathe (rather than just wash)—we were scheduled every other night, but we doubled up so everyone bathed nightly, taking turns to get the more desirable end away from the taps. She washed our hair over the bathroom sink once a week, removing tangles and checking for nits with ruthless efficiency. She made sure we were in bed at night and turned out the lights at the correct time. She monitored our talking after lights-out, turning a deaf ear unless she could hear us outside the closed dormitory door.

There was no Mr. Hagen around, but Matron had a daughter, Sally. Sally was profoundly deaf, and many years later my mother told me that Mr. Hagen, Matron's former husband, had beaten her while she was pregnant, and damaged Sally in the womb. Sally was the reason Matron had taken the job at school rather than work irregular hours in a hospital. They could both live in the boarding house, and Sally could attend the National School for the Deaf, which happened to be in Exeter, close to the school.

Sally was several years younger than I was, but when I started at the Maynard as a ten-year-old she played with us younger boarders after

161

school. At that time the Deaf School's policy was to forbid students to sign but rather teach them to lip-read from an early age, a decision that never occurred to me to question then but now seems cruel, since it kept them isolated, unable to communicate easily with either the hearing or their deaf peers. Sally's speech was guttural and difficult to understand, and we had to mouth words very distinctly to make her understand us. Her frustration frequently morphed into fierce anger, when she lashed out physically at anyone near her. We were slightly afraid of her, especially as Matron naturally defended her. Matron too had a temper that erupted if any of us tried her patience too far.

When we were sick we went into what we called The San, short for sanitorium, a room with three beds opposite Matron's bedroom so she could keep an eye on its inmates, who were kept in isolation from other boarders until they were well again. Mostly we had flu or head lice or the usual childhood ailments—measles, mumps, whooping cough, German measles (rubella)—if we had somehow escaped them previously.

In my second term at the school, before my eleventh birthday, I developed an excruciating earache. All night I tried to bury my right ear deeper and deeper into the pillow, hoping the softness would make the pain go away. It didn't. When the doctor came the following morning, he looked in my ear and listened to my description of the pain.

"I think she has a mastoid infection," he said. "She'll have to go to the hospital, and they drill a hole in her skull behind her ear to relieve the pressure." That sounded scary enough, and he didn't tell me that, left untreated, the infection could spread to my brain and I could even die.

Matron called the ambulance. The ride was slightly scary, but all I really cared about was that something was happening to help me with the pain. Matron came with me to the hospital to check me in, but couldn't stay, as she had to get back to her other duties. She had already telephoned my mother, who would get to Exeter as soon as she could, which turned out to be late that night.

I had never been in a hospital before (I wasn't even born in one). I had no idea how to behave, but went into my normal boarding school mode of doing what I was told and not asking questions. A nurse took me up to the children's ward and put me in a bed. I sat there with nothing to do except worry and try to ignore the pain. Worst of all, I hadn't brought a book to take me away from my surroundings. I was too shy to chat to the other children, all of them much younger than I was. The radio was playing "If I Knew You Were Coming I'd've Baked a Cake," a song I will always associate with pain. I waited for someone to come and take me away to have the hole drilled.

A nurse came with a bedpan. I didn't know what it was, and politely refused it. Some time later I had to pee. I tried to ignore it, but eventually it became urgent. I was too embarrassed to call a nurse, so I got out of bed to look for a lavatory, but couldn't find one. I did find a bathroom with basin and bathtub, and, desperate, I peed in the bath and flushed it down with water. Just as I was finishing, a nurse came in. She was horrified and not at all sympathetic, but she showed me where the lavatory was, before scrubbing the bath with disinfectant. I felt as if I had contaminated the hospital, and went back to my bed in shame.

Eventually the doctor came. I expected him to tell me when he would drill the hole in my skull. Instead, he sat on the bed, patted my hand, and said, "We're going to try a new drug called penicillin that might make your infection go away without an operation. I haven't tried this before, as until now only men in the armed forces could have it, but now anyone can and I think it will work. The nurses will give you an injection every four hours for ten days, and I will be watching carefully to see how you do." I was so relieved! I didn't look forward to the injections (shots), but they were a lot better than the hole.

The next morning I was overjoyed to see my mother come into the ward. Someone to protect me in this alien place! She hugged me, then too soon left to talk to the nurse and doctor. When she came back she hugged me again (an unusual event), and said, "I am sorry, but Daddy needs me at home, so I have to go. I will be back in ten days to take you home." I was sorry to see her leave and wished for her comforting presence. However, the things she brought with her partially made up for her absence. Miss Rapley had rushed to put together a box of all my favorite books from the Lamledra bookshelves (she decided the owners' children were too old to need them)—among them *What Katy Did*, *Daddy-Long-Legs*, and *Pollyanna*. My mother had also taken out the maximum number of books from the library. They didn't quite last the ten days, but Matron also visited and brought me more to read.

163

My mother also brought a cut-out doll dressing book of the characters from the film *Little Women*—June Allyson, Margaret O'Brien, Elizabeth Taylor and Janet Leigh—with their Victorian wardrobes. Miss Hyndman had just taken all the boarders to see the film, and I loved making a big mess cutting out the doll's clothes and leaving scrap paper all over my bed. One of the nurses cleaned it up with a huffy expression and clucking noises.

I got used to the shots, first in my arms, then in my legs, then my buttocks. I became a human pincushion. Some nurses were better than others, and I learned to dread the clumsier ones. But the treatment worked. The pain miraculously disappeared and my hearing was still good (I thought of Sally). I was the first child in the Devon and Exeter Hospital to have a mastoid infection cured by penicillin. It was lucky that the new National Health Service had recently been implemented, so my parents didn't have to pay for my treatment. Since it was so new, penicillin was expensive.

At last the ten days were up, and my mother came to fetch me in the car for the long drive back to the farm. I was still somewhat weak from my enforced bed rest. There were only a few weeks before the end of term, so I didn't go back to school until after the Easter holidays. I was afraid that I wouldn't pass the summer exams and be held back from "going up," as we called it, to the next year. I borrowed friends' books and studied the science, history, and geography I had missed. I needn't have worried. The exams were easy for me and at the end of term I was listed as first in my class. I was even elected form captain for the summer term, perhaps in sympathy for my illness.

When my mother came to visit me in the hospital she spent a little while with Matron. My mother had a very sympathetic ear, and most people who met her confided their life stories. Matron was no exception. To give her a break, my mother invited her and Sally to spend some time with us on the farm in the summer. They came during harvest, and Matron (I was encouraged to call her Aunty Sheila, but found it hard) gave herself tendinitis by enthusiastically pitching sheaves into wagons. Like other fatherless children such as my cousins, Sally adored my father, calling him Mit-Mit. After that Matron was kinder to me than she had been, although

164

we were both careful not to seem too friendly, as that might have invited accusations of favoritism.

That year Matron met "Ross" Rossiter, a divorced middle-aged man whose family owned a large department store in Paignton on the South Devon coast. Ross embraced Sally as if she were his own. One day Miss Hyndman called us all together in the hall. "I have an announcement to make. Matron is engaged to be married, and will be leaving us in the summer." We all swiveled around to look at Matron, standing slightly pink-faced but smiling shyly. After she and Ross married, they had a child of their own, Nigel, much adored by everyone, including Sally.

Matron did not forget my parents' kindness, and one weekend every school term I took the bus to Paignton to stay with her and her new family. I enjoyed being with a non-farming household, eating good non-school food, and playing with Sally and the baby. Eventually Sally left school and became a window dresser in the family store, a job where she didn't need to communicate much, since understanding her speech was still difficult. She married a hearing man and had a hearing baby.

Of course we got a new Matron at school. This one was older, plump, and loved to tell us about her European bus tours with Cyril, her gentleman friend, which we found pleasantly scandalous. She was warmer and friendlier than Sheila Hagen, but I distrusted her friendly exterior and never liked her as much.

SCHOOL FRIENDS

Here we are, the members of Sixth Dorm (dormitory number 6, for the youngest boarders), ready for church on a summer Sunday morning in 1950, my first year at The Maynard School. We are wearing our summer church uniform, white panama hats and gloves, and white ankle socks instead of grey knee-length ones. The navy-blue suit, white blouse, school tie, and black lace-ups remained the same year-round. I, on the right, am very surprised to see that I look the neatest of everyone. I must have made a special effort.

Someone else took the photo with my new camera, a major birthday present from my parents. I don't think I asked for it, they just thought it was time for me to have one. It was a small box camera, probably a Kodak Brownie. I soon learned to load and unload the rolls of film, but took photos sparingly, as I had to use my limited pocket money to pay for developing and buying new film at the local chemist.

166

The girl on the left is Kate Gray, a year ahead of most of us. Her mother was a war widow, the only teacher in a one-room school in a small Devon village. Kate was small, a little chubby (notice the strained suit jacket, although she may have just been growing out of it), but good at all sports. The main thing we had in common was that she loved to read. Perhaps because of the age gap and the lack of common interests, we weren't *best* friends, but that was more on Kate's part than mine. Kate was popular; I wasn't a person everyone sought out.

Anne Hemsley, standing next to Kate, was the eldest daughter of our former farm pupils and also from St. Goran School. When I began at The Maynard I was glad that she started with me. But outgoing Anne, with her sunny personality, soon became as popular as Kate, and we didn't spend much time together. After a couple of years her parents moved her to close-by St. Margaret's School, maybe because it was less expensive, but also perhaps because its academic standards were lower. I unfairly but secretly blamed Anne for what appeared to me to be a betrayal in moving to a rival school.

In the center Lois Lean stands out, tall, ungainly, and wearing glasses. Not many eleven-year-olds in the Fifties wore glasses, so they must have made her self-conscious. She has not buttoned her suit coat correctly, giving her a disheveled look. Lois was the perennial outsider, the last to be picked for a team, the last to find a partner to walk to church. I don't remember her ever having a best friend. I felt a little guilty about that—we had in common that we took the same train to and from school. We were both "brainy," at the top of our respective classes (like Kate, Lois was a year ahead of me), and we were both voracious readers. But my own social position was too precarious for me to embrace Lois. And in any case I didn't like her much.

Sue Baptist, next to me, was my closest friend. She too had been touched by war. Her father ran a Malayan rubber plantation and when the Japanese invaded during World War II he was captured and spent the rest of the war in a Japanese labor camp. He managed to survive and he and his wife stayed in Malaya after the war. Since the only way to get there and back was by ocean voyage (air travel was only for the very rich), Sue spent most school holidays with her grandparents, who lived within driving distance of the school. Sue and I enjoyed playing games together—jacks,

167

hide-and-seek, catch—and rarely disagreed about anything. Best of all, she liked me and didn't want to be friends with anyone else.

The next year we became a threesome when Wendy Boyce joined the boarding house. Like Kate's, Wendy's father had also been killed in the war, and her mother kept a sweet shop in a nearby seaside town. With sweets still rationed, Wendy had an instant path to popularity on days when we could eat our "tuck," food we had brought with us to school and could eat on Wednesdays and Saturdays at tea time, when Matron unlocked the tuck cupboard. We usually shared our bounty (everyone loved the plum preserve jam my mother made from my great-aunt's recipe), and I learned to love Barker and Dobson striped mints with a creamy interior. Wendy always brought an extra supply for me.

The photos I took over the following year and pasted into an album, writing subjects under them in white ink, illustrate our boarding-school lives. In one, Sue and Anne sit on a lawn wearing identical summer skirts we made in domestic science class. Wendy and Angela Rickards sit on the lawn winding a skein of yarn into a ball, while another group reads or sews under a tree near the tennis courts. I recorded the prize table and a skittles game with glass bottles from a fete our dormitory organized to amuse other boarders. A little more imaginatively, I posed Wendy and Sue against a background of wisteria, Wendy standing, holding out the hem of her summer dress as we imagined princesses did, with Sue kneeling before her.

The time when we were closest as a group was after lights-out, when we were not supposed to talk, the time to whisper confidences, tell stories, and share information about taboo subjects such as sex. Sometimes people retold the plots of books they had read—I will always regret knowing what happened in *Pride and Prejudice* before I read it. Sometimes the more imaginative (not me) made up their own stories. As we moved into our teens these were usually trite boy-meets-girl tales that thrilled us especially since we had no experience to draw on.

We didn't keep in touch much during the school holidays. None of us made phone calls, which were for grownups, in my family at least, and we associated writing letters with our compulsory letters home from school. Once Wendy invited me home for the summer half term and I met her mother and Clive and Rodney, her two brothers. I loved living at the back of a sweet shop and helping restock jars and even occasionally serving a customer. I also enjoyed being in a seaside town where we could wander down the main street or go to the beach by ourselves without supervision. Rodney was beginning to play golf, so one morning we went up to the local golf course when no one else was about. The course was on a cliff top with a spectacular sea view.

Rodney had one club and one ball, and Wendy and I followed him around.

"Here, you have a go," he suddenly said, thrusting the club into my hand.

"But watch out, if you slice the ball to the left we'll lose it over the cliff."

Nervous, and with no natural aptitude, I missed the ball altogether several times but then, to my amazement, managed a decent shot. We heard a metallic clunk. The ball hit a tin hut in the middle of the course and came ricocheting back. I was mortified, although also relieved that I hadn't lost the ball. That was the end of my golfing.

Later I developed a crush on Clive, Wendy's darkly handsome older brother, who was a student at Exeter University. Clive had a girlfriend, Faith, and took no notice of me whatsoever, but the two of them invited Wendy and me to the first symphony concert of my life. The opening piece was Rossini's overture to *The Thieving Magpie*, a favorite of Clive's and Faith's. Hearing it always takes me back to the thrill and heartache of an adolescent crush.

We boarders had a taboo against being very friendly with daygirls. However, we did need to be friendly enough to have someone to ask to the boarding house's Christmas party, a much sought-after invitation, since the party was always a lot of well-organized fun with excellent teatime food that appealed to our deprived sweet teeth. One of the daygirls in our form, Anne Sargent, knew that we had to invite anyone who had invited us to something, so she made a point of having the boarders in our year to tea several times to make sure of her invitation. None of us liked Anne much, and we disliked her effusive mother more, so the teas were stiff occasions. However, someone had to invite her every year and we kept strict count of whose turn it was.

The daygirl I liked most was Sylvia Budd, or Spuds. She was in my year, but in the other, parallel, section. Spuds was small and wiry, with enviably

169

curly hair. She was very athletic, but also devoted to mathematics, which eventually became her career. The only child of elderly parents, I suspect school was a lot more fun than home. Her mother sent her to school every day with a snack of a cold buttered toast sandwich. Spuds occasionally offered me a bite and I learned to love it, so was always trying to get her to share. (Fifty years later, in a compilation of memories, one of the things she remembered most about school was boarders trying to eat her toast!)

While I liked Spuds and invited her to the Christmas party when I could, the anti-daygirl taboo and the fact that we didn't have any classes together except gym and games kept us from developing much of a friendship until our mid-teens, when we began to share some classes, especially maths. By then my future looked different from Wendy's and Sue's, and closer to Spuds', and I was finally willing to defy the anti-daygirl taboo.

GAMES

When I was about thirteen I developed a sizeable wobbly lump on my right wrist. It hurt with a dull and persistent ache, so during the school holidays my mother took me to the doctor. He took one look and said, "It's a ganglion."

"This is the first thing we try." He reached for a large medical book and brought it smashing down on my wrist. I was both surprised and hurt, and the ganglion was still there.

"That didn't work," said the doctor cheerfully. "Try total rest for a month or so. If nothing happens, we'll have to cut it out."

I went back to school for the summer term with my wrist in a brace, learned to write (not very well) with my left hand, and had to sit out gym and sports. The ganglion disappeared after a couple of months.

I mention the ganglion because it was a factor, admittedly somewhat insignificant, in my lackluster sporting career. However, I can't blame it for my ineptness. I just wasn't any good. All the sporting genes in my family (there were many on both sides) went to my brother. I also tried, but even competence was often beyond my reach.

At the Maynard School, like most schools, games, as we called them, were all-important. All the popular girls were good at games. We had four sessions of them a week, two of "gym" or gymnastics, and two of outdoor sports. Four times a week we changed into our gym clothes in the school cloakroom. Although our daily wear included what we called a gym tunic, we paradoxically took them off for indoor gym. Initially we just tucked our striped school blouses into our voluminous navy-blue knickers and changed into plimsolls (sneakers), but quite soon after I started at the Maynard we got a special uniform for sports, navy shorts, also voluminous, like divided skirts, and blue Aertex shirts made of lightweight porous cotton. Aertex was actually fashionable, a featured product in the 1951 Festival of Britain.

At St. Goran School walking had been our main exercise, and I had never encountered gymnastics. One session a week was aerobic exercise

171

(we simply called it "gym"), which I didn't mind. Sometimes, when we did country (folk) or square dancing, I even enjoyed it. Having to learn the steps appealed to my classifying mind, and success depended more on doing them right than innate athletic ability.

What I dreaded was the second weekly gym session, "apparatus." We lowered the long ropes attached to the gym rafters and dragged out the leather pummel horse and the vaulting box, an elongated pyramid with sloping sides topped by a padded cushion. We placed springboards in front of them, and mats behind to catch us as we vaulted. Well, most of the others did. I was among the few who failed, and I couldn't make the excuse that I was overweight. I failed to swing my legs between the handles on the horse. Worst of all was "long-fly," when we had to run up to the box, jump on the springboard, and launch ourselves over the pad, touching the other end lightly with our fingertips and landing neatly upright on the mat the other side. I never managed it and always landed on my belly in the middle of the pad until eventually I gave it up as useless, jumped up on the box, walked to the end, and jumped off.

In my teens I looked forward to my monthly period when I was excused from gym, even if all of us menstruators had to sit out at the front like lepers. The gym teachers (coincidentally called Miss Woolley and Miss Lacey) kept track of our periods in a notebook so you couldn't fake it. To avoid the torture of gym, I once stuffed one of my gym shoes into someone else's shoe bag in the school cloakroom, hoping I could sit out until it was found. It worked for a couple of weeks until the shoe turned up in the school's Lost and Found box. Of course it had my name on it.

For my first few years I was more successful at outdoor games. Our main winter sport was netball, a version of basketball played only by girls, where you can't dribble the ball. Because boarders had a lot of time on their hands after school and homework, we practiced passing and shooting daily, so I managed to get good enough to play a defensive position in the second-ranked under-fifteen team. We actually won a tournament. However, competition was greater at the senior level, and I never got close to being picked for senior teams.

Until we were fifteen, our main summer sport was rounders, a version of softball without gloves. That was my main sporting success. Although I was never good at hitting the ball, I became a good enough bowler (pitcher) to make the school team and developed a mean fastball that helped win matches. Unfortunately my success didn't last since we switched rounders for tennis the following year.

In the summer we also went swimming in the public baths down the street from the school. Neither of my parents liked swimming—I am not sure my mother *could* swim—and no one at St. Goran School tried to teach either me or my brother to swim in the Cornish sea. I was recently astonished when my brother, an international oarsman, told me he had never learned to swim. I was also handicapped since my mastoid infection meant I couldn't go in the pool my first summer at Maynard, when most of my peers became swimmers. I did learn the following year, but marginally. I could do only the breaststroke, could not float on my back, and hated jumping in or getting my face wet. All boarders had season tickets to the baths, so, on the principle of getting our money's worth, we also went swimming every Saturday morning in the summer. Once again I followed the crowd. I hated Saturday mornings, but spent them doggedly swimming laps for years.

A rite of passage was to jump off the high diving board, and I couldn't face the ridicule of not doing it. One day I pretended to be brave, walked nonchalantly up to the deep end and climbed the three sets of stairs to the top board. I looked down, terrified, at the long drop to the water that seemed as far as from a Cornish cliff. But my schoolmates were watching and I couldn't go back. I closed my eyes and jumped. It was as bad as I expected, stinging my eyes and nose and momentarily taking my breath. But I had done it. I never went up there again.

When I was fifteen we continued with gym, netball, and swimming, but we added field hockey in the winter, and tennis and athletics in the summer. We played hockey on a field about a mile's walk from the school. We were not allowed to walk to the field in our gym clothes because we might show too much flesh to passers-by, so we had to change when we got there. The pavilion was too small for all of us to get inside, so, ironically, most of us changed by the hedge, attracting (mostly) unwanted male attention. Eventually we learned to put our gym clothes on under our uniforms, which was bulky but less embarrassing. I hated the whole performance, including hockey itself. I never managed to hit the ball

173

cleanly, and cannot remember ever scoring a goal. Mostly I ran up and down the muddy field trying to keep away from the ball.

The ganglion kept me from tennis the first year we started to play, adding an extra handicap to my general ineptitude. When we were sixteen we were all eligible for entry into the school's tennis singles championship, and our gym teachers expected everyone to sign up. Ever compliant, I did, and was drawn against the school tennis champion in the first round. I still remember her name, Jill Hoyt. We went together out onto the tennis court, where she lobbed some balls at me to warm up. I missed them all. She wasn't vindictive, and I think tried to tone down her game so the humiliation wasn't complete. She failed. I missed all her serves, double-faulted most of mine, and didn't win a single point. After that I concentrated on becoming an efficient tennis umpire.

The excitement of the first Olympic Games since the war, held in London in 1948, but also the humiliation of Britain's poor performance there, spurred an emphasis on teaching athletics in schools. Here was another form of torture. We spent hours jogging around the school fields, and then dragged ourselves up to the hockey field for practice in sprinting, high and long jump, and throwing the javelin and discus. After a couple of years the gym teachers decided we were good enough to have a school sports day. I was entered in the long jump and the discus throw (we didn't have a choice—the gym teachers decided). Somehow both my parents came to watch—they must have hired a helper to milk the cows. They probably wanted to encourage me in the face of my brother's athletic over-achievement. To my utter amazement, I won the discus throw, a total fluke. Since discus throwing was already connected in our minds to large unwomanly women and I was concerned about my seeming unattractiveness to boys, I was more embarrassed than elated, and my brother teased me about it for years.

In my last two years of school I was preparing for university entrance exams, and sports became much less important to my friends and me. I finally got the courage to stop swimming on Saturday mornings. I had only one gym lesson a week, and no one expected me to jump over things. I retired my tennis racquet. I didn't miss any of it. I must have been trying, though. My last school report card says "Quite good" for gym, and "Good on the whole" for games.

174

RELIGION

My parents didn't go to church. They were both nominal members of the Church of England, and I assume they had been christened (baptized) as infants, as were most children of their generation, but I never saw any evidence of it. As far as I knew my grandparents were not churchgoers either, unusual for Victorians. My father had embraced socialism as a young man, and although he was no longer a socialist by the time I was born, he retained at least the agnosticism he had acquired with the politics. My mother had attended the Protestant Italian church in London with her aunt and uncle as a child, but when her parents moved in her teens she stopped going. Many years later, after we had left the farm, when someone asked my mother why she baked cakes for church occasions whenever asked, but never went herself, she replied sweetly, "Because I don't believe in it."

When we moved to the farm, the local Church of England vicar must have hoped to swell his minimal congregation in an area lost to Methodism since Wesley's time. On several occasions he walked the few miles to the farm to talk to my parents. My father always disappeared as soon as he saw his approach. My mother was polite but distant, offering tea but no sympathy.

Yet my parents thought some knowledge of Christianity was an important part of our cultural education. For a while they sent Michael and me to Sunday school in the Methodist chapel down the road from the farm. I loved the pretty texts they handed out each week for us to memorize—single verses from the Bible on little strips of paper with a gold-leafed initial letter and illustrations like a medieval manuscript. I still remember some of the texts, but not much else stuck, and we stopped going when I changed schools and wasn't home at weekends.

I got most of my Christian education at school. As a result of bitter Victorian disputes over who should control education, church or state, when I was growing up religion was the only subject that was compulsory in English schools. At St. Goran School Miss Rapley didn't spend much time on it, just morning prayers and learning some Bible stories. But at the

Maynard School, Scripture, as we called it, was an integral part of the curriculum, including Bible study, complete with tests and exams. Since the teaching included Church of England doctrine, the only people excused were the very few Roman Catholics, much envied by the rest of us because they got two extra preps (study halls) a week. They were also excused attendance at the formal morning assembly, a mini-service of a hymn, a short devotional reading, and prayers, followed by announcements.

Religion permeated our boarding-house life. We took turns saying grace—perfunctorily—before every meal, usually "For what we are about to receive..." with everyone mumbling "Amen." Occasionally one of us showed off our Latin ("Benedictus, benedicat"). We had evening prayers on the boarding house landing. Girls who took piano lessons took it in turns to choose and play a hymn for us to sing, and Miss Hyndman led us in the Lord's Prayer and a benediction. All the boarders were at least nominal members of the Church of England, but Miss Hyndman was a Northern Irish Presbyterian, a term that meant nothing to us then, nearly twenty years before the Irish Troubles erupted anew and sectarian tensions turned to violence. I am sure she would have preferred to take us to a dour Presbyterian chapel, but our parents expected us to attend the established church.

Miss Hyndman had a choice of where to go. The Prayer Book was the same in all Church of England places of worship, but since the church originated as a compromise between Catholicism and Calvinism, worship could vary widely from "high church," really Catholicism without the Latin that was universal at the time, to "low church," a plain service approaching Calvinist rigor. Miss Hyndman preferred the latter. So, every Sunday we walked to St. Leonard's, a Victorian church down by the river, where the service was "low"—no drama, little emotion. We formed what we called a "crocodile," two by two, with a pair of the most senior girls at the front and Miss Hyndman in the rear. It was a ten-minute walk to the church and we provided a weekly navy, white and grey spectacle for the neighbors as we walked briskly along the sidewalks, pausing only to let other pedestrians pass.

Getting a partner for the crocodile was a little tense. If, like my cousin Penny, you had one special friend, the choice was easy, but I was part of a threesome with Wendy and Sue, and one of us always had to find another partner. That usually meant walking with unpopular misfit Lois, a cruel but obvious admission of defeat in the popularity stakes. The worst was to be left without a partner if there was an odd number through sickness or absence for a weekend. Then you had to walk at the back with Miss Hyndman. She was not an ogre, but conversation could be difficult.

The vicar of St. Leonard's must have loved us as we filed in and took up three or four rows of pews—we doubled his congregation. Ever wanting to conform, and knowing I should feel something, I tried hard to experience devotion during the hymns and prayers and did not admit to myself that the spark was not there.

The hardest part to endure of the morning service was the sermon; the vicar was not a good preacher, with a monotonous delivery and uninteresting topics. Two things made it bearable. First, someone, perhaps me, devised a game, listening for a word beginning with each letter of the alphabet in sequence. Some were more difficult than others— "J" for example, if the text was from the Old Testament and there was no reason to mention Jesus. We made a gratifying audience, hanging on the vicar's every word, although he might have been puzzled when a ripple of suppressed glee ran through us if he used a difficult letter just when it was needed. On the way back after the service we compared notes as to where in the alphabet we had finished. I don't remember anyone ever getting all the way through.

The other antidote to boredom was the curate, the assistant vicar. Sometime in my early teens we got a new and handsome curate, dark-haired with twinkling dark eyes. On the occasions he got to preach we all swooned and forgot to play the alphabet game. The poor man probably found it difficult to concentrate; we sat close to the pulpit and fixed him with wide-eyed admiration tinged with a lust we hardly recognized and certainly did not acknowledge. We also willingly attended the youth group he started on Friday nights, a welcome antidote to the tedium of boarding house life.

Miss Hyndman was usually willing to sanction any semi-recreational religious activity. In my first year at the school we started attending something called Girls' Crusaders on Sunday afternoons when there was generally nothing else to do. We were allowed to walk there in a group without an escort, an escape from the constant surveillance. We met in a

177

small hall, where we sang choruses, shorter than hymns, prayed, and studied the Bible. The main attraction for me was that if we attended for fifty Sundays we got a free Bible for ourselves. Since we couldn't attend during school holidays we had to go for nearly two years before we qualified.

I still have my Bible, bound in red crinkly leather with the Crusader badge and Greek motto stamped in gold on the front cover. The edges of the pages are also tipped with gold, and it is illustrated with soulful pictures of very white Anglo-Saxons in religious poses. More than a half-century ago I pressed flowers and leaves from the school grounds between its pages, ghostly survivors of that long-vanished world. Inside the front cover is a plate recording that I received it in June 1951, when I was twelve. The term "knighthood" describing my attendance achievement seems rather inappropriate, although suitably crusaderly. I didn't last with Crusaders much longer than it took to get my Bible. It was too much like church and scripture lessons, and once we got somewhat more latitude to go off on our own on walks on Saturday afternoons the lure of escape from the boarding house paled and my friends and I dropped out.

By that time we were attending classes at St. Leonard's in preparation for our spring confirmation by the bishop in the cathedral. I continued to try to locate some kind of spiritual feeling within me, the inner light I read about in the small devotional books the vicar assigned us, but I failed. I did not admit this to the vicar or any of my friends, afraid to be recognized as a fraud. Faith was something I knew I should have, but it never came. The only thing I remember about the confirmation ceremony was that we had to wear white veils. I had hoped for a complete new outfit, but, as usual, our school uniforms sufficed. My mother came for the occasion, and one of my godmothers sent me a handsome new edition of *The Pilgrim's Progress*, John Bunyan's seventeenth-century allegory that I already knew about from reading *Little Women*. I read it with some interest, but it didn't produce that moment of conversion I was looking for. I still have the book.

Confirmation brought extra freedom. We were supposed to attend the early-morning Holy Communion service at least once a month, but Miss Hyndman did not go and it was our responsibility to get to church by 8 o'clock. Since no one was checking on us we soon realized we could go anywhere we wanted. We began sampling every Church of England church in Exeter, at least twenty of them. My favorite was St. Pancras, a very old tiny church in the city center. It had a minuscule congregation and a high church service, making attendance that much more daring.

On a very few occasions drama and ritual aroused some emotion in me. Miss Ryan, the school's headmistress, attended Exeter Cathedral, a beautiful thirteenth-century building with a huge rose window in its carved west front. She occasionally mentioned to Miss Hyndman that she would like to see us there, her girls, conspicuous in their uniforms, taking up a solid block of seating, ever noticeable, ever under her eye so she could note any misbehavior. Her wish was rarely granted since the boarding house was outside her control, and when we asked Miss Hyndman if we could go to the cathedral occasionally, she said she found the service too ceremonial.

Just once a year on the Sunday closest to November 11, to please Miss Ryan we went to the cathedral for the Armistice Day (Veterans' Day) service. We sat under the soaring Gothic roof, just restored after a wartime bomb destroyed one wing, and as the organ played at full strength, we sang Kipling's "Recessional:"

God of our fathers, known of old,
Lord of our far-flung battle-line,
Beneath whose awful Hand we hold
Dominion over palm and pine—
Lord God of Hosts, be with us yet,
Lest we forget—lest we forget!

We blithely included the poet's references to "lesser breeds without the law." Next the organ pealed out the beginning bars of a First World War hymn:

O valiant hearts who to your glory came
Through dust of conflict and through battle flame;
Tranquil you lie, your knightly virtue proved,
Your memory hallowed in the land you loved.

We sang our hearts out, and as the final notes died away the Last Post (Taps) floated plaintively down from a bugle behind the high altar. I was

179

entranced by the emotion, the beauty of the surroundings, the sorrow. I can hear that bugle still.

After the service, still holding on to the cathartic moment in the cathedral, we filed out to the space in front of the west door. There several army regiments in colorful red and black dress uniforms assembled ready to lay wreaths at the war memorial a few streets away. My mood turned from pathos to patriotism, as we, children of war, watched each regiment in turn present arms and march off with exemplary precision. The elation of the moment lasted all day.

The other times when I felt some stirrings of sentiment were on the vary rare occasions that we attended our local parish church, St. Matthew's, opposite the school's back gate. St. Matthew's was extremely high church, and Miss Hyndman hated it. Only when it was raining so hard that we would get soaked if we walked very far, were we allowed to run across the street and into what was for us a dangerous and forbidden space. I loved the incense, the singing, the theater. Maybe I would have embraced religion if we had gone to St. Matthew's regularly.

But no spark ignited. I said my prayers, read my Scripture Union passages at night, but felt—nothing. In my teens during the school holidays I forced my mother to take me to communion on Easter Sunday, holding on to a scrap of belief that the God I couldn't relate to still somehow required me to go. But as soon as I left school I stopped attending church regularly. I went on Easter Sunday until I was twenty-one, but the next year I skipped with hardly a twinge of guilt. Lightning did not strike me—not that anyone had really threatened me with hell fire—and I abandoned religion without regret. The only thing I missed was the singing. I have no singing voice—never made the school choir—but I enjoyed the hymns, especially the rousing ones. "Guide Me O Thou Great Redeemer" sung to the Welsh tune of "Cwm Rhondda" gave me goose bumps every time I heard the crowd sing it at Welsh rugger games.

FLAPS

Her name was Janet Tremaine, but everyone called her Trem. She had long red-gold hair she wore in a thick braid most of the time, fair skin with a few freckles, a ready smile, and a stocky athletic body. She was on all the sports teams but struggled a little with schoolwork. She played the piano well, her signature piece being Dvorak's *Humoresque*, a composition that still thrills me on the very rare occasions when I hear it, as does Chopin's *Waltz Number 13*, another of her favorites.

And for my entire thirteenth year I adored her.

Schoolgirl crush. In the U.S.A. where boys and girls almost always go to school together through high school, the term usually means a girl's crush on an older boy. In Britain in the 1950s, secondary schools for those in academic tracks (selected at age eleven) were, with very few exceptions, single-sex, so a schoolgirl crush was on an older girl. At my school we called it being "flaps" on someone. I don't know where the term came from—one of the Internet's *Urban Dictionary* definitions says: "affectionate name given to a close friend...derived from the fact your heart flaps or flutters when you see you have a message from them." Our hearts certainly flapped.

Being flaps was pretty much an obligatory rite of passage in our early teens, for us boarders at least. My cousin Penny and her best friend Peta were flaps on two daygirls, nicknamed Hitch and Mello, and followed them around with adoring persistence. Penny kept a diary in a fairly simple letter substitution code. One day during the school holidays while she was somewhere else I spent a day cracking the code and reading the somewhat tame entries—"Chatted with Hitch after school. Couldn't believe my luck!" I was very proud and not a bit ashamed of my sneaky success, and I told Penny I had done it. She was understandably annoyed, and kept her diary out of my way after that.

Trem was a boarder two years older than I was. The only thing we had in common was that we were both farmers' daughters, and perhaps I was attracted to her because we were so different. On the other hand, I may

181

have picked her because she had no other admirers and I didn't want a rival. I hung over the baby grand piano on the upstairs landing while she practiced, begging for *Humoresque*. I loved to watch her in action on the netball and tennis courts, and some of my most exciting moments occurred when she asked if I could help her with her homework and our heads touched as we bent over the problem.

On the last night of the summer term Miss Hyndman and Matron turned a blind eye to what went on in the dormitories, and we piled all the mattresses on the floor to sleep (not very well) in clumps of bodies, not necessarily in our own rooms. Once I managed to end up on the same mattress pile as Trem, the high point in our relationship as far as I was concerned, although our bodies never touched. That night I persuaded her to write to me over the school holidays. I waited anxiously at the farmhouse gate for the postman, hoping she would follow through. I was overjoyed when she did, although I could read little into her trite descriptions of daily life. Mine in reply were equally innocuous.

I intercepted her letters before my parents saw them, vaguely afraid they might not approve, and not wanting to discuss Trem with them. That year, for the only time in my life, like Penny, I kept a diary, probably a Christmas present, a small brown book, appropriately published by the girls' comic book *School Friend*. There was only one small rectangular space for each day and my entries were even more uninformative and laconic than Penny's, but I ended every day's entry with TLUP, meaning "Trem's letter under pillow."

I knew nothing about homosexuality and never heard the word lesbian until I got to university. But, although I didn't realize it, I had met some. On our way to St. Austell from the farm on our Friday shopping trips we sometimes stopped to see two middle-aged women who lived together in a small cottage. They didn't own a car and my mother had learned that they needed someone to exchange their library books for them (they kept a list at the library). I saw nothing unusual about two women living together. One day they took us back to their barn to see some new kittens that had curly hair. Those kittens became the ancestors of a new breed, the Cornish Rex, named by these lesbian women.

The schoolgirl stories I read when I was twelve and thirteen—the Abbey Girls or Chalet School series, for example—had many examples of

182

ardent but sexless love between girls, and even of adult teachers as couples. Most of the ones I read from the boarding-house bookshelves were published in the 1920s and early 30s, when schoolgirl crushes had not been much demonized in the larger culture. Miss Hyndman and Matron never warned us of the possible dangers of "flapsdom." Now, I think they were aware of them. They deliberately organized our lives so that any two of us had almost no opportunities to be alone together. We were segregated by age, regimented in our bath times (two of us shared baths but with Matron always hovering), thrown together with others in designated rooms in our free time. In any case, being flaps was, as far as I knew, entirely innocent. I hardly touched Trem, certainly never kissed her, although I dreamed of doing so.

My passion reached its height the summer of Trem's letters. I discovered an organ version of *Humoresque* in our sparse and eclectic record collection that I played a lot, although it didn't have the same charm as when she played it. On our way to shop in St. Austell we usually passed a street called Tremayne Road, which gave me a small thrill.

Trem left school when she was sixteen and trained as a secretary before getting married. Her letters stopped. I missed her dreadfully for about a month, but no other girl replaced her in my affections—by that time I was moving on to more remote male cricketers. When I too had left school but returned for the annual prize-giving, someone whispered to me that several of the younger boarders had been flaps on *me*. I had had no clue, but I was certainly flattered.

THE STUDY

On Saturday mornings in the boarding house we girls between the ages of twelve and sixteen enjoyed precious free time in the study. A visiting observer, perhaps a prospective parent, might have looked in through the door from the main hall to see three large windows looking out onto the lawn, bringing in plenty of light. Pairs of girls, deep in conversation, perched on two hot water radiators under the windows, keeping warm despite the belief that sitting on radiators encouraged piles (hemorrhoids)—to my knowledge no one ever developed them. The boarding house had no heat above the first floor, and we regularly suffered from chilblains, red, itchy and sometimes blistery areas on our hands and feet, caused by exposure to cold and damp. Since few homes in Fifties Britain had central heating, chilblains were a common complaint.

Two girls sat with their backs to the radiators, reading books chosen from the miscellaneous collection in the floor-to-ceiling bookshelves on the wall next to the door, relics of many previous occupants. To the left of the windows other girls rummaged through untidy heaps of personal belongings in small square lockers (without locks—no privacy even here). Several girls sat around a table by the long pocket door on the right that separated the study from the dining room. Some were doing leftover homework, others writing in their diaries or doing a jigsaw puzzle of a mountain scene. Two or three lounged on a brown tattered sofa, chatting, and one lucky girl had managed to get the single comfortable chair. On the carpeted floor others played patience (solitaire), racing demon (war), or draughts (checkers). A couple were scooping up jacks, although the carpet wasn't very suitable for the game, and someone was winding up the gramophone as it played a record of Gigli singing the "Miserere" from *Il Trovatore*.

I could have been any one of those girls. I played all the games, did jigsaws, learned to love Verdi since the only records we had, apart from the ones we danced to, were opera and a very few classical excerpts. But most likely I was one of the readers. One other girl, Lois Lean, and I read every book on all the bookshelves, many of them several times. They ranged from schoolgirl stories to weepy bestsellers like *The Robe*, but hardly any classics. I had to discover the Brontes and Jane Austen on my own. My favorites were historical novels by D. K. Broster, three about the 1745 Scottish rebellion against the English from the Scottish point of view, and *The Wounded Name*, set in the Vendée rebellion during the French Revolution. Since most of the main characters in all the books were on the losing sides, French or Scottish, they all had bittersweet endings. Although I rarely cry over books, I sniffled a bit over the fate of these heroic men in two of history's great lost causes.

One book was a rite of passage into the study. Vera Brittain is quite well known now for her memoir about nursing in World War I, adapted for television by the BBC, but we knew nothing about her. Her only representation in the study's eclectic collection was a novel, *Honourable Estate*. On page 492 was the best description of the sex act available to us. It wasn't very explicit, but we could understand roughly what was going on, and older girls told all the newcomers to the study to read the well-thumbed and discolored page while we watched for their reactions. Of course, only Lois and I read the whole long book, to discover that the couple were not married (major scandal!), and that the sex was a last gift from her to him before he went off to war. I am sure if Miss Hyndman had ever read it she would have been scandalized and taken the book off the shelves.

During the week we didn't spend a lot of time in the study. Between the end of the school day at 3:30 and tea in the boarding house at 4:30, we changed out of our school uniforms and usually went outside to play catch or practice our netball or tennis shots unless it was raining. After tea we did our prep (homework) seated silently in the dining room with Miss Hyndman watching over us. We had to get her permission to ask someone else for help, and we had to prove we had finished our work before we could leave. Then there were evening prayers and a supper of bread, cheese and milk, after which the youngest went to bed. We were all in bed by 8 o'clock, with lights out for the oldest at 8:30, nine on Friday and Saturday.

Saturday was our big leisure day since much of Sunday was taken up with church and writing our required letter home—in yet another example of the total lack of privacy, Miss Hyndman read them all before they were

185

mailed. After Saturday breakfast we stayed in the dining room to check our week's laundry—underwear, blouses, pajamas, socks—sent out to a commercial company. It came back neatly folded, but almost always with missing shirt buttons or holes in our socks. We had to sew on the buttons and darn the socks, and then show them to Miss Myers, who came in for Matron on Saturdays. I came to enjoy darning, making a careful woven patch of wool to cover the offending hole. It appealed to my sense of order. I never developed the same feeling about missing buttons.

After we had passed the laundry inspection we cleaned all our shoes, two outdoor and two indoor, and left the pair of black lace-ups reserved for Sundays out for inspection. Then we spent our free time in the study doing what we liked until lunch, the main meal of the day, meat, potatoes, and vegetable, followed by rice pudding or something similar. After lunch we went for a two-hour walk unless the weather was bad, when we stayed in and often gathered around the dining room piano to sing popular songs like the theme songs from *Moulin Rouge* and Chaplin's *Limelight*, or the music from *Carousel*.

If the weather was fine, until we were fifteen we had to walk with Miss Hyndman as chaperone, and she chose where to go, usually down by the canal to watch boats going through the lock. Once we reached fifteen we could go in a group unchaperoned. Sometimes we too went down to the canal or river, but more often we saved a little of our weekly pocket money to take a bus out into the country and walk the lanes, enjoying the freedom, the open countryside, the wooded hills, the lack of order and constraint. Although we weren't in school uniform and couldn't be recognized, we were still very law-abiding—the most adventurous thing I remember us doing was going up to a large country house and asking for a drink of water.

More daring, we occasionally went into the city, officially off limits without special permission. Since we had very little money there wasn't much for us to do, but we felt deliciously rebellious. Once we went into the only Roman Catholic church in the city, hoping to find out why it had an aura of danger attached to it. Intrigued by the whiff of incense, we peered with interest in the dim light at the statues of the Virgin Mary and saints and the ghostly flickering candles, things we never saw in our regular church-going. They seemed more interesting and holier than the plain decorations we were used to in St. Leonard's, but Miss Hyndman the Presbyterian, had made sure we knew anything to do with Catholicism was suspicious, even threatening to our mortal souls.

Very occasionally Miss Hyndman took all the boarders to the cinema to see what she thought of as a suitable film—*Little Women*, *Robin Hood*, *The Robe*. This was a major treat since I rarely went at home. Once we sneaked into *The Barretts of Wimpole Street*, not because it might be forbidden but because we wanted the thrill of not asking first. The film was enjoyable, but nothing we shouldn't be seeing. Once we persuaded Miss Hyndman to let us go without her to *Carmen Jones*, the raunchy black version of *Carmen*, telling her (semi-truthfully) that it was the opera. When I listen to *Carmen* now, I still hear the *Carmen Jones* words: "When your love bird decides to fly, there ain't no door that you can close..." and see Dorothy Dandridge smoldering on the screen.

Whatever we did on Saturday afternoon, we had to be back by five o'clock for high tea, tea and supper combined, with sausage, eggs, baked beans, bread and butter, and cake. The combination of our favorite foods and the simple luxury of cake made it our favorite meal of the week.

Afterwards the study again became the focus of our fun. We cleared away the dishes, opened up the pocket door between the dining room and study, pushed the tables aside, wound up the gramophone, and danced the country dances whose steps we learned in gym class—Newcastle, Sir Roger de Coverly, Sellinger's Round. For others, like the Veleta and the Skaters' Waltz, we needed partners, a great opportunity to hold hands with the people we were flaps on. Miss Hyndman took some time off and didn't watch, so we twirled, skipped, jigged, and laughed with abandon until bedtime.

FEARS

In 1952, when I was thirteen, a British scientist, Sir Jack Drummond, his wife Ann, and their nine-year-old daughter Elizabeth were murdered while camping in south-west France. Drummond and his wife were shot, but Elizabeth, beaten repeatedly on the head with a rifle butt while trying to escape, died a little way from the camp. Naturally it was a huge story in the newspapers, especially as Drummond was well known, a nutritionist who devised the wartime rationing system credited with avoiding widespread malnutrition. Eventually Gaston Dominici, a seventy-five-year old nearby farmer, confessed to the crime, claiming that he had been driven to it after watching Ann Drummond undress.

I was both fascinated and terrified by the murders, especially Elizabeth's. The story that Dominici watched Ann undress haunted me—when I undress at night it still sometimes flashes briefly into my consciousness. At that time I was also beginning to read murder mysteries my parents regularly borrowed from the library—Agatha Christie, Margery Allingham, Ngaio Marsh—detailing killings that far outnumbered the norm in peaceable England. At night, with no electricity, the farm and the whole valley was totally dark apart from moonlight and the faraway stars. It was also eerily quiet, with no traffic noise, only the occasional owl. The farmhouse doors had never had locks, so anyone could walk in at any time. I feared a visit from the English equivalent of Gaston Dominici, catching us unawares.

One night, when I was sleeping downstairs in the bedroom that used to be our playroom, I woke suddenly to the scraping noise the front door just outside my bedroom made when it opened. Since we never used that door as an entrance, an old chair and a pile of newspapers were obstructing the way into the hall. I heard the newspapers falling over. A mirror on the opposite wall of the bedroom reflected the hallway, and I thought I could see a sliver of moonlight through the gap in the opening door.

The noise stopped.

"They've gone around to try the back door, " I thought. "I only have a few minutes."

My parents' bedroom was at the top of the stairs leading from the front door. I inched out of bed as quickly and quietly as I could and started up the stairs. Something moved at the top. Without stopping to think how anyone could have got past me up the stairs, I froze, then, in huge relief, realized it was our indoor cat Fluffy, her pregnancy showing through her long fur. I rushed into my parents' bedroom.

"Someone is trying to get into the house," I whispered urgently.

My father got up and went cautiously to check the back door. No one there. He got a candle and looked at the front door. It was still firmly closed, but the chair had been knocked over and the newspapers scattered. At that point Fluffy started nosing around and we realized that while she was looking for a place to have her kittens, she had upset the chair and newspapers and the chair had scraped on the door, making the noise that had woken me. We all went back to bed. I even slept. In the morning we found new kittens mewling among the papers.

My nighttime fears were of violent death, present in the news and in my chosen reading. In those days of newspaper reticence I never consciously heard the word rape except as the name of something farmers occasionally grew as cattle fodder. My parents never warned me about "stranger danger." I was somewhat afraid of our neighbor across the moor, Mr. Sanders, who was indeed abusing his daughter, but I didn't know that then and it was his gruff and confrontational manner that bothered me. No one at school seemed to worry about our safety from predators. When we were in our mid-teens and went for unescorted walks on Saturday afternoons, we were always in a group so there probably was no danger. One night a man did climb the boarding-house fire escape, opened the dormitory window and looked in. The girl in the nearest bed woke up to see his head and shoulders right next to her and screamed. He left before anyone could pursue him. I wasn't in that dormitory and the threat was remote enough not to scare me. My imaginary assassins were more real to me than an actual predator.

I had daytime fears as well. The fifties were the height of the Cold War, when there seemed to be a crisis that threatened nuclear war at least once a year. Unlike American children, we didn't have drills for what to do in a nuclear attack. No crouching under desks. I don't know whether our government thought that we children of war knew how to act in an air attack, or whether they just expected Britain's total and immediate annihilation. We did know about mushroom clouds and I had read in a newspaper that a nuclear attack would produce a series of flashes and then a bright glow. I worried at the increasing glow over cities like Exeter as outdoor lighting increased after wartime blackouts. During the frequent international crises of the fifties—Suez, Quemoy and Matsu, Berlin—I read the staid, conservative newspaper left out for us at school with foreboding, watched the skyline for a mushroom cloud, in ever-present fear of imminent nuclear disaster.

I was also worried about illness. When I had jaundice at age three, I threw up a lot, and I developed a fear of vomiting. When I was in bed in the dark I often had vague stomachaches, possibly brought on by anxiety about the very thing I feared—throwing up in front of my schoolmates. It never happened, but I lay awake willing my rumbling stomach to calm and calculating how long it would take me to get to the bathroom. Two other girls in my dormitory had appendicitis attacks, excruciating pain and vomiting, and were taken off to the hospital by ambulance in the middle of the night. After the first episode, my night fears became more specific. Was I too about to lose my appendix? It never happened.

In my mid-teens another very real fear took over—polio. Polio scares were usually in the summer when epidemics were most frequent. Swimming pools were closed, outdoor events were canceled, and parents worried and tried to keep us away from crowds. Since I spent much of the summer isolated on the farm, I was less afraid than I might have been if I had lived somewhere where the closings and cancellations directly affected me. Still, I had read somewhere that polio could start with a sore throat and stiff neck, so I worried every time my throat was a little scratchy and turned my neck anxiously to make sure it worked well. In my cohort of fifty girls at school, one died and another was crippled with polio. When the vaccine that eventually eradicated it in Britain became available in my twenties, I made sure to get the protection.

I had one phobia that I couldn't keep to myself very easily. I have no idea why, but I hated anyone or anything touching the front of my neck. I avoided clothes with high necks, and even now I wear only loose-fitting

190

polo necks. I also hated seeing people touching their necks. Unfortunately my brother discovered this and would make me squirm in agony by rubbing his neck up and down or tapping it lightly for several minutes. He didn't have to touch me to make me react. I was a sitting target, too tempting to resist.

But I did manage to avoid my mother's phobia of buttons, one she succeeded in keeping from us until we grew up. She hated buttons in any form, and the sight of them en masse made her feel faint. I didn't realize this because I sewed on my own buttons when I was home, and Mrs. Hore took care of anything on my father's clothing. My mother avoided any clothes with buttons as much as possible. Apparently a button phobia isn't that uncommon (Steve Jobs had it), and, weirdly, both my daughter and one of my nieces inherited it. It was when my daughter started to object to clothes with buttons at age two that my mother told me about it. Jane was not around my mother enough for her to have passed it on knowingly, nor was my niece.

Mostly I kept my fears to myself, never talking about them to my parents or anyone else. I have one lingering legacy. Every night, as I turn onto my side, ready for sleep, I automatically cross my arms over my chest, as I have done for sixty years. I used to do this to prevent someone stabbing me in the heart, which I knew from all the detective stories meant certain death. For a long time I also shoved a pillow down my back to protect me from behind.

CORONATION

On the night of February 1, 1952, when I was almost thirteen, I dreamed that I was in a crowded space when someone announced in a loud voice that King George VI had died. So when Miss Ryan, our school headmistress, suddenly and unprecedently interrupted our chemistry class the following morning, I knew what she was going to say. "I am very sorry to tell you," she announced, "that the King is dead."

I had seen the King and Queen a couple of times, waving at them enthusiastically as they passed in an open car, but, unlike some of my friends who had lost fathers in the war, I had no experience of death. Although I was conventionally sorry, it didn't mean much. I was more interested in my premonitionary dream, so alien to my practical, matter-of-fact mind. I have never had another dream like it.

The King was much loved for his leadership during the war, when he and his wife had refused to leave London even after Buckingham Palace was bombed. But he was a remote figure, and as a nation we soon stopped mourning and started to celebrate our new young Queen. Britain was slowly emerging from its postwar depression. The previous year, 1951, we had celebrated a Festival of Britain, when my entire high school traveled to Plymouth by train to see the Festival Ship, full of examples of British achievement like the Hovercraft. Now we had over a year of anticipation of the celebrations for the Queen's coronation in June 1953. The initials EIIR (Elizabeth II Regina) were everywhere. Every schoolchild received a coronation mug with the Queen's portrait on it and a specially struck five-shilling silver coin, larger than our half crown and not something we were meant to spend—I don't even know if shops would have accepted it. And we had a week off school.

Although the Queen worried that televising the ceremony might reduce the solemnity of the occasion, she relented and, for the first time ever, a royal occasion was to be shown on television. Many people bought their first TV to watch it, but not my parents. We had electricity by then, but no TV reception, and in any case a set was too expensive for our challenged budget. My mother and father couldn't leave the farm, but they wanted Michael and me to have the experience (it may yet be the only coronation in our lifetime). They arranged for us to take the London long-distance bus to stay with Aunty Kathleen, my father's widowed sister, the first TV owner in the family. I was in charge of nine-year-old Michael on the bus. He was a pain, fidgeting, misbehaving, and refusing to do anything I said, although I suspect I was playing the role of bossy older sister.

So it was in Aunty Kathleen's house in Chiswick, where my father grew up, that I saw my first television set, a plywood box stained to look like mahogany, with a twelve-inch screen, two knobs underneath to turn it on and control the volume, and a cloth-covered speaker behind a round plywood cut-out. It sat squatly on a small table. On June 2, 1953 everyone—Michael and I, my grandmother Nana, Aunty Kathleen, my four grown-up cousins and two of their spouses—crowded around the set for several hours as we watched the new Queen arriving in a horse-drawn carriage (closed because of the pouring rain), then the ceremony, and the procession afterwards, all in black and white.

At school we had studied the various elements of the ceremony, so we knew what to expect. We admired the young Queen, solemn and preoccupied on this most sacred occasion, as she progressed in stately fashion up the aisle of Westminster Abbey. She wore a long satin dress embroidered with the flowers of the four United Kingdoms and other British Commonwealth nations, and trailed a velvet cloak edged with ermine. The choir sang Handel's *Zadok the Priest* as the Queen arrived at the ancient Scottish Stone of Scone encased in a carved wooden throne, seat of Scotland's kings and captured by her ancestor Edward I in the Middle Ages, (the stone was returned to Scotland in 1996). As she sat there, the Archbishop of Canterbury anointed her with oil behind a screen, the most sacred part of the ceremony, and when the screen was removed, he lowered the heavy crown onto her head. Now she was truly Queen of Great Britain and the Commonwealth. Richard Dimbleby, the BBC commentator on royal occasions, described everything in reverent tones, with occasional lighter moments. As we munched our lunchtime sandwiches he told us the sandwich originated when the Earl of Sandwich brought one to sustain him through an eighteenth-century coronation.

We watched the crowds waving enthusiastically at the rain-soaked procession afterwards, especially enjoying Queen Sarotse of Tonga, who rode in an open carriage without an umbrella and saluted everyone with infectious cheer. The following day the Queen and Duke of Edinburgh were scheduled to drive through central London in a kind of victory lap, so Aunty Kathleen took us to a corner of Trafalgar Square to see them go past in an open car. They seemed a perfect couple, young, happy, smiling and doing the characteristic royal wave. For once it wasn't raining, and we saw them in living color!

Three of Aunty Kathleen's four adult children lived in London. My cousin Shirley worked as a photographer at the Dorothy Wilding Studio, photographers to the Queen. My parents asked her to take studio portraits of Michael and me, but Michael had a bad stye on his eyelid. Although I knew I shouldn't gloat at Michael's misfortune, I was quite happy that I was Shirley's only subject. She took several large portraits that she mounted on card and sent home with us. My hair is short, in a fashionable "urchin" cut that, for once, looked tidy and showed off my widow's peak. If I had any acne spots, Shirley brushed them out. I am wearing a cardigan buttoned to the neck with a shirt collar over it, similar to my school uniform (although it wasn't). I look either at the photographer or into the distance with a pensive expression, my lips just hinting at a smile. I loved those pictures, which made me look far better that I saw myself.

After the coronation, my handsome young cousin Alan and his new wife Sylvia took me in hand for a cultural whirlwind. I saw my first ballet (*Coppelia*) and my first opera (*The Barber of Seville*). I reveled in watching famous stage actors—Dorothy Tutin in *As You Like It*, and Lawrence Olivier and Vivian Leigh in *The Sleeping Prince*, which Olivier later filmed as *The Prince and the Showgirl* with Marilyn Monroe. Cornwall, or even Exeter, had nothing like this. Michael was too young to go, so he missed the excitement.

Alan was a salesman, and, on one of the days I was there, his work took him to Oxford, so he asked if I would like to ride along. Alan had spent a year at Oxford University after his war service in the Navy, but had failed his exams and been "rusticated," the euphemism for being expelled. Alan was in no way redeemed in his family's eyes by his marriage to a highly intelligent psychiatrist with a PhD. Although they were both very happy, most of his relatives viewed their relationship with extreme suspicion as against the natural order of things— "Sylvia runs Alan's life." I didn't even know Sylvia had a PhD until I was grown up, and in any case wouldn't have known what a PhD was then.

Alan delighted in showing me Oxford, which I saw through his nostalgic eyes. I was stunned by Oxford's beauty, the golden or pewter stone of the colleges, the masses of students on bicycles, the quiet walk through the meadows. Later, when we were parked illegally by a college back gate, Alan told me about his exploits. "This is where I used to climb in after the gates were locked," he mused nostalgically. "It was a lot of fun." He spoke with great regret, and I felt how much he lamented not making the most of his opportunity. Oxford's magic began to work on me.

At fourteen, I was beginning to think about my future—"when I grow up." While still at St. Goran School, after I had won a prize with my fuchsia drawing, I had briefly flirted with becoming an artist. That soon faded as, after a few more efforts and more exposure in school art lessons, I realized my success was a fluke. Instead, I decided I wanted to be a writer. One birthday my godmother sent me a subscription to *Collins Magazine*, aimed at teenagers who enjoyed reading and writing. I devoured every issue as soon as it arrived in the mail—extracts from new books Collins was publishing, interviews with authors, advice columns, contests.

With great fanfare, the magazine editors announced a contest for a novel written by one of its readers, with publication the prize. This was my chance. My model was the children's adventure stories I enjoyed myself. I had the sense to choose a setting—the farm—that I knew well, but I peopled it with children whose parents were absent, allowing them to become involved in an improbable adventure that included villainous spies, secret messages, and a final chase across Helman Tor. It ended with the children in church singing the hymn "Soldiers of Christ Arise," which contains the lines:

Ye shall o'ercome through Christ alone
And stand entire at last.

Ye Shall O'ercome became the title.

I wrote the novel in pencil in small italic script on very thin onion-skin paper, the only kind I could find around the house without asking. I was not at all confident of my ability and feared ridicule, especially from my brother, so my project was a secret. I found an old green folder that had held specifications for a brand of fertilizer and shoved the sharp edges of the clasps inside it into the fragile pages. I wrote the title on the outside in large letters, and my name as author. But to mail it I would have to ask my mother to take me to the post office and give me the postage money. I knew that my family would be looking to see if I won, and I knew my effort wasn't good enough. If I didn't send it in I wouldn't fail. So the folder stayed hidden in a chest among discarded toys until I eventually threw it away (I wish I hadn't). I shelved dreams of authorship, although they never entirely subsided.

Instead of my dreamy aspirations, I settled for a realizable ambition, teaching, like my mother and most of the other working women I knew. Most women in the nineteen-fifties dreamed of marriage, not a career, and I too saw work as filling the interval between the end of my education and my wedding. The only alternatives to teaching for middle class women that I knew of were nursing and secretarial work, neither of which attracted me. I knew I would have to go to college, but most of the older girls at school attended teacher-training colleges, not universities. Now, after my experience with Alan, I began to think about going to a university, and not just any university, but Oxford itself. I dimly knew that wasn't easy for a woman—to my knowledge, no one from my school had done it. But my dreams of Oxford began in that coronation year.

THE RED TIN BOX

In my early teens my favorite place to go by myself was what I called The Woods, a small copse of trees on the edge of the farm, separated from the moor by the road to the milk stand. I went out through what had once been the front garden, now a straggle of plants that Jemima the goat was occasionally allowed to eat, then across Foredoors, the field closest to the cow house, and into Old Field, carefully avoiding the parts cut off by the movable electric fence that rationed the cows' grazing area. At the bottom of Old Field, about a quarter of a mile from the house, I walked through a clump of patchy grass, over a small mound, and jumped across a narrow stream. I was in The Woods.

The trees were low and scrubby, although the size of some of the lichen and ivy-encrusted trunks suggested they were quite old. Close together, they made a thick canopy even in winter that made me feel insulated from the world outside. They were a mixture of native species—silver birch, alder, mountain ash, hawthorn, blackthorn. Someone had told

197

me that blackthorn or May's blossom was unlucky to bring indoors, so I just admired its white masses in spring. In autumn I ate its bitter sloes, savoring the way they made my mouth feel dry, definitely an acquired taste.

Some of the trees leaned at various angles over a small pool in the middle of the woodland. Others lined the stream in the only place on the farm where bluebells grew. When I first started exploring The Woods I walked around the edge by the stream and then circled the pond. There I made what was to me an exciting discovery—the pond and the stream made an island that I could jump to from the bank. No one else in the family ever went to The Woods, so the island became my secret place. I don't remember ever showing it to anyone else, not even my cousin Penny.

I named the island Fifteen Balls Island after the Cornish crest, fifteen balls arranged in a shield. To me it was the secret heart of Cornwall. I felt as if I was connected to the ancient Cornish land of King Arthur and of all others who had loved Cornwall before me, an almost mystical affinity. It was the closest I have ever come to having a religious experience.

I was a matter-of-fact child, not given to spiritual feelings, but at that time I was passionately attached to Cornwall as my home. I borrowed library books on Cornish history and landscape, and read and reread a birthday present book, *The Story of Cornwall* by the Cornish historian (and friend of C. S. Lewis) A. K. Hamilton Jenkin. The book I *really* wanted was written by Arthur Mee, whom I knew as editor of *The Children's Newspaper*, a weekly publication my godmother had once sent me. Mee's *King's England* series (for adults), had an illustrated volume for every English county. The Cornish volume had recently been published, but was too expensive for my parents to buy me for birthday or Christmas. Although I frequently took out the library copy, I never owned it.

As I sat on the mossy turf reading Cornish history, breathing in the solitude in this quintessentially Cornish habitat, I decided I wanted to leave a permanent reminder of my presence. I had a small red tin box decorated in honor of the new Queen's coronation that had once contained OXO (beef bouillon) cubes that we sprinkled on the cats' lunch. I filled the tin with—what? I can't remember. I think they were objects more closely associated with Cornwall than with me personally, perhaps a replica of the Cornish crest, perhaps one of Vault beach's cowrie shells. I am sure I

198

buried it on the island, digging through the moss and fairly deep into the underlying soil. A personal implant in Cornwall's heart.

I never imagined anyone finding it. About thirty years ago my son Tom and I drove around the farm and went into The Woods from the road. We walked to the place where I had jumped the stream, but the water table had risen and the whole area was submerged. Like Avalon, the island had disappeared.

NANA (pronounced Nǎnáh)

We are sitting on a sandy beach looking across at St. Michael's Mount, a small rocky island with a castle on top that used to be a monastery, the English cousin of the French Mont St. Michel. The tide is rising and will soon cover the stone causeway to the island, so we aren't tempted to walk it. The sun is out and Michael and I are building sandcastles. Nana, my father's mother, is sitting in a deck chair next to my mother with her usual disapproving expression, although we are on this beach a fair distance from the farm because she wanted to see it. My father is, as usual, back at the farm working. Nana is dressed in her customary head-to-toe black, thick brown stockings and black lace-up shoes. Her wavy iron-grey hair is pulled severely back into a bun. Michael and I pay as little attention to her as possible.

Suddenly there is a commotion close to the path that leads from the beach back to the car park. Word spreads from group to group along the beach that a boy trod on a piece of glass and cut his foot badly. We can see a knot of people surrounding him, urging him to keep calm until the ambulance arrives. Nana, a stout woman, heaves herself up from the deck chair and walks over in a slow and ominous progress. We anxiously follow at a distance. The circle of concerned people turn to look. She brushes them aside and confronts the boy.

"How could you be so careless?" she demands. "Don't you know better than to have bare feet on a beach? It's your own fault." She turns, leaves the speechless group, and goes back to her deck chair. We follow, trying to pretend we don't know her. Michael and I have bare feet. We put on our shoes, collect our things, fold the deck chair, and leave as quickly as possible.

Much later, when I was researching family history, I found that Nana's mother died when she was a teenager and she had to keep house for her father and two younger sisters, possibly leading to her later dislike of girls. For the first time in my life I felt some sympathy for her. An intelligent

200

woman, she must have felt trapped, with marriage her only escape. When she was twenty-eight, late for a Victorian woman, she married a slightly younger man. Her husband Sidney was a civil servant in the Post Office, and, my mother told me, very likeable. Their first child, born when Nana was thirty, was a girl, Kathleen. My father, a much longed-for son, wasn't born for another ten years. As soon as he arrived Kathleen was sent off to boarding school, and when she was home during the school holidays her mother expected her to look after her brother while Nana was out volunteering for her favorite charity, the blind. We used to joke that the blind tolerated her because they couldn't see her coming.

Nana's marriage lasted over forty years before her husband (his grandchildren called him Pompa) died when I was two—I have no memory of him. Nana lived on in the suburban London house where my father was born, 12 Staveley Road, Chiswick, with Kathleen, Katheleen's husband and their four children. Kathleen probably married to get away from her mother but Uncle Harold, by repute an incorrigible "ladies' man," had trouble keeping jobs. They could not afford a house of their own so moved in with Nana. Their four children grew up under Nana's baleful eye.

Every year, to give poor Kathleen a break, my parents invited Nana to stay on the farm for about a month, almost always during the school summer holidays. My father found Nana as trying as everyone else did and spent as little time with her as he could, so the brunt of Nana's visit fell on my mother. Curiously, Nana's misogyny didn't appear to extend to my mother, whom she had supported during my father's courtship of her. "You should always be good to your mother," she would tell us several times during her visits, "You don't appreciate her."

My parents tried to shield me from the full force of Nana's dislike for girls by keeping me busy with farm chores that took me outside. Although they were very aware of her spite, I didn't feel particularly singled out by her scorn which seemed to extend to almost everything and everybody. I was aware that she doted on Michael, but that seemed to both of us to be actually worse since she was always calling for his company.

Nana was in her eighties and spent most of the morning in bed. Michael and I tried hard to avoid taking up her breakfast tray. If I did it, she always found something to criticize—her boiled egg was too soft or too hard, her toast cold, her tea too strong or too weak. If it was his turn he had to stay for a while and listen to her advice on how to behave in the world. When she came downstairs for lunch the stream of criticism, mixed with unwanted advice, continued. We all spent as much time as possible outdoors.

During Nana's annual visit when I was fourteen my mother had to go to her parents in Plymouth as her mother was gravely ill. Since my father had to take over all the farm chores, including milking, that left me in charge of the household, especially meals. On Friday, when my father was ready to take me to do the weekly food shopping, Nana called me up to her room.

"I've made a shopping list for you," she announced.

"But I already have one," I protested feebly.

"Well, add these to it. Onions. If everyone ate an onion a day, the world would be a better place."

"But no one likes onions, " I muttered.

"And Chocolat Menier. Mind you get the right kind, good French chocolate. I like it in the afternoon."

Nana must have known that no store in St. Austell in the early nineteen-fifties would stock French chocolate. She also knew that I, ever conscientious, would go to every store that might sell it to make sure. A form of light torture.

Shortly afterwards, my meal planning broke down and I had to serve bacon and eggs for lunch. Nana was furious at having breakfast food for the wrong meal and launched into a tirade against me whose details I have gratefully forgotten. My father answered with an equally biting critique of his mother and announced that he was sending her back on the next train. He did. We never saw her again, and she died the following year. I can't say I mourned her.

SAILING

In *The Wind in the Willows*, one of my childhood favorites, Ratty tells Mole that there is nothing he loves more than "messing about in boats." My father agreed wholeheartedly. His parents owned a bungalow, a one-story low-roofed house, on the banks of the River Thames not far from their home. In the summers they spent most weekends and their annual holiday there. My grandfather taught my father how to sail a dinghy, to row a skiff, to paddle a canoe, and, perhaps the most challenging, to pole a punt. That involves standing on a platform at the rear of a low flat-bottomed boat and pushing it forward with a long pole. It is very easy to turn the pole the wrong way and fall in, or to get the pole stuck in mud and be stranded hanging onto it while the punt carries on without you. My father quickly became an expert punter who never lost control.

From when he was quite young my father owned his own canoe, a cedar canvas model built in Peterborough, Canada. When he moved away from home he left it at the bungalow, even when we moved to the farm, since he had no time or opportunity to use it in Cornwall. Kathleen's youngest son Brian began living in the bungalow and one day burned it down with a carelessly left cigarette. The canoe, stored underneath it, was a pile of cinders. Although my father hadn't seen it in years, he mourned it deeply.

He always hoped to get back on the water. After all, Cornwall was surrounded by the sea. He read nautical books, took sea stories out of the library, and, in his few moments off from farm chores, practiced tying nautical knots. He was especially proud of tying the intricate and time-consuming turk's head, looking like a small turban. Then, when I was in my early teens, my father's godfather, Uncle Bobby, died and left him some money, not enough to make us rich, but sufficient to have a small sailing boat built for us. We lived about seven miles from Fowey (pronounced Foy), a secluded harbor at the mouth of the local river, where there was a very active sailing community. Since my father wanted to race, he decided to commission a fifteen-foot sailing dinghy in the local Fowey River class. She would be called Roberta in honor of Uncle Bobby.

We sometimes went to watch Roberta's progress at the boat-builders, across the harbor in Polruan, Fowey's neighboring town. We crossed the harbor on the ferry, climbed the steep hill to the boat yard, and stood in the workshop full of sawdust and smelling of pine and linseed oil. Gradually our boat took shape, from its ribbed shell to its planked exterior, and, finally, to its carefully sanded tapered mast. The dinghy was completely open, no half-decking, just a seat that ran round three sides of the stern, with another crossing the center.

While we lived on the farm we rarely did anything together as a family since someone had to be home to tend to the chores, especially at milking time. Also, the boat was built for two people, three at a pinch. To my surprise, my father chose me, not my brother, to train as his crew. Maybe it was just that I was older, or perhaps he hoped it would be something athletic that I, rather than Michael, would be good at. Also, although I didn't realize it at the time, Michael couldn't swim—Roberta was very stable and never capsized, but there was always the possibility.

So my father started to teach me how to sail. First I learned to raise and lower the sails, to thread the sheets (ropes) through the cleats and coil them neatly. He was patient and gentle, never raising his voice even when I made elementary mistakes. Then we started sailing.

"Watch your jib all the time. Keep it tight to the wind. If you see the edge flutter, pull it tighter," he said as he kept his eye on the mainsail, his eyes wrinkled in concentration.

"When we go about, move as quickly and smoothly as possible. Don't let go of the one sheet until you have got hold of the other so you can pull the sail across quickly without it flapping."

"When we are running with the wind the jib should billow out over the bow. You can change sides if it works better, with the main on one side, the jib on the other."

"Watch the surface of the water. If it is smooth, that means there is no wind. Let the jib out a little to catch what wind there is. If it has rough ripples that means a squall. We need to be ready to sit out on the boat's edge for when it hits."

Those things I learned to do. But I never learned the harder stuff— steering the boat, managing the main sail, being the captain. In a crisis I tended to turn the tiller the wrong way, making things worse. That made me afraid of doing the wrong thing, of capsizing into the deep unfriendly water beneath us. As with other sporting things, I was not a natural sailor, but it was my timidity, my fear of failure, that prevented me from fully trying to master the skill.

My father never said anything to make me feel inadequate. He was frustrated when we did not compete well and were usually in the last three boats in races. In our first year we won the silver spoon for the boat with the least points. We laughed and used it in our sugar bowl, but I knew by his semi-joking references to it that my father felt the hurt. It can't have been just my ineptitude because once my father lent me as crew to the sailor whose boat usually won, and he still came in first, despite my nervousness about jinxing him. Maybe my father wasn't as good a sailor as I thought, or maybe the boat just wasn't fast.

Still, we were not deterred. Every Saturday afternoon in the summer we drove to Fowey, down the hill through the narrow streets crowded with tourists, and parked as near as we could to the small yacht club where we were members. (We couldn't afford the fancy one further toward the harbor mouth.) We rowed out to our mooring in the club dinghy, baled out the inevitable accumulation of rain, put up the sails, and cast off. If there was plenty of wind we raced in the harbor, if the wind was light we went out into the open sea beyond the harbor mouth. When there wasn't much wind we were sometimes out there with the race unfinished when it was time to go home for milking. Then we had to row back.

My father disliked the photo at the beginning of this piece because it shows some of our shortcomings, although he thought enough of it to make a frame and it always hung somewhere in the house. The main sail isn't high enough up the mast so it is wrinkly. I, the only person visible, have the jib nice and tight, but I should be sitting on the other side of the main. Still, it was a beautiful day and we are at least moving quite well. I may even have been enjoying myself, although I was usually too tense to feel the full pleasure of the quiet, purposeful swish of a sailboat with a good wind. That I never admitted to my father. I didn't want to disappoint him, or miss the time we had together.

CRICKET

Tyson runs up and bowls to Harvey. Ooh, it's a fast one! Harvey jabs at it but doesn't connect and it goes through to Evans, standing well back. The ball goes back to Tyson, who polishes it on his trousers as he takes the long walk back to the beginning of his run.

The soothing Hampshire burr of John Arlott, the premier BBC radio cricket commentator, describing England's match against Australia.

Somehow I heard Arlott's voice on the radio during the winter of 1954–55, when I was about to turn sixteen. I don't know who would have tuned it in—not my parents, who didn't follow cricket, and it was before I got my own radio. I certainly wouldn't have chosen it by myself. I knew nothing about cricket. Although some girls' schools played the game, my school didn't. My brother played at school, but it wasn't his favorite sport, and he never talked about it. But Arlott's voice, soft even at exciting moments, a buzz like a bee if it could speak, mesmerized me. It felt as if he was speaking to me personally, intimately, drawing me into a world he felt passionately about. I started to listen carefully.

Cricket is not a game for those seeking instant thrills, the constant roar of the crowd, the immediate excitement. It is a sport that makes the term "leisurely" seem almost too fast. In those days all international matches took up to five days, first class county matches three, playing from 11 a.m. to 6 p.m., with intervals for lunch and tea. Even village cricket games lasted all afternoon.

In England cricket is always played on a large green field. Two batsmen from the batting side, wearing white, equipped with large leg pads, and carrying wide wooden bats, each stand at a wicket, three sticks with two smaller rounded pegs (bails) balanced on the top. A bowler runs up to one of the wickets and bowls the ball to the batsman at the other. The ball bounces once. If the batsman hits the ball far enough the two batsmen exchange sides for a run. If the batsman misses and the ball breaks the wicket the batsman is out. The fielding side's aim is to get all eleven players on the batting side out while allowing as few runs as possible.

Obviously this is a very simplistic overview of a complicated sport—there are many terms for different batting strokes and fielding positions, and there are more ways of being out than just having the ball hit the wicket. What sets cricket apart, and what drew me in, is its slow pace. Most of the time the bowler bowls, the batsman plays a defensive shot that is picked up by a fielder, or he misses the ball altogether, either purposely or inadvertently. The ball goes through to the wicketkeeper behind the wicket, and the bowler bowls again until he has bowled six consecutive balls, called an over, after which the fielders change positions and a different bowler bowls to the batsman at the other end. All this is what takes time. The same thing happens monotonously, sometimes for hours, until there is a sudden flurry of activity when someone makes a lot of runs, or is out, before returning to the same rhythm as before. Listening to the radio commentary, always aware that something could happen even if it often didn't, I found it provided the perfect minimal level of excitement, moderate, not feverish, that I preferred in all things, books, movies (the few I saw), school netball games.

I started listening to John Arlott during England's tour of Australia. All other countries playing international cricket were current or former British colonies—at that time Australia, New Zealand, India, Pakistan, South Africa, and the West Indies. The England/Australia rivalry is the oldest and was at that time the greatest. They play for the "Ashes," a name coming from a journalist's mock obituary of England after the team's loss of the five-match series in 1882: "the body (i.e. English cricket) will be cremated and the ashes taken to Australia." In the winter of 1954–55 (summer in Australia) England was winning, largely because of the success of their fast bowlers, Frank Tyson and Brian Statham. I developed a crush on Tyson, nicknamed "Typhoon Tyson," possibly the fastest bowler ever. Perhaps his balding head and gaptoothed smile made him appear accessible to plain Jane me. I made a scrapbook of Tyson's newspaper cuttings from our daily papers at the farm and dreamed of meeting him and even marrying him, although I had no idea how that could happen.

I had never seen a cricket match, not even at the village level, since the game was not very popular in Cornwall. No one I knew was interested in the sport. We had no television, so the only visual images I had were black and white newspaper photos, emphasizing the brilliance of the "whites" that all cricketers wore. I learned by ear from the radio. As I listened to Arlott and other commentators on the BBC, I gradually sorted out the terminology and the finer points of the sport, the techniques of fast and slow bowlers, the names of the fielding positions, the different strokes batsmen made. I would not have learned them so fast as a spectator, although I took cricket books out of the library and read them cover-to-cover. I also learned the sounds—the comforting thwack of the bat hitting the ball squarely when the batsman made a good stroke, the duller thud when his bat merely blocked the ball from the wicket. I, who am easily bored, never tired of the long periods when nothing much happened. I still had the commentary to listen to, and it enthralled me. I had a little game where I rolled special tokens to simulate a cricket match. I played it by myself, learning how to record the score.

Once I was hooked I spent summers glued to the radio every time a Test (international) Match was on. Even my parents listened in July 1956, knowing they were hearing history, when the spin bowler Jim Laker took nine out of ten Australian wickets (that is, dismissed the batsmen) in the first innings and all ten in the second, an unsurpassed feat. One of my most vivid memories is of us sitting around the kitchen table listening in disbelief as one Australian after another fell to his almost unplayable bowling.

My obsession with cricket was unique among all the people I knew. I had no one to talk to about it, and little desire to play it myself, although one summer my brother taught me a little on a very rough pitch we laid out in Dairy Field. I wanted to be a bowler, but was as inept at that as every other sport. But I didn't really mind not seeing a cricket match. John Arlott was enough.

RESISTANCE

In the boarding house we got up at the 7:30 bell, came down to breakfast at 8, leaving our dormitories tidy for Matron's inspection, changed into outdoor shoes for the short walk across to the main school, came back for lunch (changing shoes again), returned for afternoon school, came back for tea and homework, attended evening prayers, ate supper, bathed and went to bed at the allotted times. If anyone challenged the routine, or at least failed to conform, I don't remember it. It was impossible to oversleep when other girls were getting up. Matron checked that we changed our shoes to go outside. At the outer edge of wartime austerity no one thought of skipping meals.

Bells punctuated our life. Miss Hyndman kept a big one in the boarding house hall that she rang for meal times and evening prayers, and Matron used it to wake us up in the morning. In the school building a prefect standing at the bottom of the main stairs rang an even larger one to signify the beginning and end of school and the end of each period.

We were thoroughly trained to conformity. Once or twice a term Miss Hyndman blew a shrill whistle (to distinguish it from the bell), signifying a fire drill, when we had to close all windows, leave the house as quickly as possible via the metal fire escapes, and line up on the lawn outside. She often picked the time when we were about to get up in the morning.

Once in late spring some workers started digging the foundations for a new gym across from the boarding house lawn. On their first day the foreman blew a whistle to begin work at 7:30. We jumped out of bed, closed the windows with emphatic thumps, and rushed down the fire escapes in our pajamas and curlers to line up on the lawn in front of the bemused men. They must have been amazed and then entertained by the sudden appearance of thirty girls in their decorous nightwear. After a short interval Miss Hyndman appeared on the boarding house's flat roof to ask why we were lined up out there. The foreman explained that his whistle had caused the commotion. We were embarrassed when we realized what had happened, but were then consumed by giggles. It took us a few days to get used to the early morning whistle.

We conformed to daily expectations. We also kept to rules. There were two sets of rules, one for the boarding house and another for the school, the first enforced by Miss Hyndman and Matron, the second by school prefects, teachers, and, as a last resort, by Miss Ryan, the headmistress. Neither set of enforcers had any jurisdiction over the other. At school, prefects could report wrongdoers to teachers, who could issue order and (worse) conduct marks, imaginary stains that Miss Ryan announced in a stern voice at morning prayers along with our fortnightly class lists. I never got one. In the boarding house we lost privileges—no "tuck" (that is, our own extra food at teatime), no shopping on Thursday afternoons, no permission to go into the city, banned from special treats like a visit to the cinema. In most cases rebellion just wasn't worth it. It got you nowhere.

Very occasionally someone in the boarding house, usually a new girl, got so homesick she thought of running away. It was pointless. We had no money for travel—Miss Hyndman doled out our pocket money on Thursdays only in the small amounts we needed for a comic and a bag of sweets. Even our suitcases were locked away until the end of term. Miss Hyndman read our weekly letters so we couldn't ask our parents to take us away. Phone calls in the red telephone box near the shops cost more than our pocket money.

We weren't totally trapped. Older girls had the freedom of the Saturday afternoon walk and Sunday morning communion, when we were out of Miss Hyndman's watchful eye and could do things like go into the city without permission. Sometimes a daygirl would ask one of us to her home at the weekend, or a teacher took us on an excursion. Mrs. Bennett, my history teacher, had me to tea at her house every so often.

Our main form of resistance, an oasis of daring in our regulated lives, was the midnight feast. Midnight feasts took a lot of planning. Every member of a dormitory was necessarily involved, whether they liked it or not. First we had to get food together, not easy with our limited pocket money and nowhere to store it that wasn't subject to Matron's scrutiny. One of the girls stored what we had collected in her personal locker, but it couldn't be for long. To make the challenge greater, a major requirement of a proper midnight feast was hard-boiled eggs and canned fruit salad. This

211

meant someone had to sneak into the kitchen while on the dish-washing crew after supper when the cook had gone home, open a can without getting caught, and boil the eggs. Once someone didn't dare leave the eggs in long enough and I later bit into a cold soft yolk. It was unexpectedly yucky and I have never liked soft eggs since.

We didn't have alarm clocks to tell us when it was midnight so we listened for when Miss Hyndman and Matron went to bed and then waited for as long as we could bear it before getting out of bed as quietly as we could—usually before the actual midnight hour. Most feasts were in the dormitory but occasionally a group was more daring and tried to go downstairs past Matron's bedroom to the study. They usually got caught. We had no plates, so we served the fruit salad in furtively washed soap dishes, giving it a certain acquired taste. Once we heard Matron coming just as we had dished it out. We leapt into our beds the moment before she turned on the light. Gladys spilled her fruit salad under the bedclothes and started to laugh. "What are you laughing at?" Matron barked. "Oh, Matron, I am swimming in fruit salad."

Caught having a midnight feast called for the highest penalties. Gladys spilled the fruit salad the week before our time off for the Queen's coronation, and Miss Hyndman threatened to keep us at school. Of course she didn't, since she would have had to stay with us. Another time we were caught when the school was participating in a BBC quiz contest called "Top of the Form." As a punishment we were forbidden to be in the audience. I was an alternate for the team, and I was devastated not to be there and join in the excitement. Our school lost. I knew the answer to the question that caused them to lose, which made me more indignant, although of course it wouldn't have mattered.

I didn't want to rebel. I wanted to conform, to be like everyone else, or even better than others so I could be popular and successful. I was never a star, but I always had friends. I got by.

CRUSHED

I spent two thirds of every year at The Maynard School—I didn't go home at weekends as I had at Miss Rapley's. It was too far, and in any case nobody did. Life at school was my real life and home on the farm my vacations. My family's lives were increasingly remote. My friends were my school friends, and I missed their company when I was home. In the Christmas and Easter holidays my cousins lived with us, and Penny and I did things together, but she was two years ahead of me at school and as teenagers that gap began to matter. In the summer Penny and her family lived in Polperro and my company came from visitors, especially the Wylie family and Tim Nelson, who came, usually separately, every year.

Alan Wylie was the accountant at RFD, where my father had worked during the war. It became a tradition that they visited every summer until we left the farm, and the senior Wylies were, like most of my parents' friends, honorary uncle and aunt—Uncle Alan and Aunty Peggy. They had two daughters, Jill, who was my age, and Carol, three years younger. About two years after their first visit their son Adrian was born. Michael and I thought Aunty Peggy spoiled him dreadfully. We called him A-Drain when no one was around.

Carol was only interested in girls' games, as we thought of them, so Michael took little notice of her, but Jill became my good summer friend. I envied her slightly frizzy, well-behaved blonde hair and was a little in awe of her biting wit, more noticeable as we moved towards our teens. Even when we were young she always seemed to be the epitome of sophistication, telling me about shopping, movies, and girlfriends in Guildford, her home town. It was far from anything I knew.

To us, the Wylies were rich. They had a relatively new car, a Standard Vanguard, that could go sixty miles per hour, which I thought meant it could take off imminently, although there were few Cornish roads where we could get to that speed. They had new clothes—one photo shows Carol and Adrian in very well-tailored outdoor coats. By the 1950s Uncle Alan made the occasional work trip to Malaya and brought back trinkets that he

213

distributed liberally. For years I wore a plain fake gold bracelet I thought was the height of elegance.

Michael and I looked forward to the Wylies' two-week visit because we got to go somewhere with them every day. We five children bundled into the back of the car, kicking each other to make room. On sunny days we went to the beach, often a different one each day. We splashed in the sea, climbed in and out of one of RFD's rubber dinghies that Uncle Alan had brought with him, poked tiny fish and sea anemones in rock pools, and made elaborate sand castles. We ate sandy sandwiches of a jarred mash called fish paste, or egg, or jam, and drank thermoses of tea. There was less to do when it rained, but usually we went out to wander around a town and have a Cornish cream tea (two scones, strawberry jam and clotted cream). My parents rarely joined us since summer was always busy on the farm.

When I was about ten I started going back to Guildford with the Wylies, returning by train a week later. To me the journey was hugely exciting. It took a very long day, up the A30, a two-lane road that was notorious for traffic bottlenecks in the summer. We started by crossing Bodmin Moor, then skirted the edge of even larger Dartmoor, occasionally driving across the middle of the moor, passing the forbidding walls of the notorious prison and watching out for the wild ponies native to the area. Sometimes we branched onto the A303 that took us past Stonehenge and Jane Austen's house. We stopped for picnics along the way, a welcome respite for Jill, Carol, Adrian and me, squeezed into the back. I don't remember us squabbling, but surely we must have sometimes.

The Wylies lived in a fairly large house on a main road outside the Guildford town center, on a corner by a traffic light. Jill's bedroom, which I shared, was on the side by the light and I lay in bed listening to the unaccustomed traffic noise and watching the red, yellow and green reflections alternate on the ceiling. At that time Cornwall had only one traffic light in the entire country, a fair distance from the farm.

In Guildford I got to experience some of Jill's sophisticated life (to me). We walked to shops. The family had a television set even before the Coronation, so we watched sitcoms and quiz shows. We listened to the latest music. I first heard Elvis with Jill—*Heartbreak Hotel*—raw, primitive-sounding, utterly unlike anything I had heard before. Uncle Alan and Aunty

Peggy sometimes took us to a show. I saw my first musical, *The King and I*, with them.

In our early teens Jill astounded me by acquiring a boyfriend. Costas was Greek, had oily black hair and wore a velvet-lapelled jacket, very tight pants, and sharp-toed shiny shoes—the uniform based on early twentieth–century Edwardian dress worn by groups of urban teenagers called Teddy Boys. Respectable middle class people feared and despised Teddy Boys, so Uncle Alan and Aunty Peggy banned him from the house, but Jill kept on meeting him in one of the coffee houses that had begun to appear in Britain's incipient youth culture. I couldn't see the attraction, but then I had no experience of boys and little chance of getting any. For years Jill's stories were the closest I got.

Tim Nelson was one of the people whose lives my parents tried to better in some way, strays who arrived for varying lengths of time to rest, relax, or recover from some temporary or recurring trouble. His next-door neighbors, old friends of my parents who sometimes came to the farm for vacations, were sorry for him as the only child of elderly and restrictive parents, and one day suggested he come with them to have some fun. After that he came alone every summer for several years. The only photograph I have of him is from behind, giving me few clues about what he looked like, and I have no mental picture. Since we were roughly the same age, we did things together around the farm in easy companionship.

Tim was passionate about cars and engines. He could identify the make and model of any car from a distance. Between his first and second summer visits I, ever competitive, studied cars in traffic and parking lots until I could recognize them as well as he could. That was Tim's lasting legacy to me—wherever I have lived I can't stop myself noting makes and models and idly checking traffic.

Tim's other skill was draughts (checkers). He played regularly with his grandmother, who gave him money every time he beat her. He became invincible, at least to me. However much I practiced at school, where I could beat most of my friends, I never managed to win a single game against Tim.

Because I was at school for most of the year I knew none of the few local boys, all of whom were firmly taken by local girls early in their teens.

215

In any case I was separated from them by class and education. Tim was the only boy I knew at all well. He showed no sign of being interested in me, but in my mid-teens I fantasized about him as my regular boyfriend. Then, one summer, Tim's visit coincided with the Wylie family vacation and Jill met him.

I don't know why I confided in Jill. Probably she was telling me about her adventures with Costas the Greek, very tame by today's standards but way beyond me then, and I was trying to compete.

"I think I'll marry Tim one day," I said.

"Oooh," Jill giggled, "I'll have to tell him that."

I was horrified. I could imagine nothing more embarrassing. I tried to persuade her not to reveal my secret, but she wouldn't promise. So then I tried to be with them at all times so she had no opportunity.

One day we went to Port Quin to go to the beach and have tea at the Doyden Café. Somehow as we walked up to the tea house Jill and Tim escaped from me. I saw them coming back toward me on the cliff path between clumps of purple heather. Jill was smiling gleefully, but I couldn't read Tim's expression. I knew she had told him. On top of the Port Quin cliffs, one of my favorite places on earth, I had failed to stop her.

I don't know whether that was when I stopped telling *anyone anything* about my personal life. I certainly learned not to trust friends, not even Penny. I think by then I had stopped telling my parents more than superficial details about life at school or my own inner feelings. If I ever did tell them. I do know that I still bury feelings deep and find it hard to excavate and articulate them.

After that Tim spent one more summer with us. One day, when we were standing together on a cliff top and no one else was nearby, he put a tentative arm around my shoulder. I angrily shook it off. I was sure he felt obliged, that Jill had pushed him into it. He didn't try again.

The following year Tim joined the Air Force and eventually became a crack pilot, flying with the Red Arrows, the British equivalent of the Blue Devils. He lost touch with the family. The crushing embarrassment stayed with me.

216

WALCOTT

For most of my teen years Tim was our summer visitor. The rest of the year was Walcott's. The photo shows our cousins Nick and Richard on the left, patting the rump of Buttercup, the matriarch cow. They are all standing in the dirty in its normal state. The boy on the right with the tentative look, whose hand barely touches the cow, is Walcott Hamilton.

Walcott was the only child of Canadian and American parents living in Bermuda, where his father was a photographer. His grandfather was one of the first Americans to build a house in Bermuda, and his parents moved there when he was six, since his lawyer mother was recovering from tuberculosis. Walcott was already there, living with his grandmother. Many Bermudan parents sent their children to school in England, the US, or Canada, and one of Walcott's friends was going to Rosehill school, where Nick and my brother went from ages eight to fourteen. Walcott's parents didn't think much of American or Canadian education, so they decided to send to Rosehill there as well. He was twelve years old.

My brother soon discovered that Walcott had nowhere to go during the Christmas and Easter school holidays (in the summer he went back to Bermuda), so, in the welcoming tradition of my parents, he suggested Walcott come back to the farm with him. Initially Walcott found the farm far more alien territory than the school. The dirty, in particular, terrified him. He had never seen so much mud in his life. In a piece my brother read at my mother's funeral, Walcott recalled his first encounter:

> *The farm was a new adventure, all cows and kale and mud. Mud. A lot of mud. I had become something of a cleannik in those days and there was all this mud. All of us had gum boots and everyone else seemed to walk about in it with impunity. But I knew that it was different for me. I knew with the certainty of a twelve year old that if I set foot in the stuff I would be swallowed whole never to be seen again or, at the very least, it would get in over the top of my boots and I would be stuck with squishy feet which was just as bad.*

He described how my mother stepped in:

> *Joan was kind, gentle as she urged me outside to play. I stood at the door like a cat contemplating a swim. We were well into the second day before faith in boots and she won out. It was a revelation. Mud has a bottom upon which one can make one's way. Farms were OK. After that there was no turning back. I was squooshing about with the best of them. We swept out the barns and rode on the tractor. Life was good.*

In the casual way of children, we teased Walcott for his American accent. Initially the farm food was also alien and he would only eat bananas, which he pronounced with the short American "a" rather than the English long middle "a." But he won—the family always used the American pronunciation after that, with the faintest hint of quotes around the word. (Curiously, now I am an American, I have reverted to the British pronunciation.) After a few days of the banana diet he became more adventurous about food:

218

Mornings we would eat cream so thick we could spread it on toast like butter. I had never heard of cholesterol, which was just as well. Some days Michael and I would go for long hikes off the farm. Joan would make us Cornish pasties for lunch on far away hillsides. Perhaps it was the Aga stove which made them so good, but more than likely it was her warm smile which gave them that special quality that cannot be found again except in those memories of those days on the farm.

My parents had rescued friends dealing with post-war stress, taught pupils how to farm, and taken in my aunt and cousins. My father was a surrogate father to my cousins, and now my mother took on a similar role with Walcott. He became part of the family for four years until he returned to Bermuda and joined the US Air Force. We missed him.[§]

[§] My thanks to Walcott for providing me with the text of his remarks, and for using some of my pieces in his English class for Argentinians.

DORM PHOTO

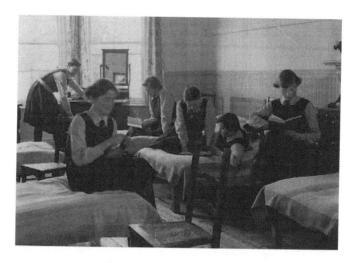

This is my boarding school dormitory in 1955, when I was sixteen. I am fourth from the left, sitting on the bed sharing a book. Usually we weren't allowed to sit on the beds unless we were about to get in them, but this photograph was posed for a publicity brochure. I am surprised to find a London address for the photographer on the back. London was light years away.

Our Spartan existence is clear. No carpet, no spring mattresses, no pictures, no frills (although the edge of a vase of flowers is visible—who put that there?). There was also no heat. We hadn't put in any extra effort to make the room tidy for the photograph—it had to be like that at all times. Even when we turned our beds back to air before going down to breakfast we did it neatly. The comfortless chairs were not for sitting; we put our neatly folded clothes on them at night.

It must be early summer. There are leaves on the trees outside the window (barely visible in the photo); the sun is pouring in, it looks like lilac in the vase, and we don't have sweaters on. However, we aren't wearing summer dresses yet, waiting for a directive from the headmistress that came unpredictably when we had sweated enough to warrant it. We are wearing the winter school uniform: gym tunic, blue-and-white striped blouse, school tie, and black stockings in the days when no one *ever* wore them. Underneath the tunic are two pairs of voluminous knickers, one inside the other. What on earth was the purpose of the double layer? Preservation of chastity? We were certainly chaste. We are all unnaturally tidy, especially me. Usually I was in trouble for untidiness, a major sin in our little world. At this point I still have my hair scraped back in my pre-perm ponytail.

I can date this photograph because I am wearing a form captain's badge, a visible sign of popularity and probity. I was elected captain by my classmates in my first year at the Maynard School when I was eleven, and then not again until this year. At both of those stages of our communal existence it was smart to be smart; in between it wasn't. Now, this year, I was enjoying school. I felt an insider, that I had crossed some invisible barrier into the elite.

Academic ability was suddenly worth more because it was about to be tested—we were preparing to take our O Levels that summer, national public exams. Once they were over Gladys, sharing the bed with me, Sue, on the right, and Sandra, at the back on the left, would be leaving school forever. Sue's parents sent her to "finishing school" to learn the ladylike behavior the school had failed to instill, while Gladys went back to help out at the farm. Sandra was a year ahead of the rest of us and was probably going on to further training — secretarial, perhaps? Wendy, at the front on the left, stayed one more year before entering a teacher training college. Only Alison, behind me on the left, and I planned to stay two or more years to take Advanced Level and university entrance exams. It must be against the odds for a small group of women in the 1950s that we both eventually finished our doctorates.

In other ways we were typical, sharing values and assumptions that were almost universal among middle-class families. The hothouse atmosphere of boarding school reinforced our common ethos. We had little privacy and experienced most things together. We shared baths, meals, sick rooms, books, maths answers, confidences. Wendy and Sue were my particular friends, but I also spent one half term break at Sandra's home—I can't remember why, since we weren't particularly friendly—and was struck by the formality of a doctor's household and the loneliness of an only child with older parents. I must have compared my somewhat ramshackle farmhouse existence to their neat house with all the amenities—and, despite the loneliness I detected, perhaps envied their orderly existence.

I know I envied Alison, who had it all—looks, brains, and athletic ability. Yet she was not as popular as others with similar gifts. I am not sure whether this was because it was generally agreed that she had a tendency towards arrogance, or because she had committed the ultimate and quite irredeemable sin of starting out as a daygirl and only joining what we firmly believed was the boarding elite when her parents moved to Nigeria.

For five years, and longer in some cases, I spent considerably more time with these girls than with my own family, yet the bonds were remarkably fragile. Wendy I saw occasionally while she was in college but not after she graduated. Sue turned up at a Cambridge party one day quite unrecognizable until I mentally scraped off the layers of make-up and discounted the affected accent. When I married in 1962, seven years after this photograph, I didn't invite any of the people in it. I no longer knew any of them. What we shared was the little world of school and when we stepped outside it our differences far outweighed the ties of our common experience. At school our lives were circumscribed, our conversations restricted. When, in the dark after "lights out" we defied rules against talking and discussed love, sex, and boys, we had little actual experience to report, and I am not sure we would have told anyway. There was a taboo against real revelation. The reticent and stoical male ethos of the stiff upper lip was ours as well. That at least lasted—I have never entirely erased it.

THE RADIO

I saw it during the Easter holidays.

My mother and I were leaving the greengrocers in St. Austell with our week's worth of vegetables and fruit when something in the next-door shop window caught my eye. A small blue suitcase with silver fasteners, its crinkly surface flashing in a sunbeam that momentarily lit up the drab street corner. I looked at it more carefully. The shop sold electrical goods, not luggage, and the suitcase was open to show what was inside. It was a portable radio!

Portable radios were a new phenomenon. Transistor radios were just beginning to be sold in Britain in the mid-1950s, but this one was a precursor, still working with valves, but small enough to be carried around and using either batteries or an electrical cord. I wanted it badly! The only radio available to us in the boarding house at school was in Miss Hyndman's room, where she occasionally invited us for cocoa on Saturday evenings to listen to the BBC's *Saturday Night Theatre*. If I had a radio we would have a choice. We could listen to anything the BBC in its wisdom cared to offer us, at least until our bedtime.

But the radio cost £12 5s. 2d., about the same as a month's worth of groceries for a family of four. It was far too expensive for a Christmas or birthday present, and way beyond anything I could save for with my meager pocket money. Then I had an idea. I didn't often ask for things, but I knew that if I did my father would be easier to persuade than my mother. When we got home I approached him with a broad smile.

"Daddy, I saw this super portable radio in St. Austell. I could take a radio like that to school. If I pass all my O Levels, will you buy that radio for me? Please?"

My father never used superfluous words. His telephone conversations, on the few times he had them, usually went something like this: "Yes. Yes. Bye."

This time his response was, "All right." I was amazed. Was it that easy? Did he really mean it?

"Promise?"

"Promise."

Once my father had agreed, my mother didn't object. Since I had no doubt that I would pass all my O Levels, I thought that next August the radio would be mine.

In 1951 the British government introduced a new more flexible General Certificate of Education (GCE), replacing the School Certificate exams my parents took. The GCE had two levels, Ordinary (O) Level and Advanced (A) Level, and students could take a wide variety of academic subjects, with none specifically required, although almost everyone took English language and maths (as we called it), and at that time no one could go to university without passing Latin. Many students at less academic schools than ours left school at fifteen, still the official school leaving age, without taking national exams, but at the Maynard we were all expected to sit for them.

When I was fourteen, I had to make choices that defined my academic future—specifically, whether to go on the arts or science track. One year of physics and one of chemistry had left me cold, and although I did well in both subjects I gave them up without a backward glance. I didn't totally abandon science, however, since for the next two years we all had to study biology, partly because this was the time our teachers thought it right for us to learn about rabbit (that is, by extrapolation, human) reproduction. I found biology fairly boring, and spent time in class adding segments to the impressive tapeworm I had drawn as a homework assignment.

We prepared for the O Level exams over two years. The school allowed us to take only seven subjects, perhaps to make sure we passed them all. When I was fifteen, I, together with my teachers, had to decide which seven I would take. As I was planning to go to university, my teachers advised me to leave Latin and English literature until Advanced Level. So I was set to take English language, history, French, German, math, biology and...art. Immediately I realized the radio was in jeopardy! Although I enjoyed art class, I knew I didn't have a lot of talent and didn't expect to be examined on my ability. But my teachers insisted, maybe to give me some breadth beyond academics. I wrote to my parents asking them to intervene, but they responded tactfully that my teachers knew best. I had to accept my fate.

224

Our teachers had no compunction about teaching for the test. We studied past papers as if they were scripture and practiced every aspect of every subject—in-class essays, foreign language translation, maths problems, literary critiques, science practicals, drawing and painting. In the spring of 1955 we took mock exams, actual papers from previous years. Then early in the summer those of us taking French and German had oral exams, when someone came to the school and had a brief conversation with each of us. We also endured a biology practical, dissecting frogs.

Late in May we stopped having indoor gym in the school hall. Now it had to be made ready for a more serious purpose. The school caretaker emptied two classrooms of their desks and chairs and carried them into the hall. He set them in rows, not too close together, and facing the stage. A few weeks later the paper exams started. We had no more formal classes and didn't have to go to school unless we had an exam. I spent my time going over my notes and past papers (we called it revision), practicing maths problems, memorizing historical facts. I took some time out on sunny days, but I knew I couldn't relax for long.

Each morning and afternoon the teacher proctoring the exam laid out sheets of the official O Level writing paper, lined, with a hole in the left corner, on each desk. She also distributed scrap paper, blotting paper, and short pieces of official string to tie the pages together. She laid a name card on each desk in alphabetical order next to the string and placed the printed exam paper on each desk, turned over so the content wasn't visible.

On the morning of the first French paper we filed into the gym, carrying only the equipment we needed—fountain pen and bottle of ink (the school didn't allow us to write with ballpoints, believing they ruined our carefully taught italic handwriting). I found the desk with my name and sat down. The first part of the exam was a dictation in French. Our French teacher read a passage slowly, including punctuation, and repeated it once. My task was to write it down correctly, including catching all the silent verb endings and making adjectives and nouns agree. Then the proctoring teacher told us to turn over the exam paper. In this section I had to translate a passage from French to English, then one from English into French. I wrote feverishly for an hour before the order to stop and put down our pens, fasten our papers together with the string through the holes, and leave them on the desks to be gathered up and sent with an official seal to the examining body. The next day I came back for the second French paper, with grammatical questions and an essay (in English) on a text we had read.

On a later day I lined up nervously by the art room door for the first Art exam, drawing the human body. The room was set up with easels and paper, and I picked up charcoal from a box as I went in. A clothed female model was ready to pose in the position required by the examiners, and I had an hour to draw her. We had had a lot of practice in life drawing, and my effort looked reasonably like the posed figure. I was somewhat encouraged. Maybe the radio was in reach.

That afternoon I came back for another hour to make a pencil drawing of a single lily in a vase. I enjoyed drawing flowers, and felt somewhat confident of my ability to do well enough to pass, so I was able to relax a little and even enjoy the break from writing. However, I was very nervous about the next day's exam, free drawing and watercolor.

This time I had to draw a picture illustrating one of five subjects and paint it in watercolor. I rarely managed to get watercolor right. My washes were either too thick or too thin, and my colors tended to bleed into the wash. My perspective was also usually a little askew. But this day my luck was in. One of the topics was a street scene, and with St. Austell in mind, I drew a Cornish shopping street, with both shop fronts and shoppers. I particularly remember drawing a little girl with a hoop that actually looked right. For once, I didn't ruin it with the watercolor. I had done much better than I thought I could.

Because of the large number of subjects students could take, many of which my school didn't offer, and because each subject had multiple papers, the exams were spread over about six weeks. For the rest of June and into early July I followed the same routine—exam, revise for the next one, exam. I exhausted my right hand writing five history essays in two and a half hours. In English Language I wrote a précis (summary) of a passage, answered grammar and reading comprehension questions, and wrote an original composition. I performed maths computations, solved quadratic equations, drew geometry figures, decoded geometry problems. I never saw a multiple-choice question.

The best part of O Levels was the freedom we had from the school's daily routine. So, when the exams were finally over, we were in no mood to go back into the classroom and our teachers wanted any excuse not to have

226

us for the month before the summer holidays. Instead there was a tradition of putting on some kind of entertainment for the rest of the school. As a group we decided to do a skit based on the Odyssey, calling it *The Oddity of Sessylu* (Ulysses backwards). Using a Penguin translation of *The Odyssey* as our guide, we picked out episodes in Ulysses' journey that most appealed to us, including the Cyclops, Scylla and Charybdis, Circe, the Sirens, Calypso, and his return home. A few of us collaborated on writing the script, making Ulysses a naïve bumbler, and playing most of the scenes for laughs, which largely succeeded with our friendly and non-critical audience. Everyone did something, either on stage or behind the scenes. I played the small part of Hermes, the messenger of the gods, who forgot his messages and constantly fiddled with wings on his sandals that threatened to fall off. I enjoyed myself and got some laughs, but I felt awkward on stage and realized I was not much of actor.

O Level results didn't come until sometime in August. At the beginning of the month I began to watch anxiously for the red post van to turn into the farmyard. I rushed out to get the mail and looked through anxiously for the brown envelope with the official examiner's logo. The postman soon realized what I was looking for, and told me in advance that it hadn't come. Then, one day in mid-month, he was smiling! I snatched the official envelope from the pile of mail and tore it open apprehensively, pulling out the single sheet of beige paper, and scanning down the list of subjects. At that time there were no grades, just pass or fail. I saw a solid line of "Pass." I had passed Art!! I hadn't worried about the others. The radio was mine!

"WE CAN'T AFFORD IT"

We can't afford it. Our parents' normal reaction whenever Michael or I asked for something extra— piano lessons, a new dress, a book we wanted to own rather than forever check out from the library. My parents' response was true. We couldn't.

By the time we were both in our teens, our parents were paying fees for two boarding schools, including the expensive uniforms and the cost of travel to and from school twelve times a year. It was becoming more difficult to make a living from a small farm—ours was sixty acres—when farmers with larger areas could make economies of scale. Prices were going down for the milk, eggs and pork that provided our staple income, and our land wouldn't support more cows or pigs.

Our relative poverty meant that any new clothes were almost always school uniform. After school and in the school holidays I usually wore my cousin Penny's cast-offs. In my mid-teens I rebelled.

"Why can't I have something new that Penny hasn't worn? Something I choose for myself?" I asked my mother sulkily.

"Well," she said, "We can't afford to buy you new clothes. It's all we can do to keep up with your school uniform. If you want a new dress you'll have to make it yourself."

Although I had shown no aptitude in sewing classes in Domestic Science at school, I was desperate enough to try it. Next time we were in St. Austell we bought a pattern for a pinafore dress (jumper) and a length of woolen material (fabric), lime green with black flecks. Ever the puzzle lover, I found cutting out the material and following the pattern intriguing and satisfying. Then I had to tackle the actual sewing. Our sewing machine had belonged to my grandmother, an aged treadle model that sat gathering dust in a corner of the passageway between the kitchen and the dairy. It took me a while to master keeping the machine going with my feet, but I learned that having two hands free while my feet pedaled away was a great advantage over a school machine where my right hand had to turn the wheel.

228

The pinafore was a success. I wore it over a black sweater and my school friends admired it—even I thought I looked good. It had cost very little, and I hoped my mother was willing to buy more material. She was. I got more ambitious, and soon had a new floral summer dress and a gray winter skirt. By the time I left school there was no stopping me, and all through university I made almost all my own clothes, including coats and ball dresses.

Meanwhile, to help with our school fees, my mother got a job teaching kindergarten at a small private school in Par, about six miles away. On the few days when her school holidays and mine didn't coincide, I used to enjoy going to school to help her. She was a good teacher, friendly, patient, and willing to have fun. Occasionally, she slipped up, like when she drew a seal on the board. It was pretty good, except she gave it two flippers and four feet. On the way home in the car, I said tentatively, "I think seals have two flippers and two feet." "Oh dear," said my mother, "Do you think I need to correct it tomorrow?" We decided she didn't. There may still be a few confused adults.

Going to school with my mother cemented my growing ambition to be a teacher. Most girls of my generation were destined for one of three careers, secretary, nurse, or teacher. On my school's 350th anniversary in 2008, twenty-four girls in my year responded to a request for information. Half of them had taught at some time in their lives. However, although almost all my teachers were single, my generation expected any career to be temporary, before we married and became housewives. Teaching seemed to be a good career since if something happened to your husband and you had to go back to work, you would have the same time off as your children. Unlike my mother, I didn't want to teach all subjects at the elementary level, but a single subject at the secondary level, like my role models at school. That meant a university degree, and that meant A (Advanced) Levels, the essential prerequisite for university entrance. Here my parents' poverty made a difference.

Since I was on what we called the arts (humanities) track, I would prepare for three A Levels (scientists took four). So, when I was sixteen, my parents, my teachers, and I had to decide which three I would take. My best subject was French, but to do well enough at A Level I would need to go to France for a while to immerse myself in the language and perfect my accent. During spring half term, as we were all sitting around the kitchen table after lunch, my father broached the subject.

"We've been talking to your teachers, and they tell us you need to go to France. I'm really sorry, but we just can't afford the money for you to go. We really would if we could, but we just don't have it."

I knew the "We can't afford it" refrain. I knew my parents wouldn't deny me something important unless they had to.

My father went on, "I know you have already decided to take A Level Latin and English Literature. You're good at history, so we wondered if you would agree to do history instead?"

This was more than just a decision for the next two years. At British universities students "read" (the usual term) one main subject, and, everywhere except Oxford and Cambridge, one subsidiary subject. I would eventually be teaching my main subject. I didn't want to teach English or Latin. I would become a history teacher.

What could I say? I liked history well enough. "Yes, that'd be all right," I agreed. I certainly didn't want to ask my parents to make even greater financial sacrifices for my education than they already had, even if they had offered. Which they hadn't. There were no other arts subjects that appealed to me as much as history. I was used to accepting decisions made by others—large ones like where I would go to school down to small ones like when to get up in the morning or what to wear to school every day. I conformed.

It was just as well. I learned later that I don't have a real facility for languages, and I would have found that out too late. Reading French and understanding its grammar is very different from speaking it. I would never have done as well in French as I did in history. I was lucky not to have tried.

When I was seventeen, I caught sight of a letter on my school's letterhead that was lying around on the kitchen dresser in the usual pile of mail waiting for my parents to address. I was curious why the school would need to write to them, especially as they had said nothing to me. The letter wasn't in an envelope, and since no one was around I read it, although I knew I shouldn't. It reminded my parents that they were in arrears on my school fees. Until that moment, I had never thought about how expensive my brother and I were, or whether the farm brought in enough to pay for us. I thought the problem was probably temporary and wasn't worried that I would have to leave school, but I vowed to myself that I wouldn't let them support me once I went to university. I was able to keep that vow.

In the 1950s money was not a consideration in applying for a university place. Getting admitted was very competitive, and if I got a place I would be funded, with either the state or my local authority paying my tuition and a living allowance based on my parents' income. Our poverty was actually an advantage. Inspired by my trip to Oxford with my cousin Alan, I decided that I would try for the top—Oxford and Cambridge. This was a stretch—the Maynard girls who went to university at all went to the University of London or one of the newer "red brick" universities, as they were disparagingly called then. But the year I started my A Levels, one girl two years ahead of me got into Cambridge. It was possible.

THE SIXTH FORM

The Maynard School photo in 1956 shows a total of forty-nine sixth formers. I can tell the numbers easily from the photo, because we stand out from the rest of the schoolgirls. We had left our gym tunics behind and are wearing the Sixth Form uniform —the striped school blouse and tie and a skirt that was not subject to the same length regulations as the tunics. We could finally adopt the calf-length hemlines of Dior's "New Look," only seven years after it was introduced, and our black stockings could be nylon instead of the thicker lisle, although they laddered (ran) easily and replacing them was expensive.

The Sixth Form was the name given to the two school years between ages sixteen and eighteen. About a third of my year had left school after O Levels. The ones who stayed on prepared for entrance to various forms of further education, including elementary teacher training, nursing, or secretarial school, most of which required entrants to be seventeen, so they needed one more year at school. Those of us hoping to go to university had to spend two years of study for A levels.

The more grown-up uniforms and slight relaxation of standards were one hint of greater laxity in the Sixth Form. No one checked on our whereabouts all the time. If we had free time during the school day, instead of being supervised in a classroom, we could go anywhere within the school grounds, although most of us just headed for the library. Things were also more relaxed in the boarding house. There too the numbers in my year were depleted. Of the six girls in the 1955 dormitory photo, only three of us were still at school—Alison, Wendy and me. By 1956 only Alison and I remained. I was never particularly friendly with Alison, and with the smaller numbers the taboo against boarders being friendly with daygirls disappeared. My new best friends were Sylvia Budd (Spuds), whom I had wanted to befriend for years, and Angela Beaven, both of them mathematicians. I yearned to have Spuds's sporting ability, but that became less important in the Sixth Form and my lack of ability was no longer a barrier to friendship. I greatly admired Angela for her persistence and

232

daring in forcing the school to allow her to take two arts subjects and maths, at A Level, a hitherto unheard-of combination that the school at first claimed was impossible to schedule—I too would have liked to do it if I had known it was possible before I committed myself to the arts.

In the boarding house we had more privacy, not in the dormitories where Matron still reigned, but in the Top Study, a small room on the top floor of the boarding house reserved for Sixth Formers, where even Miss Hyndman had to knock on the door. It was sparsely furnished with a table, a small sofa, and not enough comfortable chairs for us all, but it was our domain. There we did our homework without supervision, relaxed, gossiped, complained, ate. We toasted crumpets, a sort of flat muffin with holes that soaked up butter, on the small gas fire. Here my radio became indispensable, as we listened to comedies— *The Goon Show, Hancock's Half Hour*—and quiz shows, and, daringly, smuggled it into the dormitory so we could huddle over it and listen to the Top Twenty on Radio Luxemburg on Saturday nights from 11 to midnight. The only problem was that I couldn't plug it in to the electricity since Miss Hyndman claimed it would add to the house's bill, so we had to club together to buy batteries.

In the school building during the day we became responsible for helping with discipline. Miss Ryan, our headmistress, chose twelve of the most worthy Sixth Form girls to be school prefects, with one of them given the honor of being named Head Girl. Prefects wore special school badge tiepins and wore unusual hats— black velour tricorns in winter, and flat straw boaters in summer. They were mainly responsible for maintaining discipline in the school's corridors. At the beginning of the school day, one prefect stood at the top and another at the bottom of the stairs shouting out, "Don't run," or, "No Talking," as the girls rushed from the cloakrooms to their form rooms before morning prayers. A minor and pleasurable power trip was to ring the bell to change classes. At morning prayers prefects filed into the gym in a row at the back of the stage, looking down on the rest of the schoolgirls in the body of the gym, while the Head Girl preceded Miss Ryan up the center aisle, carrying her books and papers.

Miss Ryan chose most prefects from the second year of the Sixth Form, but a few were younger. At the end of my first year I waited anxiously as she announced the new prefects for the autumn term at the end-of-the-year assembly. I was very nervous. I badly wanted the

233

recognition, but feared I was not popular or sporting enough to be chosen—academics counted more, but maybe not enough. I sat at the back of the gym trying not to look worried. Then Miss Ryan called my name, I went up to the platform to get my hat and badge, and joined the other prefects at the back of the stage. I was supposed to look dignified, but it was hard to disguise my happiness, and I am sure I beamed at everyone as I walked to the back of the stage. Finally I had really joined the elite.

The prefects had their special room at the bottom of the main school stairs. Like the boarding house Top Study, this too was private, and teachers very rarely came in. The twelve of us became close friends, and my relationships with Spuds and Angela, also prefects, deepened. We developed our own rosters for stair duty, our main responsibility, studied when we weren't in class, and exchanged confidences, jokes, opinions. Someone had left a game of tiddlywinks in the room, and we developed a tiddlywinks sports league using the room's rug, whose design had defined lines at each end. We put the cup at one end and raced against each other, pressing the tiddlywinks as fast as we could to get to the cup first. We hoped no one knocked to catch us on our knees in hot competition.

In the Sixth Form, academic work became concentrated and serious. For two years my classes were predominantly in my three A Level subjects. We had eight sessions a week in each, most of them double periods. The rest of our time was taken up with one double period of exercise of some kind, the compulsory period of religious instruction, one class of civics, some art and music, and a good sprinkling of preps (study halls) so we could at least make a start on the enormous amount of required homework.

Our history teacher was Mrs. Bennett, a clergyman's widow known behind her back as Ma B. She seemed immensely tall, over six feet, with a booming voice. She wore her short dark hair curled backward into a roll over her forehead, and dressed severely in serviceable straight skirts and sensible flat shoes with plain solid-color blouses, topped by a cardigan. She brought her two adored dachshunds, Fanny and Maud, to school with her in her car. Once she left a pile of exercise books in the car and the dogs shredded them, a twist on the perennial excuse, "My dog ate my homework."

We didn't encounter Mrs. Bennett as a teacher until we were in our mid teens and preparing for O Levels, but her reputation as a strict disciplinarian, plus her overbearing demeanor, meant we were all inclined to be afraid of her. But one day she came into class and announced that she had just read an article about how students no longer learned the dates of the kings and queens of England, and she would give a Mars bar to the first one of us who would recite them correctly. I wanted that Mars bar, but even more I wanted to win the contest. I studied overnight and in the next history class named all forty-three of them correctly in sequence. I won! After that, Mrs. Bennett seemed friendlier and I enjoyed history classes.

For A Levels Mrs. Bennett chose to have the five of us in the A Level class study British and European history from the fall of Rome to 1216, an unusual choice of period that few others studied (most did the Tudors and Stuarts). I think it helped us to stand out when applying for university. She also chose our required special subject, monasticism in England in the twelfth century. Mrs. Bennett was not much interested in the nuances of interpretation, and gave us the "facts" as gospel. Our classes were mostly lectures, with us taking notes, but we also studied past A Level papers, discussing how we would answer the questions (all essays). For homework we went over our notes, read additional material, and practiced writing our responses. I was glad I had agreed to study history. It appealed both to the romantic side that enjoyed historical novels and Cornish history and to the more analytical part of my brain, seeing patterns in past events.

We spent an equal amount of time with Miss Anderson, our Latin teacher. We learned to translate passages both from and into Latin and identify aspects of Latin grammar. We had two set texts by Virgil and Cicero that we also had to translate and critique in essays. Miss Anderson expected a lot from the four of us taking Latin. We studied the texts until we could almost recite them verbatim and practiced translation endlessly. I particularly enjoyed translation, approaching it as I would a jigsaw or crossword puzzle, looking for the right solution.

We had two teachers for English Literature. Miss Lane, a genial white-haired woman with a twinkle in her eye behind her glasses, was responsible for the two required Shakespeare plays, *Hamlet* and *Henry IV Part II*, and two of the optional texts (chosen by our teachers from the examining body's list) by Milton and Lamb. I was not good at critiquing literature, always nervous that I had missed something. I was used to there being a right answer, not a range of what appeared to me to be equally valid

235

opinions. Our other teacher, who taught us the compulsory Chaucer selections and works by Marlowe, Browning and Hardy, was an exciting new arrival. Miss Hooper was fresh from university, curly-haired, dressed less conservatively than other teachers, in swirling skirts and frilly blouses Most intriguingly, she was engaged to be married, actually marrying in the summer of her first year. I noted the possibility, the first in my experience, that a married teacher could continue working.

Finally, at the end of the two years, we sat for the exams, three three-hour essay papers in history, two translation papers and one literature paper in Latin, a paper on Chaucer and Shakespeare, and another on the optional texts in English.

When I got my results that summer I was both glad to find that I had passed in Latin and English, and surprised that I got a distinction in History. I was on the right track. But A levels were not the end for me. I had never forgotten my visit to Oxford with my cousin four years before, and longed to walk those streets in my own right. While almost all the rest of the Upper Sixth were leaving for universities, I had decided, with my parents' agreement and some encouragement from my teachers, that I would be coming back to take the even more rigorous exams required for entry to the Oxford and Cambridge women's colleges. Mrs. Bennett wasn't sure of my chances, but I was determined to try.

A portion of the school photo. I am second from the right of the row of Sixth Formers behind the teachers.

CRISES

If my school life was extended for another term at least, home was about to change radically. We were leaving the farm.

Sometime in my middle teens my father got allergic to cows. His face swelled so badly he could hardly see out of his eyes, and his arms and hands swelled up as well. He couldn't go near our main source of income. My mother took over everything to do with the cows, getting them in from the fields, feeding them, milking them, helping them with difficult births, working with the vet when needed. The most my father could do was take the milk to the milk stand every morning.

My mother's day became: get up early, milk the cows, drive to Par to teach kindergarten, come home, prepare lunch, milk the cows again, prepare dinner, and fall into bed. At least Mrs. Hore did the cleaning and laundry, and helped out with lunch. My father did all the other farm chores—pigs and chickens, growing crops, general maintenance— but he couldn't do much to relieve the strain on my mother. When I was seventeen, she, who was never ill, suddenly had a severe asthma attack and was admitted to the local hospital, scarcely able to breathe.

It is a measure of how detached I had become from my family and the farm that my recollection of these events is very sketchy. I never actually saw my father's swollen face during an allergy attack. I don't remember being asked to do extra work to relieve my mother, although once we got a milking machine I usually helped with the cows when I was home.

I was home when my mother had her asthma episode during the summer holidays, yet the actual event remains almost beyond my recall. I know we didn't call an ambulance, because it had to come from Bodmin, which would have taken too long. My father took her in the car to the Bodmin hospital's emergency room, where they admitted her. In those days the National Health Service didn't provide hospital gowns, and my father had to rush off to buy a nightgown because my mother didn't have one. I faintly remember visiting her, dismayed to see my capable mother lying in bed in that unfamiliar nightdress, not doing much and still struggling for

237

breath. I worried about her recovery, especially as she had been given penicillin and had a violent allergic reaction that further sapped her strength.

While she was in the hospital Mrs. Hore and I were in charge in the house. Michael and I milked the cows since my father couldn't. That summer Michael was moving schools, to a high school in Truro, Cornwall's capital, about thirty miles from the farm. He needed a complete new school uniform, so my father drove us to Truro and put me in charge of buying all the required items, from underwear to sports equipment. I was nervous about the responsibility and appalled at the cost, but also glad to be useful. I spent the next few days sewing on the necessary nametapes, a little resentful that my brother didn't have to do it himself as I had done.

After more than a week my mother came home from the hospital, still weak and not ready to take up all her duties again. She was most worried about her kindergarten class—school was about to start and she didn't think she was up to it. Since I had helped her on a few occasions, we decided that I would go back to my own school late so I could cover her class for the first few days—my first experience of teaching on my own. I had begun to learn to drive, but had not advanced beyond practicing on the farm driveway, so my father took me there and back each day. I did my best to emulate the things I had seen my mother do with the class of about fifteen four-year-olds, all of them just starting school. We played games, I read to them, organized finger painting, and generally kept them happy. I was exhausted at the end of the morning, but proud that I could do it.

Not proud enough to boast about it when I got back to school just under a week late. I was embarrassed at having to miss classes, and worried that I had done something wrong. However, my parents wrote a letter explaining my absence, my teachers accepted my return without comment, and I soon settled back into the normal routine that was now so much more part of my life than the breaks at the farm.

But the crises at home had enormous consequences for me as well as my parents. In the autumn my parents looked at their lives. They loved the farm, my mother especially, but they weren't making enough money, and the work was making them ill. Although they rarely talked about any of their struggles, that Christmas holiday, as we sat at the kitchen table for lunch, my mother approached the subject.

"We have something to tell you. We've decided to sell the farm. It's hard to make money on small farms now, and we haven't been well. Daddy is going to look for a job. We are sorry to leave this life, but we think it's best."

I sensed how difficult it was for them to give up farming, but to me this was liberation, and, although I tried, it was hard for me to hide my elation. We would be moving to what I though of as civilization! No more having to be home every day at milking time, no more isolation. I could live a life I thought of as "normal." I couldn't wait!

My father started to find a job back in the industrial world he had left thirteen years before. It wasn't easy at age forty-eight, but eventually he was hired as a manager at a plastic foam factory in High Wycombe, a town about thirty miles west of London, famous for furniture manufacture. I looked forward to radical change.

SELLING

My father began his new job in High Wycombe at once, leaving my mother to preside over the end of our farming life alone, as she had at its beginning. She embarked on sorting out and selling the accumulation of thirteen years of our lives.

When I came home for the summer holidays after I took A Levels, my mother said to Michael and me, "We'll be having the farm sale at the end of August. Everything must go, and it all has to look as good as possible. Without Daddy here, I'll need a lot of help. Jenny, you'll paint everything that needs painting, and Michael, you'll do all the chores that Daddy used to do. It'll be a lot of work, but it'll be worth it."

I was vaguely aware that my mother loved the farm more than my father did. She never said anything about it, but I suspect that the closeness of their relationship and the freedom of their life when they were together all the time were hugely important to her, more important than the farm itself and the work it involved. But although it was immensely painful for her to contemplate leaving, she didn't show it. Anyway I was in no mood to notice or listen. I looked on the move as liberation, repatriation, a return to a normalcy that I had, in fact, never experienced. I set to work with enthusiasm.

I had to clean and paint everything paintable—machinery, fences, doors, gates. Painting was new to me, but I enjoyed it. Every morning I wrapped myself into my faded blue school art overall and gathered my scraper, paintbrush and paint. I began with gates. I sanded the peeling entrance gate, gave it three coats of shiny white paint, then carefully traced over the still faintly visible GUNWEN FARM in black letters on the top bar. Many of the other gates had never been painted, but the two that led into the area surrounding the house became a similar shiny white. I was out alone, occupied, happy, pleased with a job well done.

The gates done, I moved to machinery—we would plant no more crops. First I removed years of oily grime and rust, then repainted in the original colors that were just visible in protected places. The Wylies arrived

240

for their usual summer holiday, and Jill and Carol joined the effort. We assembled everything in the field behind the house dairy, opened the window to plug in my radio, and painted all day. We painted old farm machinery my parents hadn't used in years. Michael used the tractor to free old harrows from patches of fallow grass in the fields and dragged them over for rejuvenation. The tractor was a challenge, covered with years of oil and grease and with a slight split in the oil casing that we did our best to disguise with new blue paint. Our bodies and hair became a rainbow of smudges as the plow, the hay rake, the fertilizer spreader started gleaming in their second youth. We also helped with farm chores—cows got milked, pigs and chickens fed, eggs collected. And still we painted.

On the sale day everything stopped except the morning milking and feeding. The auctioneer had advertised the sale in the local papers, and cars and cattle trucks (in anticipation of purchases) started to fill the fields along the drive. We learned how respected and even loved my parents had become in our community. Friends and neighbors came from miles around with no intention of buying, just to support them. They and many total strangers wandered around checking on the equipment and animals, waiting for the auctioneer to arrive. We followed them nervously, trying to assess their interest.

The auctioneer set up first in Dairy Field, where we had displayed all the equipment. He started the usual auctioneer patter, rather like a very vocal human turkey—"Twenty, twenty, do I hear twenty-one? Ah, thank you, Sir! Twenty-two? Do I hear twenty-two?" We noticed that friends bid up things if they thought interest was flagging, all of them managing to get out before they bought something they didn't want. When the tractor came up for sale, one of our neighbors, whom we knew had no interest in it, kept bidding and only bowed out at a price more than we had paid for it. Our painting had its reward!

The auctioneer moved to the area outside the cow house, which could be closed off so nothing could escape. One by one we drove the cows out for their turn in the ring. Even Buttercup, the senior cow, had to go. The pigs followed. The chickens had already gone, sold for meat, and we even sold the battery.

After a long day, by dinnertime it was over. My mother, Michael and I stood together in the weed-infested front garden and watched sadly as cows and pigs we had known for years were loaded into trucks and driven off. We didn't talk about it, but even I, however much I was joyfully anticipating our new life, couldn't help a few tears. My mother, as ever, stood stoically, but I could sense the sadness in her uncharacteristic lack of vitality. For the first time in thirteen years she didn't have to milk the cows.

Yet we had something to celebrate. Everyone agreed it was one of the best sales in memory, raising more than a thousand pounds. My mother telephoned my father with the good news. She gave Michael and me £10 each, the most money I had ever had at one time in my life, as a reward for our hard work. The only animals left were our thirteen farm cats, which my mother was planning to euthanize. I couldn't bear to contemplate that and used some of my money to advertise for a home for them in the local paper. My mother was skeptical, but to my great joy a young farmer answered the ad. We rounded them all up at feeding time and he collected them, pleased with his instant rodent protection. It was hard to see cats I had named and loved leave, but I comforted myself that I had saved them from a worse fate. They were tough cats, survivors of feline enteritis and used to living in barns, so I hoped they would adjust to their new surroundings.

Shortly afterwards my brother and I went back to school, and my mother was left to put the farm itself up for sale. She faced long days alone with no farm chores and no companionship beyond her morning kindergarten class. I was shocked to discover at half term that she had begun to smoke, although she stopped as soon as she was reunited with my father after the three months it took to complete the farm sale. After half term I didn't see the farm again for more than thirty years.

HEAD GIRL

When I returned to school in the autumn of 1957, I was one of only a few who were staying in the Sixth Form for a third year to prepare for Oxford and Cambridge entrance exams. At that time there were five Oxford women's colleges and two at Cambridge, with a third just starting and admitting only five girls a year. The competition for admission was fierce, and all of them had entrance exams that were more demanding than the A Levels we had completed in the summer, but I was determined to try. My parents encouraged me, and it never occurred to me to worry that, already short of money, they had to pay at least another term's school fees. If I didn't get into either university in the fall, as was likely, I would stay at school in the spring to take one more Oxford entrance exam, and complete applications for the University of London as a fallback.

My more immediate concern was who would be chosen to be Head Girl, a considerable honor, and one that Penny had held before me. I knew it would be between the two most senior prefects—me or Alison Brading. I also knew who it would be—charismatic, highly intelligent, athletic Alison. But as soon as I arrived at the boarding house I heard that Alison, who had been spending the summer in Nigeria, where her father was the head of a large hospital, had contracted polio. She had been flown back to England in an iron lung, and was lying immobile in an Oxford hospital.

I couldn't help feeling a twinge of excitement at my rival's removal, before suppressing it in a larger twinge of remorse. To make amends I made sure I wrote to Alison weekly. The following year, when we had moved relatively close to Oxford, I took an hour-long bus ride to visit her every week. The first postcard she managed to write was to me, a picture of the hospital with "Hi, Jenny" in very shaky print. I still felt guilty because we had never been close friends, and I had envied her, and I was so glad when she began to breathe on her own, and eventually walked without assistance. She was determined to recover enough to do biology practicals, and a few years later got her Oxford place, her PhD, and a career as an Oxford professor.

Meanwhile, I enjoyed the prestige of being Head Girl. The duties weren't onerous. I had to carry Miss Ryan's books into prayers every morning, and once a week select and read a bible passage at the assembly. I organized the roster of duties for the other prefects, and took a turn myself. I chaired the school's student council, although I can't remember that we ever did anything significant.

More importantly, I concentrated on my academic work in preparation for the November exams. My school report for that term shows that my curriculum had shrunk to a bare minimum—mostly history, Latin, and essay, for exam preparation, leavened with the perennially required gym, games and scripture. I and another girl, Josephine Rutter, who was also aspiring to read history at Oxford, had daily lessons, just the two of us, with Mrs. Bennett. She tried to widen our horizons, both in history itself and in general. One day she said to me, "I think it would be good if you knew a little about art history. Here's a book." She loaned me *The Story of Art* by E. H. Gombrich. It immediately grabbed me although my experience of fine art was confined to the very small collection in Exeter's museum. I devoured the book, read others, and longed to see the paintings and sculpture featured in the illustrations. It was the beginning of a lifelong pleasure. The following summer I asked for *The Story of Art* for my school prize for the best A Level results. I still have it.

Mrs. Bennett was careful not to raise our hopes too much. We had heard that four hundred girls took the exams for every one admitted. Just getting an on-campus interview, the next stage after the exams, was an honor. Mrs. Bennett once said to me that she thought Josephine was more likely to get an interview than I was. I became more determined. In particular, I practiced the general essay, my weakest point, with Miss Anderson, the Latin teacher. My secluded life at home on the farm and in the boarding-school hothouse meant I had limited life experience to draw on. I feared my common-sense, prosaic approach to life had stunted my imagination, so it was a challenge to think of anything original to write. I just hoped for inspiration in November.

When November came I was ready. The history papers tested both our knowledge and our understanding of history. We needed to show a more sophisticated knowledge of the periods of British and European history we had studied for A level, including interpretation of different sources. One of the questions on the Cambridge exam asked us to evaluate a number of fictitious sources for an event and come up with a convincing narrative, taking into account all the evidence. We also had to explain why we had chosen one conflicting source over another. Synthesis was my greatest strength, and I greatly enjoyed that question, which appealed to my puzzle-solving mind.

Then the dreaded general essay loomed, but I was lucky. The Oxford exam asked us to comment on a quote that contrasted art and music: "Art is art and must have a meaning, but music is music and can mean nothing." After a couple of months of my art obsession and the good music education all of us had received at school, I felt I had something to say. I decided to define "meaning" as appealing to the intellect rather than the emotions, and agreed that art was more likely than music to provoke an intellectual response, although I disagreed that either of them "must" or must not mean something.

The Cambridge exam gave us more choice, including one asking us to describe the sea to someone who had never seen it. After years at Lamledra, seeing, hearing, smelling and watching the sea, here was something within my limited experience! I asked my readers to picture themselves standing at the highest point they knew of, looking out and imagining all they could see as water. I described the colors, from vivid blue to steel gray, the sighs of the waves and the boom of the surf, the salty, seaweedy odors, the changes as the weather changed. Once again I enjoyed myself. I came out of the exam room proud that I had done my best, but hardly allowing myself to hope. The odds were too great.

Of all the girls who took the exams, only a few were called for an on-campus interview. We knew it would take a couple of weeks to hear anything, and then only those invited for an interview would get telegrams. The others would get formal rejection letters a good time later. I tried not to hope.

Then, two weeks later, while I was at lunch, Miss Hyndman was called to a ring at the door. The vital telegrams had arrived! She came in with two yellow envelopes, and I tore them open with everyone at lunch watching. Both St. Hugh's College at Oxford and Girton at Cambridge wanted to interview me in early December. I was ecstatic, but tried not to be too obviously excited, as Josephine didn't get interviews and I didn't want to gloat. We were classmates rather than friends, and we both went on as if nothing had happened between us.

The question now turned to what I would wear. My mother came up from Cornwall to take me shopping for a suitable outfit. A couple of Christmases before, my godmother had sent me a book by Noel Streatfield, one of my favorite authors. Called *The Years of Grace*, it wasn't one of her usual novels about talented girls and boys acting, skating, or dancing, but an advice manual for teenage girls. She told us how to stand, how to keep our skin pure, to use a little makeup, how to talk to boys, how to behave in adult company. And she advised us how to dress. I read the book several times and believed everything she said, but had few opportunities to follow her advice in any detail. Here was my chance. She maintained that every girl should have a gray flannel suit with a pleated skirt. That was what I wanted.

My mother had other ideas. She took me to Exeter's major department store, where they stocked such suits, but refused to let me try a gray one on, saying it was dull and wouldn't suit me. She was probably right, but I sulked. Instead my mother chose a suit in a subtle yellow and green tweed with a straight skirt. She also picked out a suitable hat.

I hated that suit. I told my mother I would never wear it after the interviews, a threat I kept. She tried to persuade me that I looked my best in it, but I couldn't see it. All I wanted were gray sunray pleats. My mother wouldn't give in and she had the power. We bought the tweed suit. Since I had nothing else suitable, I was doomed to wear it.

Me (left) and Josephine Rutter

INTERVIEWS

In early December I put on the tweed suit and hat, with nylon stockings and brown lace-up shoes. I packed my overnight leather suitcase, and took the train to Oxford. St. Hugh's was a rather unassuming red brick building in a residential neighborhood, very different from the gray stone of the men's colleges in the city center. Inside it was dark and gloomy, more like a Victorian house than a college. The female porter met me at the door and showed me to a Spartan, private room for the night. Interviews would be the next day.

More than one hundred girls had been invited for interviews in different subjects. We all had dinner together, the kind of institutional food I was used to at school. Competitors for the very few places available, we eyed each other warily, not speaking much. I was far too shy to initiate conversation. A few other girls exchanged basic information—school, hometown, subject. Most came from well-known schools and seemed confident. No one was wearing a hat. I scrunched mine into my suitcase.

The following day about twenty of us who wanted to read history or what Oxford called PPE (philosophy, politics and economics) sat in a small waiting room, with a large bay window overlooking a garden with a few leafless rose bushes and a brick wall, waiting to be interviewed by a professor in our subject and by another professor in charge of undergraduates' general welfare. Most of us sat in silence, not looking at each other, and trying not to show how nervous we were, but one self-assured young woman sitting on the window seat talked animatedly to her neighbor in an impeccable upper-class accent.

"I couldn't bear another term at school," she said, mentioning one of the top girls' boarding schools, "so I left and went to a crammer in London to be coached for the exams. It's a lot more fun in London and I don't have to waste my time on dreary things like gym. I'm sharing a flat with some other girls." Living independently in London at age eighteen was so far beyond my experience it had never occurred to me to be possible.

She turned to the rest of the room. "Are you planning to go to St. Hugh's if you get in?" she asked. We all nodded. "I'm not, she said, "Unless I have to. My sister's already at Cambridge, and I'm going on there for interviews tomorrow. She loves Girton and thinks Cambridge is tons better than Oxford. Also, I can do just economics there, which is what I really want."

Then she spoke the words that would tie us together for thirty years: "Anyone else going on to Cambridge from here?" I looked around. No one else stirred. "I am," I said tentatively.

"Oh, good. Some company on that tedious train journey. Let's take a taxi to the station tomorrow morning."

I agreed, although I had no idea what I could say to her face-to-face on the train.

At that point I was called in to talk to the history professor. She sat at her desk in a gloomy room, her clothes covered by her black gown. She greeted me without much warmth. After some general questions on history, she asked about an exam answer I had written dealing with the reign of Edward I. She suggested that there could be a different interpretation of events than the one I, taught by Mrs. Bennett, had given. This was the first time I realized that history wasn't a fixed collection of facts, but a matter of interpretation. I struggled to answer the professor's questions, but hoped I had conveyed that I could at least have an open mind.

Next I talked to another don (professor). Somewhat friendlier than the history professor, she asked me about myself and I told her a brief narrative of what I saw as my unadventurous life so far. She particularly emphasized that at Oxford we didn't just have to do our best, we had to do better than the men. I had no idea about the struggles women's colleges at Oxford and Cambridge had endured to get accepted as full members of the university. Even then, in 1957, the Oxford women's colleges were negotiating for full university status, which they didn't receive until 1959. The Oxford professor had good reason to feel insecure, but I wasn't interested in competing with men. I just wanted to know some.

At the end of the interview the don asked me, "Are you also interviewing at Cambridge?"

I said I was. "And if you get into both, which will you choose?"

"Oxford," I said firmly. I wasn't hedging my bets, I wouldn't have dared. After my day out with my cousin Alan four years before, that was indeed my intention.

"Have you ever been to Cambridge?" she asked.

"No."

"Ah," she said enigmatically.

Judy (I had found out her name by that time) and I took the taxi the following morning. The train from Oxford to Cambridge meandered for three hours through the countryside, stopping frequently, which gave us plenty of time to talk. I had never met someone my age like Judy, worldly, sure of herself, fashionably dressed, able to talk freely about many things. I was dazzled and contributed very little to the conversation except responding to her direct questions. Judy told me how her sister was enjoying both academic work and a busy social life in her last year at Cambridge. "Wait till you get there. You'll find Girton is much nicer than stuffy old St. Hugh's." I had to admit that I had a similar impression of St. Hugh's, but was not ready to change my mind.

We took the bus from Cambridge station to Girton College. It was three miles from the city, further than St. Hugh's from the center of Oxford, but a woman would need a bicycle in either. The building was more imposing than St. Hugh's, red stone, set in a large garden and park area that made it seem more like the men's colleges. It had taken the pioneering women many years to raise the money to pay for it, but I knew nothing about that as I walked up to the gatehouse.

My interviews the next day were with two historians, Mrs. Lindsay and Mrs. Chibnall (no one called them Doctor or Professor, perhaps because, unlike most women dons, they were married). Neither asked difficult questions, to me at least, or suggested we were in competition with men. Mrs. Lindsay was particularly friendly and welcoming, a motherly figure who made me feel less alone in a sea of unfamiliarity.

I had enough time between interviews to take the bus into Cambridge by myself and wander along the famous Backs, where the River Cam runs along the back of several of the men's colleges. I gazed at the lawns framing the soaring gray stone Perpendicular facade of King's Chapel. It was peaceful since the university term had ended, and the beauty of the place overwhelmed me. It was the same feeling I had when standing on a

Cornish cliff looking out over the ocean. As I stood there I knew that this, not Oxford, was the place for me. If I had the chance. Back at Girton, when Mrs. Lindsay asked the inevitable question about my choice, I replied, "Cambridge."

BOYS

In my early and middle teens I had very little contact with boys. My local male acquaintances were limited to six. My brother and my cousins Nick and Richard, and my brother's friend Walcott, were all younger than me. I didn't like Mrs. Hore's son Colin and felt guilty about teasing him. I didn't even want to think about Tim after Jill had exposed me, and in any case he no longer came to the farm. Although I dreamed of romance, I wasn't alone in my lack of experience. None of my school friends had what could realistically be described as a boyfriend.

At school our contacts with the opposite sex increased somewhat in the Sixth Form. We had one period a week of civics when we studied a specific topic, usually connected to national politics, like world hunger or refugees. A different teacher covered the class each year and I imagine it wasn't a popular assignment since we didn't take it seriously, regarding it as a chore that kept us from our A Level work. The topic was common to all the high schools in Exeter, and every term we had a day when all Sixth Formers got together to hear relevant speakers. That part was occasionally quite interesting—the torture came with the evening's dance or "social." We girls, in our best dresses, hung around the edge of the school gym in groups, trying not to look at the similar knots of boys in equally awkward poses on the other side. Only the best looking and most confident boys dared approach the girls, and they chose the pretty ones, usually blonde and vivacious, to partner them on the sparsely populated dance floor.

Some daygirls opted not to participate in the evening's torment, but Miss Hyndman insisted that boarders attend. Never once was I asked to dance. I stayed in a group with other similarly spurned girls, pretending we didn't mind our rejection, half afraid that some boy might actually approach us, since we feared we wouldn't know how to react if one did.

Part of the problem was that we didn't know how to dance. Those were the days before any vaguely rhythmic wriggle would do—the few who could (they must have had lessons) waltzed, quick-stepped and foxtrotted. The most daring could also tango. We listened to rock'n roll on the

251

gramophone, but the band at these occasions never played it, and in any case we didn't know how to dance to that either.

That changed in my third year in the Sixth Form. For some inscrutable reason Miss Hyndman decided that the Sixth Form boarders needed more contact with the opposite sex, in carefully controlled environments of course. She talked to her counterpart at Exeter School, the local private school for boys. Together they arranged for us to have weekly mixed-sex ballroom dancing lessons.

Every Saturday evening we went over to the school gym and met with a dance teacher, an enthusiastic and bubbly blonde who brought with her a series of records for the various dances. First, we had to get over the fear of dancing with a boy. Initially the teacher assigned us partners, but as time wore on the boys chose their own. We still had to wait to be chosen, but, to my surprise, I didn't lack for partners. I usually danced with the school's Head Boy, tall, bespectacled, approachable, in what seemed a natural connection. Sometimes, much to my excitement, Hodge, the most popular boy, handsome, with curly hair and laughing eyes, chose to dance with me. I also had a third fairly regular partner, although I can't remember much about him.

Instead of watching from the sidelines I learned to dance all the steps I had envied others doing at the "socials." Like most physical things, I wasn't all that good, but I did well enough to feel confident on the dance floor, especially if my partner was competent. We even learned how to rock'n roll, moving on the off-beat as our instructor told us. We also got used to talking to boys, still awkwardly, since we didn't see each other much, but with increasing confidence as we exchanged A Level experiences. I started to look forward to Saturday evenings.

Miss Hyndman also allowed us to go to cheer on the Exeter School debate team in their contests, especially as the team was made up of four of our dance partners (there was no similar contest for girls, and we were too acclimatized to inequity to think about it). The debates often went on quite late, and there was a little socializing over cocoa afterwards. We got back to the boarding house well after lights out, but Miss Hyndman didn't seem to mind.

Later in the term the Exeter School boys had a dance, and we all hoped to be invited. I was astonished to receive three invitations, from the Head

Boy, from my third partner, and from Hodge, which I didn't expect since he could have his pick. I really wanted to go with Hodge, but the Head Boy had asked first, so I felt I had to choose him. Hodge actually seemed disappointed. I was amazed—three boys taking an interest in me. My confidence blossomed.

The boys' dance was a formal affair, with programs and a full band. At the same time as we had shopped for the hated suit, my mother had bought me a strapless blue dress with an ankle-length bouffant net skirt and matching dyed blue satin shoes with heels. I loved it, and felt almost pretty. When the much-anticipated day came, in total contrast with the dreadful "socials," I danced every dance. It was all very decorous—strictly chaperoned, and no touching beyond what was necessary on the dance floor. That was fine by me—I had no idea how to negotiate the next step.

THE LAST DAY

December 19, 1957. The last day of school. We had packed and sent off our trunks, with the only things left behind ready to go into our small suitcases. On the last day boarders always wore our Sunday navy blue costumes, making us stand out from the daygirls in their normal school uniform.

There were no classes on the last day, only the final school assembly in the morning, after which we cleared out our desks and left. As Head Girl I carried Miss Ryan's books and papers into the gym and up a center aisle through the ranks of girls standing silently. They brimmed with the suppressed excitement that accompanied every last day. I felt it too. I placed Miss Ryan's books on the table in the middle of the platform and went to join the other prefects in line across the steps at the back of the stage. Soon I would go down to the lectern to read the last scripture lesson, always I Corinthians 13 from the King James Bible: "Though I speak with the tongues of men and of angels, and have not charity, I am become as sounding brass, or a tinkling cymbal..."

We started with the school hymn, an adaptation of John Bunyan's poem from *Pilgrim's Progress:*

> *He who would valiant be*
> *Gainst all disaster;*
> *Let him in constancy*
> *Follow the master;*
> *There's no discouragement*
> *Shall make him once relent*
> *His first avowed intent*
> *To be a pilgrim.*

We all knew the words by heart, and the anticipation of the Christmas holiday encouraged us to sing to the top of our lungs. After several prayers and the lesson, Miss Ryan read the cumulative class lists, so everyone knew who was top of her respective form. She gave out prefects' badges to new prefects and new carriage girdles. Finally, with even more gusto than the Pilgrim hymn, we sang the school song, never questioning its placing sports before academics:

When the match is lost or won
And we are homeward wending,
When the long term's work is done
With mirth to greet its ending...

We ended with the rousing shout of the untranslatable school motto, "Manus justus nardus."

I walked down to Miss Ryan's table, picked up her books, and preceded her down the center aisle to the double doors and up to her room. I had heard nothing from Oxford or Cambridge, so I assumed I had not got a place and planned to be back in January for University of London entrance exams. I wished Miss Ryan a happy Christmas and went back to the boarding house for lunch.

While I was eating lunch a telegram arrived for me. I tore open the yellow envelope and quickly read the brief capitalized sentence pasted onto the buff-colored form. "OFFERING YOU A PLACE GIRTON FOR AUTUMN 1958. PLEASE REPLY AT ONCE." I rarely showed my feelings in public and I appeared outwardly calm as I passed the telegram to Miss Hyndman so she could read it. But I was inwardly ecstatic, probably the happiest I had ever been. The telegram was reply-paid, and I sent an immediate acceptance. Miss Hyndman let me telephone my mother to tell her the news. My mother was the most excited I could remember, and promised to tell my father as soon as he finished work. I went back over to the main school to tell Miss Ryan and Mrs. Bennett, who were still there. They too were excited, both for me and since my success reflected on them and the school. I also said goodbye. Since I had nothing to come back for, this was truly my last day of school.

While most of the boarders left for home after lunch, I and some other sixth-formers stayed on an extra night to go to the school dance. Although there was a dance every year, I had never gone before because I had no partner to invite and had no desire to be a "wallflower." Now, because of our dancing lessons, I actually had a choice. Once again I wanted to invite Hodge, but felt obliged to ask the Exeter School Head Boy, since he had invited me to their dance. I put on my blue dress and shoes and someone helped me put my hair in a Greek chignon. I returned to the gym that evening in a cloud of delight. People crowded to congratulate me. I danced every dance. My dress flounced around me as I twirled, and my feet in their matching blue satin shoes flew in time to the music—I never missed a step. I don't think I have ever been happier.

Later that week another telegram arrived for me from Oxford. St. Hugh's also wanted me. I was flattered and encouraged to be offered a place at both universities, but I was set. Judy and I had exchanged addresses, and I let her know I had chosen to go to Girton. She had too, but I was too much in awe of her to do more than have an occasional chat until our final year, when we both dated men from the same college who knew each other well. After we married our boyfriends, we lived near each other in Norfolk, and became lifelong friends.

As I was tearing open the telegrams on my last day of school, my mother was watching as those of our possessions she hadn't sold were loaded into a van. They would be stored until after the new year when we moved into our new, much smaller, home in Marlow, a town about forty miles outside London. A young couple had bought the farm and were anxious to start work.

The next day my mother started the long drive to our new life. She had already picked up my brother from his Cornish school, and she collected me in Exeter late that morning. We went on to meet my father at my godmother's where we were staying for Christmas. For the first time, at the end of term I went east, not west. We left Cornwall and farming behind.

My new life began.

EPILOGUE

IN TRANSITION

It was the classic tourist trap. The photographer leapt out in front of me on this London side street just off Trafalgar Square, called out "Smile," and snapped me before I had time to protest. Not that I was good at protesting. I even paid more than I could really afford for a copy, giving him my address so he could mail it. I wonder if I would resist if it happened to me now, but I'm afraid not. I am the same compliant person in an older body.

I was in London on a Saturday morning sometime around my nineteenth birthday, checking out the art galleries and doing some shopping. The bag I'm holding contained fabric for a new dress. I could afford it because for the first time in my life I was earning money. I spent the first two months of my freedom from school working in Foyle's, a large London bookstore that employed and underpaid many young people in transition from school to university, and advertised in national newspapers to attract them. I liked the idea of working in a bookstore, although the reality was much less glamorous that I had imagined.

We started in the mailroom before being assigned to a department. To my disappointment, I wasn't to work in a book section, but the record area, where I eventually did all the ordering since Maggie, our manager, preferred chatting to coworkers and customers, and soon noticed that I actually enjoyed the responsibility. The most popular single at the time was Perry Como's "Magic Moments" (flip side "Catch a Falling Star"), and I can still remember its number, RCA1036, since I ordered it practically every day. I learned a lot about pop music, as we called it then, and built up a small eclectic record collection of my own, ranging from a Saint-Saens piano concerto to jazz drumming.

I commuted into London from Marlow, our new home, six days a week, more than an hour's travel time each day, including negotiating the underground in the rush hour, all new experiences for a sheltered boarding-school girl. Although the Tube was less crowded on Saturdays, I dreaded that day since a young West Indian man came in every week all afternoon, wouldn't be served by anyone else but me, and tried to proposition me over the desk. He asked me to play records he could hear in a booth, but never bought anything. My colleagues found it highly amusing, but I had no idea how to put him off and tried to endure the pestering, at least secure in the sales counter that separated us.

The best part of each day was my lunch hour, which I spent in the National Gallery, just down the road with free admission. I gazed spellbound at the paintings I had read about in my last term at school. My favorite was Leonardo Da Vinci's *Virgin of the Rocks*. I still have the reproduction I bought and had framed. It sits in our attic, but I haven't the heart to give it away.

The commute and working six days a week was exhausting, but a greater problem was that by the time I had bought my rail season ticket and underground pass and paid for my lunch, I had practically no money left. So after a couple of months I quit, went to the local unemployment office, and found a job as a clerk at Harrison's, a factory in High Wycombe, the next town to Marlow and an easy bus ride from outside our front door. The factory printed all the stamps for Great Britain and the British

Commonwealth. Security was tight. It always amused me when the supervisor of the room where they assembled books of stamps sent me down to the Post Office to buy stamps because she couldn't get them in the factory.

My job was to keep track of the hours worked in one of the printing rooms so the men got their correct wages, something that would be done today by one computer, but then employed six women to deal with the different areas of the factory. All except me had left school as soon as they could, and they regarded me with some suspicion as an alien creature. After I had been there a few weeks Gladys, the most assertive, sat down by me during our lunch hour and asked,

"How did you learn to speak like that?"

"Er—my parents do," I replied politely and with the best friendly expression I could muster.

"Did you have elocution lessons at school?" I said I didn't.

"Do you live in a house?" was her next question. I assumed she meant something other than an apartment, where some of them might be living.

"Yes."

"Why are you working here?"

I explained that I was filling in time before going to university. My replies must have satisfied Gladys. After that I was her friend, and if we ever had to go anywhere in the factory she always introduced me in a proud tone as, "Jennifer, who is going to university." When I left the girls presented me with an expensive fountain pen.

Working at Harrison's gave me enough time and income to enjoy myself, hence my almost weekly Saturday excursions into London. I further developed my passion for art, not just in the major galleries, but also in the smaller ones exhibiting contemporary work, like paintings by John Bratby, the founder of the "Kitchen Sink" school. By looking and reading I educated myself to appreciate a wide range of art.

In the photo I am probably on my way to the National Gallery after shopping at my favorite fabric store in Regent Street. Now what strikes me most are my clothes. The coat was a bargain from Peter Robinson on Oxford Street. It was really no bargain since it had no fastenings and hung open, so was useless in cold weather and too hot in summer. It sat mostly unworn in my closet for years. But, in choices I am sure were unconscious,

260

underneath I have on clothes hardly distinguishable from my school uniform. The navy skirt I made myself, and I paired it with a striped T-shirt very similar to our school blouses. I am even wearing a hat like we wore at school, although a lighter color. Only my shoes, with their short heels, suggest emancipation.

GUNWEN FARM, 1989[**]

I wouldn't have seen it if it hadn't been for my partner Connie's insistence.

That morning we had driven over the hill above where the milk stand used to be, and Gunwen Farm appeared ahead of us as it always had, a cluster of low gray buildings on a slight rise. I felt that thrill of gratified recognition when something is just as you remembered—a totally familiar landscape. We drove between the farm's boundary and the moor on the narrow road that follows the stream, the three bumpy crags of Helman Tor rising to the right. We parked at the bottom of what we used to call Strawberry Lane and walked the short distance to the farm gate, the same one I had opened countless times forty-something years ago. The wild strawberries we used to pick in profusion every summer were still there, and we tasted a few as we walked.

"Well," I said to Connie as we leant over the gate, "This is it."

"Aren't we going to see the farmhouse?" she asked, puzzled.

"No, it's private property." She gave me a scornful look.

"I don't care; I've come this far and I'm going to see it." She opened the gate, and I followed, protesting ineffectually. We do this often; I see the obstacles, she disregards them. I have come to see this as a useful symbiosis rather than a fundamental flaw, a creative tension between impatience and caution.

We walked down the same dirt drive through Entrance Field, now separated from the road by a new rail fence, and turned the corner, passing a lane on the left, choked with undergrowth. My father had kept it clear; in its hedges my brother and I picked the violets my mother crystallized for our birthday cakes when post-war austerity meant there were no candles. A little further on, we saw the big open Dutch barn where we stored the hay. On its right was the oak tree in whose low branches I read for hours. A few steps more and we were in the farmyard. The barns, built of irregular

---

[**] A longer version of this appeared in *Biography* (March 2002).

chunks of Cornish granite held together by mortar, were as I remembered them, their cars in the same shed, the house behind, and further ahead, the barn my father had turned into an efficient milking shed.

There were a few changes. The farmyard was all clean concrete, not the muddy area my little brother had christened "the dirty." A barn next to the cowhouse and another beyond were new to me, and, I noticed as I scanned the yard, so was a dark gray slate plaque set low in the big barn wall, a little above and to the right of the door. No one was around, and I crossed the yard just far enough to read its inscription. We have a photo of me standing tentatively, aware I am trespassing, leaning forward, shoulders hunched, relying on my long sight to relieve my curiosity. I learned that on February 6, 1778, William O'Bryan, founder of the Bible Christian church, was born on this farm and died in Brooklyn, New York, a month before his ninetieth birthday.

We had never known this. I had never heard of the Bible Christian church, and, as far as I was aware, it had left no trace in the Cornwall of my childhood. As we returned to the car, back up the familiar drive and down Strawberry Lane, I pondered this discovery. Then we drove the short distance to where I once went to Sunday school in the small Methodist chapel at the end of a row of cottages— the only public building in the valley's apology for a village—and found that the plaque bearers had preceded us. We learned a little more: William O'Bryan gave the land and helped to build the first Methodist chapel on this site around 1796, when he was eighteen years old.

Back home, I looked up the Bible Christians and found they were a small Methodist sect, and their most distinguishing feature was that they had an unusual number of women preachers. I was busy with my dissertation on another topic, but the Bible Christians intrigued me, and a few years later I began to research both them and the O'Bryan family. That became a major topic and the subject of an academic book.[††]

In a library in Manchester I found William O'Bryan's diary, fifteen bundles of closely handwritten paper, clumsily sewn together. When he was living in Brooklyn, he recorded three dreams of the farm. They are happy

---

†† Jennifer M. Lloyd, *Women and the Shaping of British Methodism: Persistent Preachers, 1807-1907* (Manchester University Press, 2009).

dreams; in 1856 he is with his father and delights in the field called Well Park, "so richly covered over with corn almost ripe for harvest, and especially at the higher end those springs and such clear water." In 1863 he is sitting on a hedge next to "Grand Field" with his daughter Catherine. They went to the bottom of the field, where there was a pool of water and "It seemed we were in heaven. I felt it, and said, now we are in heaven."

Less than a year later, in the third dream, the pool is large enough to swim in, and "tho waking, I never ventured to swim yet now I courageously plunged in and worked my arms briskly, without any fear, and pushed on courageously." I knew exactly where he meant. When we lived on the farm there was a duck pond on the edge of the field we called Foredoors, probably the same as Well Park. Perhaps the name we knew came from its position in front of the main door of the present farmhouse, which O'Bryan never lived in.

For I also discovered that O'Bryan would scarcely have recognized the farm as it is now. In the library of the Cornish Museum I found a plastic folder with two pieces of waxed paper on which someone had traced outlines of old maps of the farm in 1775, three years before O'Bryan's birth, and 1842, nearly thirty years after he left. The first tracing was a sketch rather than a map, showing a large building that was probably the big barn where the plaque now sits; even we knew it was the oldest building on the farm. But although the barn was the one building O'Bryan would have recognized now, it was not the same. The fire during our first year on the farm had destroyed the roof and everything inside, and my father had rebuilt it, filling in an upper story door with concrete blocks and replacing the slate roof with sheets of corrugated iron.

Standing in the farmyard that day in 1989 I had privileged knowledge. I was the only person in the world who knew both of William O'Bryan's existence and of the barn fire, who knew that the barn was not exactly the one he had known. This matters to no one but me, but the fragility of the slender thread of memory, a blip that survived by mere coincidence, brought me closer to O'Bryan, ultimately sparked my interest in a name I might have passed by in any other location. For I too have a past, and mine and O'Bryan's intersect in interesting and suggestive ways. We grew up in the same place, and both settled in New York State. Like his wife and daughters I experienced involuntary displacement, and, like them, I learned to be American.

For the first time I felt a real connection with the past. This was not just O'Bryan's space, it was also mine. Like him, I knew where to find the violets, the strawberries, the hazelnuts, the sloes. Perhaps he too read in the oak tree's branches and spent hours on his own in the small woodland area in the far corner of the farm. He claimed he was "born in the shadow of Helman Tor," and he must have crossed the moor, as we did, to climb to the top of the first crag and on clear days see the distant sea on both Cornish coasts. We had the binding thread of a shared but private location, the extended space I still know best in the world because it was circumscribed, remote, and I had thirteen years to explore it, to know its intimate landscape.

I wonder why we didn't know about William O'Bryan, when there must have been people still alive in our community who remembered when the chapel where I briefly went to Sunday school belonged to the Bible Christians. Since we were always outsiders, however much my parents were liked and respected, probably no one thought to mention him, especially as we weren't chapel goers. Yet the effect of the plaque on me remained. Shortly after I saw it I began to write memoir pieces that have, twenty-five years later, resulted in this book.

I have preserved my own memories of Gunwen Farm, to record our presence— to people it with myself, my parents and brother, our friends and and relatives, and the pigs, cows, chickens, and cats who shared that unforgettable time and space.

VAULT BEACH, 1996[#]

My grown-up children and I sit apart from each other on the sand.

It is sand only by courtesy, a false promise gleaming seductively from the cliff walk. In fact it is tiny white and gray pieces of gravel, coarse to the touch, unpleasant to walk on barefoot. Close up it is a dull gray on the surface but sparkles in the dampness we uncover when we comb it gently with our fingers, looking for a glimpse of pale pink. We are searching for cowry shells no bigger than my fingernail, folded mounds, crimped at the edges, tiny pink-striped calzones. I am the person who knows they are there, who brings that knowledge back to Vault Beach where perhaps it has been forgotten.

I spent many childhood days staring at surely not this very sand but its ancestor, eroded from the granite Cornish cliffs. Perhaps it is the same sand—it seems indestructible. No other Cornish beach I know of has granite sand. Why not? Perhaps some quirk of the tide sifts the fine from the coarse, and dumps the gravel here, on the long curve from the rocky Gorran headland to the smooth gaunt Dodman point, a deceptively long distance I don't think I ever walked. Is there a connection between the granite sand and the cowry shells, also unique to this beach? They are smaller and squatter than the ones I have seen in American necklaces, the ones Africans once used for money. I have never found a cowry shell with a creature in it. Do they float here only when their inhabitants are dead? Is Vault Beach perhaps the Sargasso Sea of cowries, and our shells the relics of those that did not make it back?

In my memory we found cowries easily. We carried a small handful up the steep path to our cliff-top school, a gray slate house with small-paned windows reflecting the ocean's moods, snuggled in a hollow on the cliff top, protected by a hedge of fuchsias. Today I find many other small shells that I remember—yellow or terracotta snails, limpets shaped like coolie hats, my favorite spiral winkles—but no cowries. Were they this rare fifty

---

[#] A version of this was published in *The Big Brick Review* 1 (2014.

years ago? Or has something changed? Perhaps the tides have shifted with global warming, although the granite sand is still here. Perhaps cowries are dying out in Africa. Maybe someone gathers the shells and glues them together into tourist souvenirs. It could be that the ocean deposited a finite number millennia ago and we picked up most of them. The beach is shelled out.

I look ahead to where Tom and Jane have staked their claims. I showed them how to sift for shells in Majorca when they were small children twenty-five years ago. A storm the night before had left our hotel's beach a shrunken mess of stinking seaweed so we rented a double stroller and walked to a tiny inlet sheltered from the still-brisk wind. We hunkered down between rocks like Vault's, where the ebbing tide uncovered pools with sea anemones and salt-water shrimp. The Majorca sand had a hint of coarseness and an area of fine pebbles that reminded me of my childhood siftings. I showed Tom and Jane how to rake the sand, to look carefully and slowly, to distinguish shells from pebbles, to be patient. We excavated a small pile, enough to satisfy, and took them home as souvenirs, spread out on shelves for years.

Tom and Jane have not forgotten. We haven't traveled together for a while, but have as usual fallen into easy companionship. I am still the guide, I control the itinerary, and we resume as adults the pattern we had on vacation in Austria, in France, in Majorca those many years ago. All I taught them in their childhoods I learned here in mine. In the mornings, in the schoolroom atop the cliff, Miss Rapley encouraged me to love learning and let me surge ahead by myself. In the afternoons, on this beach, walking along these cliffs, I learned to appreciate the astounding beauty of the place, and to look for and name flowers in the hedgerows, sea creatures in the tide pools, shells. I instilled these passions in my children, I prepared them to hunt patiently for cowries. They choose to do so because I learned here that it was fun. I am passing on Miss Rapley's legacy.

Connie grew up without beaches, without shells, across the ocean from where we sit. Her memories are of horses, high school pranks, family gatherings with her Polish grandparents. I have no claim on her past youth, no influence; it is the present we share. She chooses not to join the cowry hunt, clambering over the jagged rocks covered with sharp barnacles to watch the ocean break at the edge. I look across at her familiar silhouette in

267

this unfamiliar place, linking past to present. I have sat in that precise place many times, but better she is not aware of this, is not my follower, claims it as her own. It is enough that she indulges my nostalgia; she cannot share it.

I shift locations a little and turn my attention to an area of tiny pebbles. I begin to sift again—and just then, a flash of pink, a cowry, exactly as I remember. I brush off the sand and jump up to show Tom and Jane, who are encouraged. A family passes by, parents, two small children, and ask me what I am doing. Looking for cowries, I say, and show them my find. They are interested—they come here often but never knew to look. They drop their bags and join the search. But we find no more and decide to give up and go look for a Cornish cream tea. I call Connie, open my clenched hand to reveal the lone pink treasure, and we wind back up through the yellow gorse, pink vetch, and rosy ragged robin that have bloomed here in summer far longer than I remember. I look over my shoulder and see the family has recruited others to the hunt. The tradition is safe. I have passed it on, a small piece of my childhood inherited by another generation. If there are cowries left to find.

ACKNOWLEDGEMENTS

For more than twenty years of my adult life I wrote nothing more than letters. Then I took a job as a teacher of the gifted and found I had to teach creative writing, for which I had no training or experience. I enrolled in a summer course for writing teachers, where, apart from learning teaching methods, we also wrote for ourselves. I found I enjoyed it.

Sometime later, when I had returned to graduate school, a friend took me to hear Amy Tan speak at an event organized by Rochester's literary organization, Writers and Books. The staff distributed catalogs and I saw a class in autobiography that called to me. Fin Drury's class was the beginning of this book, and I benefited enormously from her detailed, insightful, and delightful critiques. Like several others, I took Fin's class every session until she retired, and I still meet monthly with five other Fin graduates, Elizabeth Osta, Pamela Pepper, Maxine Simon, Jane Shosten, and Kathy Van Schaick, to share writing, friendship, and Christmas cookies.

When I started teaching at the College at Brockport I was very fortunate to become a colleague of Judith Kitchen, who allowed me to take her Creative Essay class, where her guidance and encouragement helped me move away from the academic writing required of a historian. To my delight Judith asked to join a writing group originally connected to the class and continued to offer penetrating critiques of my work until she moved to the West Coast. The most recent members of the writing group, Amy Andrews, Margay Blackman, Bill Capossere, Geoff Graser, and Gretchen Stahlman, and former members Len Massineo and Georgia Whitney, have provided me with sympathetic but rigorous feedback that has improved my writing enormously.

I also benefited greatly from feedback and fellowship over several years in the 1990s from members of the Feminist Women's Writers Workshop (FW3), especially Joan Dickinson and Mickie Grover.

Sadly, Fin, Judith and Joan are no longer with us, and I miss them.

A class from Sonja Livingston was crucial in helping me to develop the format of short and not necessarily chronological pieces that form this memoir. Sonja recognized that I had a viable project, and without her advice and inspiration I would never have organized my disparate pieces, written over many years, into the collection you read here. Sonja also invited me to join a writing group she was forming. My very grateful thanks to her and the other group members, Gregory Gerard, Lee McAvoy, and Elizabeth Osta, and former members James Graves and Sally Parker. Their support, encouragement, and feedback helped me believe in my project and bring it to fruition.

Finally, my partner Connie Gates has provided unfailing support and critique. She has read every word several times, and is my final reader and critic over a glass of wine in the late afternoon. As always, my love and thanks.

Made in the USA
Middletown, DE
22 November 2015